# More Than a Footnote

## Canadian Women You Should Know

### KARIN WELLS

Second Story Press

**Library and Archives Canada Cataloguing in Publication**

Title: More than a footnote : Canadian women you should know / Karin Wells.
Names: Wells, Karin, 1949- author.
Description: Includes bibliographical references.
Identifiers: Canadiana (print) 20220204063 | Canadiana (ebook) 20220204098 | ISBN 9781772602661 (softcover) | ISBN 9781772602678 (EPUB)
Subjects: LCSH: Women—Biography. | LCSH: Women—History. | LCGFT: Biographies.
Classification: LCC CT3202 .W45 2022 | DDC 920.72—dc23

Printed and bound in Canada

Edited by Andrea Knight

Second Story Press gratefully acknowledges the support of the Ontario Arts Council and the Canada Council for the Arts for our publishing program. We acknowledge the financial support of the Government of Canada through the Canada Book Fund.

ONTARIO ARTS COUNCIL
CONSEIL DES ARTS DE L'ONTARIO
an Ontario government agency
un organisme du gouvernement de l'Ontario

Conseil des Arts du Canada     Canada Council for the Arts

Funded by the Government of Canada
Financé par le gouvernement du Canada

Canadä

Published by
SECOND STORY PRESS
20 Maud Street, Suite 401
Toronto, ON M5V 2M5
www.secondstorypress.ca

MIX
Paper from responsible sources
FSC
www.fsc.org    FSC® C103567

*To Olivia Duwyn, Anna Dobie, Amelia Lyon,*
*and all the young ones carrying the torch....*

PRAISE FOR *MORE THAN A FOOTNOTE*

"Wells has crafted an essential, engaging read, filled with captivating tales of inspiring women who deserve much wider recognition. With extensive research woven into sparkling prose, this book provides an engrossing window into the lives of women who dared to step beyond the bounds of acceptability. But the book goes beyond mere historical biography to lift the curtain on the research process. Wells makes the astute observation that men's lives are saved in the public record, while so many women's stories remain ensconced in family storage. That means uncovering the full stories of women's lives often involves tracking down relatives, knocking on doors, digging in closets and chests, and wiping away a lot of dust."

—Olivia Campbell, *New York Times* bestselling author of *Women in White Coats: How the First Women Doctors Changed the World of Medicine*

"Nobody brings history to life quite like Karin Wells, whose work on the page is as vivid and compelling as her work on the radio. Her subjects in *More Than a Footnote* leap right off the page to challenge our notions of Canadian history and its characters, illuminating the accomplishments of remarkable women in arts, science, politics, and more. These stories are a gift."

—Kerry Clare, author of *Waiting for a Star to Fall*

"A brilliant astrophysicist, a world-renowned cellist, a pioneering computer programmer—you've never heard of these early twentieth century Canadian women? Karin Wells makes their stories sparkle; I burned with indignation to read of the chauvinist oppression they endured, but my heart leaped up—and yours will, too—to learn of such intrepid women whose light has been hidden until now."

—Michele Landsberg

# TABLE OF CONTENTS

# INTRODUCTION

*None of us want to be in calm waters all our lives.*

—Jane Austen, *Persuasion*

I once had a closet that was more tunnel than cupboard. It stretched a long way back under the eaves of the house, getting darker and darker as it went. When I opened the door in the morning, the light shone on my everyday jackets and pants and shirts—familiar, comfortable clothes. Every so often when necessity demanded, I plunged into the tunnel, bumped my head on the sloping ceiling, and dug around in the dark for something seldom worn, sparkly perhaps. Beyond the seldom-worn, in the deepest recesses of the tunnel, were the absolutely forgotten—battle-scarred dresses hanging from one shoulder on an old wire hanger, blouses and skirts that had fallen on the floor years before, now crumpled, missing a button—often lovely things I didn't know were there. Not to stretch a metaphor, but there are an awful lot of untold women's stories stuffed in the back of our collective closet, stories that deserve an airing.

Biography, individual stories of men or women, has all too often been dismissed, particularly by historians, as fleeting and frivolous, stories that shed no light on the ways of the world. Biographies of the powerful have their place—prime ministers and the very rich, soldiers and Nobel Prize winners, and the stories of women one step removed from power—Clementine Churchill, wife of Sir Winston, Eleanor Roosevelt, and, in Canada, Sandra Gwyn's *The Private Capital*, on the wives and mistresses of Sir John A. Macdonald and Sir Wilfrid Laurier. But reshaping the world and all its parts often rests in the hands of the less powerful. What about those stories?

In her book *History's People*, historian Margaret MacMillan quotes the nineteenth-century polymath Thomas Carlyle, who asks, "Which was the greatest innovator, which was the most important personage in man's history, he who first led armies over the Alps and gained the victories of Cannae and Thrasymene or the nameless boor who first hammered out for himself an iron spade?" It's an even bigger question when "he" is changed to "she" (or "they").

In 2019, The Rooms, the provincial art gallery of Newfoundland and Labrador, mounted an exhibition called *Future Possible*; simply put, it was an art history of the province with a twist. History through paintings has all too often been full of dark gold–framed portraits of overstuffed, unsmiling men intent on looking Important. "Here I am," they said, "the embodiment of History." And true to form, curator Mireille Eagan began this exhibition with a cluster of those somber paintings, then the exhibition took a deep breath and said, "Now we're moving on," and walked away from those men, and looked at the people of Newfoundland and Labrador who had very little, if any, power and what they accomplished. Fishermen, men who worked on military bases, and women and their work. Around another corner and high on the wall were several Grenfell mats, the floor mats that women in tiny, scraggly communities on the Labrador coast made and sold, that kept communities alive when the fish failed. Those women reshaped their world.

We know the names and stories of queens, empresses, and rulers—Elizabeth I of England, Catherine the Great, Margaret Thatcher; "heroines" like Laura Secord (and her cow); merciful, good women—Florence Nightingale comes to mind, who was far more than merciful; feminists and suffragettes like Emmeline Pankhurst, Susan B. Anthony, and in Canada, Nellie McClung and the Famous Five.

These are women who accomplished big things, whose stories are told and images cast in bronze. But not frequently enough.

In the UK, where they count statues, 85 per cent of the hundreds of statues scattered throughout the country are of men; in Edinburgh, it's 95 per cent. The other 15 per cent, the women in granite and marble, include a lot of nameless naked nymphs and a great many Queen Victorias, leaving around forty statues of women who are heralded for their own accomplishments. In London, there are more statues of animals than women—but then, it is England.

In Canada, there is a new statue of a woman hockey player outside the Hockey Hall of Fame in Toronto, we have put Viola Desmond on the ten-dollar bill, and there are more women on the list of Persons of National Historic Significance, a somewhat dutiful and obscure government list. But who even knows that there is a list of Persons of National Historic Significance? We need to meet women whose stories sing and to find out what they are singing.

Information about women tends to be thin on the ground and hard to find. The majority of women in the Western world have changed their names when they married, hiding themselves away and making it next to impossible to follow their lives, to discover where they lived, what they did, who were their sons and daughters, and, particularly, who were their mothers. Charlotte Small and Anne Louisa and Nancy Mackenzie, all Métis women, would seem to have no mothers. The women who gave birth to them and brought them up are nameless, noted in whatever records there are by a question mark or generically as "native woman."

I looked hard for the name of the mother of cellist Zara Nelsova. Surely Ms. Nelsova, in one of those many press interviews that performers give, would have mentioned her mother—no, not once. Manitoba birth records give her a name, but there are no birth records of any of her siblings, born in the same city two and four years earlier, nor of her younger brother. Did someone go into the records after Zara became a little bit famous and add her mother as an afterthought? Who knows?

A biographer tracking down Christian women has a fighting

chance of finding something in a family Bible or church records, but what family records are there of a Jewish girl whose ancestors fled the pogroms of central Europe? First Nations women come from an oral culture. There were no written records, and when settler governments began keeping track, Indigenous people were often numbered, not named, or were given new, "white" names.

Class makes a difference. Louis Riel, the martyred Métis leader and founder of the province of Manitoba, and his sister Sara, whose story must wait for another time, came from what might be considered Métis aristocracy. Not only did Sara Riel receive a good education, but because she was a Riel, her letters were safely filed away. Elizabeth Simcoe, wife of Governor Simcoe, kept a fulsome and valuable diary—her housemaid, probably not. Then again, many literate but self-effacing women did not keep diaries—three cheers for Mina Benson Hubbard (and everyone in her canoe) who managed the expedition into northern Labrador so well that she (and her Métis guide, George Elson) had time and energy enough to sit in their tents at night, listening to the sound of the river, and writing in her diary. Those diaries, a little ragged and watermarked, have survived. On the other hand, Zara Nelsova finished four hours of cello practice every day and her fingers were throbbing, sometimes bleeding. She had neither the inclination nor the time to pour her heart out in a diary. Luckily, she was a tireless self-promoter, and there are scores of press interviews. Computer scientist Beatrice "Trixie" Worsley, as far as we can tell, kept no journal and gave no interviews. As well, she was a compulsively tidy person who dumped anything she did not need straight into the wastepaper basket, keeping only the most essential professional correspondence and her lecture notes (comprehensible only to mathematicians and other computer scientists). Fortunately—at least for anyone looking to tell her story—Trixie Worsley died suddenly before she had a chance to throw *everything* away.

There is more that gets in the way of digging out women's stories. In 2021, the McMichael Canadian Art Collection mounted *Uninvited*, an exhibition of the work of women who were contemporaries of the Group of Seven, the men whose painting has come to define Canadian art. Many of the Group were supportive of these women and admired their work, yet they never included any in their "club." According to the McMichael's chief curator, Sarah Milroy, simply *finding* the work these women created was difficult. "In part," she wrote in the show's catalog, "the dearth of information results from the way in which families and friends have held their legacies close. And, she adds, "a male artist belongs to history, it seems, a woman to those she loved and cared for."

Astrophysicist Allie Vibert Douglas created a well-written memoir full of stories of the life of a young woman scientist in the first half of the twentieth century, but it stayed in the family. Douglas was a woman with an international reputation, yet nothing has been published about her life beyond respectful obituaries. The same is true of Dr. Jean Rumney, Canada's first woman veterinarian and a woman who had to deal with the disabling effects of polio; her family put together their own record of her life, but it has not gone any further. Then there is this country's second woman veterinarian, Dr. Edith Williams, who along with her partner, Dr. Frieda Fraser, are major figures in lesbian history in Canada. These are two more stories that must wait.

Some women have deliberately stood in their own way. Margaret Lyons, a woman of Japanese heritage who became first a BBC journalist and then ran Canadian public radio, told her daughter in no uncertain terms that when she died, she did not want a fuss. After Margaret died, her daughter discovered that Margaret had kept everything going back to her first contract with the BBC. Fortunately, neither she nor her husband ever got around to sorting and throwing things out.

These women were each able to push through and do what they wanted. For some, it was a matter of timing. Thousands of men were in Europe in the trenches fighting World War I when Allie Douglas arrived in London, and she made the most of the opportunity; she got a job in the civil service that never would have come her way had the men been at home. Trixie Worsley arrived in England and worked with Alan Turing, "the father of computer science," just before he died. Isabel Brown Crook, a committed socialist, was living in China as the revolution unfolded and dared enough to stay.

Zara Nelsova and Margaret Lyons both had ambitious fathers who did not seem to notice that their firstborns were daughters, not sons. Allie Douglas had an older brother, George, and she followed in his wake, even overtook him at times. Trixie Worsley had a mind that could not be stopped, as did Dr. Vera Peters. Peters was both the most socially conventional of these women—she married and had children—and the most inventive. At home, she was Mrs. Lobb, who made jam and sat in the passenger seat on family vacations; at work, she was Vera Peters, pioneer radiation oncologist. Vera Peters turned herself into two different women to make it all work.

Above all, these women were daring, insatiably curious, and not afraid to offend. Mina Benson Hubbard and Charlotte Small wanted to know what was around the next bend in the river. Painter Paraskeva Clark went head to head, philosophically, with the Group of Seven. Margaret Lyons put the future prime minister of Singapore, among others, in his place. She knew she would never get anywhere if she was polite.

I had, by luck and good fortune, a small connection with several of these women through my work with CBC Radio: I spent time with Mina Benson Hubbard's daughter-in-law and granddaughter; I have worked with Vera Peters's daughter, Dr. Jenny Ingram, and, two years before she died, I made the trip to the hospital that surgeon Lucille Teasdale had established on the border of Uganda and Sudan. My good fortune gave me a closer view and, I thought, added to my insight. But then again, I worked with Margaret Lyons every day for two years, yet I had no idea of her life as a Japanese internee until more than thirty years later.

It has become a trope to say that we and our history are defined by our stories, but it's true. These women lived good stories fraught with drama. Often as not, they battled forceful foes; many lived in spectacular, often dangerous, places; invariably, they were made miserable by setbacks; they cherished their victories; and no one lived happily ever after. They are not princesses.

Look at all the stories we have missed. We know only half of our history. There are the women who ran cattle ranches in Alberta a hundred years ago; there is Elisabeth Mann Borgese, who led the push for the United Nations Convention on the Law of the Sea from Halifax; labor leaders like Madeleine Parent and Nancy Riche; Mary Two-Axe Earley, who began the fight for First Nations women's status recognition; the BC-born doctor Victoria Cheung, whose statue has pushed Norman Bethune into a corner in some Chinese hospitals.

So many stories. Here are ten.

—Karin Wells
Lac du Morency, Quebec

# AUTHOR'S NOTE

There are only two things that would be useful to know before you read any further. First, you will find quotations from a myriad of letters, diaries, and memoirs throughout almost every chapter of this book. Some of these first-person writings have been previously published and have the benefit of editing and annotation. Others came to me more or less "raw." I decided, as much as possible, to let them all stand in their original form, therefore, you will encounter a number of archaic modes of speech, creative spellings, and grammatical idiosyncrasies that reflect both the times in which they were written and the personalities of the women and men who put their often-spontaneous thoughts on paper.

I have noted all sources, both published and unpublished, in the bibliography, which you will find on the Second Story Press website.

And second, in the interest of consistency, all measurements, distances, weights, and temperatures have been converted to metric.

# 1. MINA

*…an aching sense of my own littleness and unimportance.*

The younger woman drags a chair across the room and draws it up to the door of the big oak wardrobe.

"They're up on top, at the back." Betty Ellis, then nearly ninety, stays put in her chair and waves her hand in the general direction of the wardrobe. "There should be two or three." Judith, Betty's daughter, Mina's granddaughter, feels her way across the top of the wardrobe.

"Got them!" She holds her breath, stretches her arm, and teases the heavy paper roll forward. It falls off the wardrobe into her hands, and she neatly tucks the roll under her arm and climbs down. "They've been up there a long time." Betty laughs. "Photographs that Mina took. Labrador."

The old woman gets up from her chair and moves to the table by the window. Betty Ellis knew Mina Benson Hubbard better than anyone in England—she had married her son John in the late 1940s. Now, gently unfurling the roll, she puts her elbow on one end while her daughter wipes her hand on her sweater and holds down the other. The late afternoon light coming in the window falls on the old photographs. "Labradoooor." Betty stretches out the last syllable and gazes down on this far away, long ago place.

Two long, narrow photographs, panoramas, one of a wide, silvery river slithering through the landscape; the other of tall, pointed water reeds reaching up and reflected down in the water. They are huge, low vistas. The George River is wide, its valley so much wider. The rocks are worn and smoothed by the ages. No jagged peaks. The landscape is vast, the colors are muted. This is the North.

Mina took those photographs in 1905, more than a hundred years before that Yorkshire afternoon, and she must have taken them at the end of the day when the light was low and diffused. Grays and blues shift darker toward the horizon scores of kilometers away. The two Ellis women and their visitor look—no one speaks—at the strength of that landscape, at the loneliness of it all, and think about this woman standing in her heavy skirt, flecked with grass and dirt from the climb up the hill, looking through the viewfinder.

The moment passes, and Judith Ellis takes the photographs from her mother and rolls them back up, this time sliding in a sheet of tissue paper for protection. The old lady pours another cup of tea and watches Judith climb on the chair and put Mina's photographs back on top of the wardrobe. Not a particularly secure place to store old photographs, but no one looks worried. They might still be there, on top of that wardrobe in the little Yorkshire village of Scalby in the north of England.

In all likelihood, they are not. This visit was in 2005. Betty Ellis, the last living direct connection with Mina Benson Hubbard, died a few years later.

Betty Ellis knew Mina as a well-spoken, well-dressed, well-heeled middle-aged Canadian woman. But in the Labrador landscape of those photographs, even a century later, Mina remains a bit of a mystery, a bit of a marvel.

+++

In 1905, Mina Benson Hubbard was in Labrador to mop up her husband's mess—although she never saw it as a mess. To her, it was a heroic odyssey gone tragically wrong. When she took those photographs, she was on her way to finishing the trip that he had started.

The world was watching, at least the world that read Canadian and American newspapers, when "the plucky comely widow" and her crew stepped into their canoes and headed north. Did anyone really expect her to come almost casually paddling down the George River into Ungava Bay two months later? When she climbed out of the canoe, carefully lifting her skirts—she had found a compromise in her clothing and wore thick knickerbockers under those skirts—and shook hands with the Hudson's Bay agent, she had traveled nearly a thousand kilometers through the interior of Labrador and had made her mark in the annals of geography. And just as she had created a new practical wardrobe that let her be both a lady and an outdoorswoman, so, in the course of two months in the bush, had she reinvented herself.

None of this ever should have happened. A little more than ten years earlier, she had been an inconsequential farmer's daughter in Bewdley, Ontario, a teacher in a one-room schoolhouse destined for a predictable, dreary life. When she took those photographs on that summer's day in Labrador, and when she took another "observation" with her sextant and her compass, she was a woman bent on a scientific purpose. Those "observations" were the raw material for her maps of northern Labrador that became the definitive maps of the region, the maps that guided trappers, explorers, and rescue missions through northern Labrador for decades to come. There was a Métis man standing beside her on that hill, George Elson. He held a crude, hand-sketched map that other Indigenous people had given him when they set off, and there was an "official" map of the region that left a great deal to the imagination. That's all there was. Mina Benson Hubbard's maps were accurate, and they held up until the 1930s and the advent of aerial photography.

Less tangible but more important, Mina Benson Hubbard was one of the very few women in Canada—ever—to mount a successful exploration into the bush. There were no major mishaps, no one died, no one was injured, and when she and the four Métis men with whom she traveled paddled up to Kangiqsualujjuaq, the old Hudson's Bay Post in Ungava Bay, they had become a tight traveling family.

There is another, much earlier photograph that speaks volumes. Looking back at the camera is a slight girl in a black dress, six-year-old Mina Benson. Her weight is resting on her left elbow, and she is gazing almost disdainfully into the middle distance. Disdain is not an emotion common to many six-year-olds, but there it is. Disdain and defiance, with her from the beginning. Her father was one of seven brothers and sisters, Protestant Irish immigrants, who climbed off the lake steamer at Cobourg, Ontario, in 1846. The Bensons headed north into a land of scrub oak, brushwood, wild grapes, lupins, and tiger lilies. The three Benson brothers cleared the land and established homesteads around Rice Lake. Mina, born in 1870, was a seventh child of a seventh child. Her father, James Benson, and her mother, Jane Wood Benson, were the less prosperous Bensons—they had less money, less farmland than the other Bensons, and they lived in a one-story, plain little house. All the Bensons were conservative Christians, several believing that higher education was a corrupting influence—not a promising setting for a bright little girl. Fortunately, Mina's parents were not only less successful but they were also a little bit less zealous and made room in their thinking for Mina to go beyond the local one-room school. She was sent to high school in Cobourg twenty-seven kilometers away and in so doing became one of only 5 or 6 per cent of young people in Ontario, most of them boys, to learn something more than basic reading and writing. But, at the age of sixteen when she finished high school, her life came to a screeching halt. Women in the late nineteenth century had few options. Mina showed no inclination to settle down and marry the farmer next door, so instead she took over the local one-room schoolhouse. It seemed to be the only alternative. There she stayed for the next ten years, a Protestant spinster schoolmarm, until, at the age of twenty-six, for no apparent reason, she changed careers.

For a woman to have one career in the late nineteenth century was unusual enough, but to have two was remarkable. Her sister and two cousins had become nurses. Until the mid-nineteenth century, nurses tended to be either religious sisters, upper-class do-gooders, or jumped-up hospital cleaners. Then came Florence Nightingale, the British woman who professionalized nursing with her attention to diet, dirt, and drains as she looked after soldiers in the Crimean War. The first Canadian Nightingale-inspired nurses' training started in 1874 in St. Catharines, Ontario. Whatever the reason, the Benson women skipped over St. Catharines and went to New York to learn nursing. Mina followed them in 1896. Nurses' training back then meant hard labor, scrubbing floors and cleaning windows fourteen hours a day, intended to weed out the weak and the lazy. There was nothing weak or lazy about Mina Benson. She graduated at the head of her class and was keen to find a job. (There were some who objected to paying nurses anything for fear that the profession would only attract "careerists," women who were in it for the money.) The Smith Infirmary on Staten Island snapped her up. Her nursing career was brilliant but short (brilliant and short would become the hallmark of the phases of her life). Not long after she put on her starched uniform and cap for the first time, she was assigned a typhoid patient. His name was Leonidas Hubbard, and he was the man whose well-intentioned ineptitude would define her life.

Hubbard was a dreamer, a romantic, with an innocent enthusiasm for adventure. He was hardworking enough, but his head was in the clouds, the northern clouds. It was full of stories of "the North"— Labrador—at a time when most people had no idea what or where Labrador was. Like Mina, he was a farmer's child (from Michigan); like Mina, he was brought up a conservative Christian; and, like Mina, he had been a teacher. He was also a kind man who was undoubtedly transfixed by this nursing angel who restored him to health. At the age of twenty-nine, Mina fell in love with her "Laddie," as she called him. He was two years younger, a slight man never weighing more than 130 pounds. Had he been a man of a little more substance in every way, things might have turned out differently. She was in love with his kindness, his romantic visions, and his idealism. Young love. You cannot help but wonder how their relationship might have changed as their love seasoned and matured, but it was not to be. They married in the winter of 1901; two years later, he was dead.

***

Having rejected teaching in fairly short order, Leonidas Hubbard went after a career in journalism, beginning at the Detroit *Evening News*, then moving on to New York. After Mina nursed him back to health, he got a job writing for *Outing*, one of the many outdoor adventure magazines that were captivating the American public. Hubbard did well with *Outing*, eventually becoming assistant editor. The magazine cashed in on public appetite, ran articles on the North, and published northern fiction, including Jack London's *White Fang*. America in the early twentieth century was preoccupied with stories of adventure and exploration. There were legions of "gentlemen explorers." Colonel Willard Glazier, a Civil War hero, had "discovered" what he claimed was the true source of the Mississippi River. He got two books out of that voyage. Future US president Teddy Roosevelt, who had been a frail and sickly child, "explored" the West in his youth, then later, in 1913, after he was president, undertook his biggest voyage of discovery up the Amazon, a trip that nearly killed him. Roosevelt called it his "last chance to be a boy." And that is what these tales of adventure were all about—a Peter Pan world for boys who did not want to grow up but at the same time were desperate to prove their manhood. There was an adolescent spirit of derring-do, man against the wilderness. In his Labrador diary, even as food was running low and things were going from bad to worse, Hubbard wrote, "This promises to be a hungry trip. But it's a man's game." Leonidas Hubbard wanted to win his "man's game." The problem was that adventures are not games.

Mina and Leonidas became engaged. She gave up nursing and journeyed back to her family in Bewdley, Ontario, in the fall of 1900. Hubbard came to Canada, spent Christmas with the Bensons, then returned to New York. Come January, when Mina, her sisters, and her mother were up to their eyes in white lace and wedding cake, a telegram arrived from Laddie telling Mina that *Outing* magazine had assigned him a story on the backwoods of the southeastern United States. He was told to pack up his camping equipment and get moving.

Mina Benson Hubbard,
upstate New York, c. 1901

Mina, leaving the Bewdley Bensons open-mouthed, dropped everything and headed back to New York. They were married within days. Off they went on their honeymoon, camping and boating through Virginia, North Carolina, Tennessee, and down the Mississippi River. Both of them loved their days in the woods, on the river, and there were more work trips together, including a canoe trip north of Lake Superior. As they traveled together, Hubbard made notes and experimented with mapmaking: taking "observations," calculating angles of the sun to the horizon, and working out latitude and longitude with his sextant. Mina watched and learned.

She also watched Hubbard's fascination with the North grow stronger by the day. It was one of the last frontiers, knowable to none but the brave, or so the thinking went. The North Pole was the ultimate challenge; men risked life and limb, planted national flags to prove they had reached the ends of the earth. Polar expeditions became an international and deadly sporting event, a roaring test of masculinity. Hubbard's obsession, resting as it did with Labrador, seemed more realistic. He dreamed about paddling through the heart of the region all the way to Ungava Bay on the edge of the Arctic Ocean. He saw himself coming back with stories of wild rivers, of the unknown Indigenous Naskapi people, and of the great caribou migration. He would not be the first white man to make the trip—far from it, Hudson's Bay Company men had traveled across Labrador seventy years earlier—but he expected to be the first to bring Labrador to the outside world. This trip would make his reputation, Hubbard thought, as indeed it did.

Dreams turned into plans, and he recruited a partner, Dillon Wallace, not an explorer nor an "outdoorsman" but a lawyer, a sensible, feet-on-the-ground man, even more an amateur explorer than Hubbard.

Wallace and Hubbard talked and planned for months while Mina cooked and chimed in supportively. Wisely, they decided that they needed a third man, someone who knew backwoods life and canoes. The man they found was George Elson, son of a Scots father and a Cree mother, around the same age as Leonidas Hubbard, and born and brought up near James Bay in Northern Ontario. They could not have chosen better. Elson became far more than a guide for both Hubbard expeditions. He was the linchpin. (Writing about the Hubbards in 1978, Pierre Berton argued that in the same spirit that Sir Edmund Hillary's ascent of Mount Everest was eventually referred to as the Hillary-Norgay ascent, crediting both Hillary and his Sherpa companion, Tenzing Norgay, Mina Benson Hubbard's subsequent expedition to Ungava Bay should be known as the Elson-Hubbard expedition.)

They had it all worked out. They would travel by boat up the coast of Labrador to the settlement of North West River, then west by canoe to Grand Lake, where they would make a ninety-degree turn and go due north to the George River, meeting on the way the elusive Naskapi people and seeing the great caribou migration. That was the plan. Once they were on the George, they reckoned, it would be clear paddling to Ungava Bay. Nearly a thousand kilometers.

In June 1903, Leonidas Hubbard, Dillon Wallace, George Elson, and Mina set sail from Brooklyn for Halifax, then on to St. John's, Newfoundland. Hubbard was thrilled when he discovered that one of their fellow passengers out of St. John's was William Brooks Cabot, the reigning expert on Labrador. Like some eager puppy, Hubbard overwhelmed Cabot with every detail of his plan. The older man later wrote in his diary—with disturbing prescience—"I am afraid H[ubbard] will get nervous and overdo and even barring accidents will fail to justify his hopes."

When they reached Battle Harbour in the south of Labrador, Mina disembarked and waved good-bye as the boat took her husband north. Yes, she would be lonely waiting for his return, but she had no major misgivings. After all, she had watched the plans take shape, seen his enthusiasm for the challenge. As she wrote in her diary two years later, "all men or most of them love to do things that are hard to do which they can do well." The men on the boat watching her figure on the shore receding into the distance, worried more about her than she about them. To them, she was a woman in danger of pining away waiting for her hero to return. Dillon Wallace wrote in his diary that Mina was "very brave." Leonidas knew that she would feel incomplete without him. "Poor little woman," he wrote.

+++

Summers are short in Labrador. Winter snow and gales that turn men into icy scarecrows can be upon a traveler in August. Hubbard, Wallace, and Elson pushed off from North West River on July 15. They were in trouble by the second day. As planned, they paddled west through Grand Lake watching for the mouth of the Naskaupi River that would take them north. What they did not realize was that there was not one but four rivers that emptied into Grand Lake. They overshot the Naskaupi—others before and after them have done the same thing—and they went up the wrong river. It was that simple. They missed the turn. There they were, three men in one canoe heading up the much smaller Susan River, a brook rather than a river, and when the Susan dribbled away to nothing, they kept going overland deeper and deeper into nowhere. One canoe meant less room for provisions. Optimistically, Hubbard and Wallace were relying on game for food, but 1903 turned out to be a bad year, and by the end of July, Hubbard, slight man that he was, was losing weight—rapidly. Sitting by the campfire at night, he noted in his diary that they read poems by Kipling and inspirational Bible passages. Neither Rudyard Kipling nor the word of God assuaged their hunger, and a few days later, Hubbard wrote, "All hungry all day." They had no fishing net and no shotgun for small game. Hubbard and Wallace had provided themselves with light rifles, but Elson, who was a far better shot, had to ask to use the rifle.

Hungry turned to starving, their moccasins were rotting, and it was starting to snow. There were decisions to be made. But this was Hubbard's expedition, and George Elson, the Métis man who knew the bush, also knew enough not to overstep his authority. He began speaking in parables, telling Dillon Wallace stories of "Indians" starving to death in the woods. Too late, Hubbard made the call that was only his to make: "Boys," he said, "what do you say to turning back?" Even then he did not comprehend the trouble they were in and wrote in his diary, "I think I'll get a bully story out of it despite our failure to reach the Nascaupees." They turned around and trudged back down the trail for four more weeks. The wind blew, the snow flew. Hubbard became weaker and, on October 17, realized that he could not continue. The next morning, George Elson and Dillon Wallace, weak from hunger themselves, left Hubbard as protected as they could in his tent and went for help. Somehow, despite the snow that was by now a blizzard, Elson snared rabbits and ptarmigan and staggered on for more than sixty kilometers. When he stumbled across a trappers' cabin, he was almost barefoot, and his clothes were barely holding together. The trappers took him in, then went back up the trail and found Wallace, frostbitten and smoke-blind from the fires he had made to keep warm and wandering in circles.

Leonidas Hubbard lay close by, frozen dead in his tent. He was thirty-one.

+++

Back home in Bewdley, Mina waited three months for word of the expedition, not for a moment expecting bad news. When the telegram arrived, she was stunned, overwhelmed with grief, and all but incapacitated. Her sister literally propped her up for weeks. His dreams had been her dreams; she not only loved him but had lived through him, and now she was without a path, unable to see a future. Returning to New York in May 1904, she was barely able to put one foot in front of the other.

Money was an immediate concern. Destitute widows were all too common. Mina had a profession, she had two, but it was barely more acceptable for a widow to be a nurse than it was for a married woman. She could go back to her one-room schoolhouse and move in with the family in Ontario, but Mina was not one to go back. Her Laddie had not anticipated his tragic end, yet it seems that there was a life insurance policy, and Mina Benson Hubbard wound up with, it's estimated, $15,000—half a million in today's dollars—enough to tide her over. For now, she could not see past tomorrow.

What she did know and believe was that Laddie's story must be told, his mission completed. She immediately turned to Dillon Wallace, who had retrieved both Hubbard's body and his diary. When the recovery team returned to the campsite, Hubbard lay buried under two-and-a-half meters of snow. Wallace kept the diary and told Mina that he would write the story of the expedition, as he said Hubbard had asked him. This would be the tribute that her husband deserved, Mina felt, and believing in Wallace, she handed him a thousand dollars to begin work.

But Dillon Wallace had already begun the blame game. The northern expedition had been a news story when the two men set out; it became a bigger story with Hubbard's death. Even before his body was brought back to New York, the *New York Times* ran a front-page story based on a letter Wallace had written to his sister. "We plunged madly into the interior of an unknown country," he wrote, "into regions never before trod by white man, with almost no provisions.... We should have taken 200 pounds of bacon or pork, we had 25 pounds...." Hubbard was the author of his own misfortune, according to Wallace, as he worked frantically on the manuscript of *The Lure of the Labrador Wild.* The final draft was handed to Mina in the fall of 1904. It's difficult to imagine a woman angrier than Mina when she read what Wallace had written. Dillon Wallace not only demeaned her husband but left no doubt that he, Dillon Wallace, intended to go back to Labrador and finish the expedition. "Perhaps," he wrote, "it is God's will." Not only was she furious, but she also became convinced that Wallace, having been found close to Hubbard's tent, was responsible for his death. Few agreed with her, pointing out that Wallace himself nearly died in Labrador when his frostbitten feet turned gangrenous. Mina could not see it that way. Looking at the fate of Leonidas Hubbard in the cold light of day, it was his incurable romanticism, his lack of experience, and, ultimately, his bad judgment that killed him. But Mina would always see her Laddie as a hero. Her hatred of Dillon Wallace never abated.

In the year after her husband's death, Mina Benson Hubbard was determined that *someone* should see her husband's work completed, and she was adamant that it would never be Dillon Wallace.

But if not Wallace, who?

+++

*...I suppose no one will ever quite know with what a sickening sense of limitation I longed to be a man, so that I could go away and do the work to which my husband had given his life, and which his death had left unfinished. But I was a woman and it did not occur to me that I could do anything until that January day when, as I sat looking out of the window, aching with a sense of my own littleness and unimportance, suddenly something thrilled my whole being. I could not tell you what it was. I could not in any definite way describe it to you, but it came like a sudden illumination of darkness and it meant "Go to Labrador."*

The scales fell from her eyes. She, a woman, could and would take up the work of her husband. Mina Benson Hubbard knew all too well that in the early years of the twentieth century, there were things a woman could do and things, if she wanted to maintain any decorum and respect, that she could not. Mina Benson Hubbard, at the age of thirty-four, was no social revolutionary. Clever, curious, full of gumption, yes, but she had never struck out on her own. She longed to "do the work to which my husband had given his life," but first she had to get past being a woman. Negotiating the social terrain of the early twentieth century took as much care as negotiating the terrain in Labrador. There was no beaten path.

Nobility of purpose was the key: devotion and dedication to a dead husband. One, like Leonidas, who had died a hero's death. That's what bolstered her courage and justified her audacity. To be an adventuress, a thrill-seeker, and plunge into the unknown for her own excitement was not acceptable. Motivation was everything. Mina Benson Hubbard cast herself more as a Joan of Arc, a woman on a God-given mission, than an Annie Oakley, a brazen woman of the new frontier. The planning for the second Hubbard expedition began.

When Mina arrived in Halifax ready to depart for Labrador in June 1905, two years after her husband's death, she stood before the press in full mourning, a tiny figure in a black dress and black hat, widow's weeds. Mrs. Hubbard, as the *New-York Tribune* duly reported, was going to Labrador to complete the work her husband began, not to "explore new lands." Once underway, she went below deck, changed into her knickerbocker skirt, and started to see herself in a new way. It was weeks later, when she was well into her journey, with the sound of rain tapping on the canvas of her tent, that she

George Elson, photographed by
Mina in Labrador, 1905

wrote in her diary, "Now begin to feel just a little like an explorer."

The "something that thrilled her whole being" and convinced her to make the trip might well have been the voice of George Elson. At her invitation, Elson journeyed from James Bay to New York in the winter of 1904 ostensibly to give his account of the last days of Leonidas Hubbard. It was Wallace she blamed for her husband's death, never Elson, and he in turn felt an obligation to the dead man that over time was equaled by his respect for his widow. It's easy to imagine Elson saying to her, "Mrs. Hubbard, it's you who should be the one to go to Labrador." Once she let him convince her, she bent to the task with the same energy she had put into scrubbing floors in her nurse's training, determined to put Dillon Wallace in his place. He was blindsided, had no inkling that Mrs. Hubbard was planning her own Labrador expedition. Wallace and his crew sailed to Halifax and on to Labrador on June 4, 1905, with Mina only a few days behind.

The Widow vs. Wallace. "HUBBARD EXPEDITION IS RIVAL OF DILLON WALLACE," blared the Halifax *Herald*. The newspapers had a brand-new story, a second chapter to the story of the death of Leonidas Hubbard, and they made a meal of it. The two expeditions were a "spectacle," they wrote, the dead man's lieutenant against the comely widow, tragic and grief-stricken. The newspaper accounts fed into public opinion that the comely widow was not merely grief-stricken but grief-crazed. Surely, only a deranged woman would plunge into the same wilderness that killed her husband. In reporting the failure of the original expedition, the papers had criticized Hubbard for arriving late in the season, for not hiring a local guide, for being ill-prepared, and for endangering the lives of all three men in his unrealistic determination not to turn back. Mina, consciously or not, met every criticism and then some. She and her crew stepped into their canoes in Labrador three weeks earlier than Hubbard and Wallace had two years before, and this time they were a team of five: Mina, George Elson, and two men he had worked with in Northern Ontario, plus a local man. The two Ontario men's canoe expertise was unparalleled. Joe Isheroff, who was Cree and Russian, and Job Chapies, a Cree man who spoke very little English and for whom she had a particular soft spot—"Wish I could understand Indian," she wrote. "He is full of fun." Finally there was Gilbert Blake, still only a teenager, one of the Labrador trappers who had rescued George Elson and Dillon Wallace the first time out. He knew the territory. There they were—a white woman traveling with four "Indians," yet another slap across the face of social convention.

This time out there were two canoes. That meant they could bring almost four hundred pounds of flour—Leonidas Hubbard had taken only a hundred and twenty—and two hundred pounds of bacon compared to Hubbard's twenty-five. All the men on the second expedition were given pistols, and Mina had her own revolver. They also carried with them the instruments she needed to record and map what she saw: two new Kodak portable cameras, a sextant, an artificial horizon, and a compass. Mina took a "rubber shirt" for warmth, a floppy hat, that stout knickerbocker skirt hemmed to her ankles, and netting to keep out the flies. There were even a few luxuries—a feather pillow, a bottle of brandy, and five kilograms of chocolate.

Less than a year earlier, Mina Benson Hubbard had disqualified herself from an expedition through Labrador because she was a woman. Now here she was setting sail from Halifax, more than ready for whatever came next.

+++

*Did not feel in the least uneasy or unnatural going off. Only glad to be at least off on our trip, really started.*

Betty Ellis had come to expect Canadian visitors inquiring about Mina, and in the 1990s, she had poured tea for an earlier visitor.

That time it was Anne Hart, Mina Benson Hubbard's biographer. They had talked for several days when the conversation drifted to Mina's diary, and Betty said off-handedly, "We still have it, and her husband's, both diaries. They're upstairs." Anne Hart nearly dropped her teacup. She, and everyone else, had assumed that the Hubbard diaries were long gone. Now here they were—Mina's handwriting, words added, words crossed out—within reach. Those diaries now rest, only to be handled by white-gloved hands, in the archives of Memorial University in St. John's. Anne Hart brought them back to Canada.

The Hubbard expeditions are two of the best-chronicled Canadian wilderness treks. Both Leonidas Hubbard and Dillon Wallace diaried the ill-fated 1903 trip, and Wallace kept a journal throughout his second expedition. Mina's 1905 diary, which has been published, runs to more than two hundred pages. It was hauled in and out of canoes a few hundred times, bounced over eddies and rapids, written in by the light of a campfire, perfumed by wood smoke, frozen in the Arctic air, and packed up and hauled by Mina between a score of houses over ninety years, yet it remains perfectly legible.

There is still another diary, unpublished, that made the same river trip through Labrador. George Elson also kept his own record of the 1905 expedition. Something compelled him to write and he began keeping notes about his life as a young man living near James Bay in the late 1800s. His 1905 expedition diary began the day they arrived in the settlement of North West River.

> June 25th, Sunday: We arrived at N.W.R. [North West River]. The mountainer [Montagnais] Indians tells me that it will take us 3 months to go up to Mishakamau [Michikamau] Lake and that we will not be able to find it without a guide and that the Nescaupee River is very hard to go up and lots of bad rapids.

What the Montagnais told him was not reliable—it took them five weeks, not three months, to reach Michikamau Lake, the halfway point, and they found their way without a guide.

The warning about the rapids, however, was all too accurate—they were fierce and there were plenty of them.

Mina, Elson, and crew knew that Dillon Wallace and his crew

Gilbert, Joe, and Job butchering caribou

were taking a different route, and they set off from North West River a day after Wallace, yet they were convinced and confident that they would get to Ungava first. The travelers climbed into their two nineteen-foot canoes, Mina in one with Job Chapies in the stern and the other three men, George, Joe, and Gilbert in the other. When they pushed off, it was the last anyone from the outside world saw of them for nine weeks. This was a trip into the unknown.

On June 28, Mina wrote in her diary, "Must harden up if I can.... George caught sight of a huge bear. Great chase.... First wild bear I ever saw.... Killed porcupine and had him for supper." She plunged into her adventure like a very keen Girl Guide, up for anything and excited about everything. "June 30.... Mice ate holes in my felt hat last night; July 1...saw two seals in rapids; July 4...bears at this time of year are apt to be dangerous.... I rather hoped one would come along but none did; July 6.... Men much amused over my attempts at 'Indian ....' Neck & face bitten & swollen & sore. Must look awful; July 10.... Coldest night yet.... Heard sound of wolves about 4 am."

She ate whatever was plucked, gutted, and put in front of her. "July 9...two partridges stewed and pancakes. Delicious breakfast; July 18.... Late breakfast. Had boiled muskrat...and boiled rice. Muskrat very nice. Does not taste at all as it smells; August 12.... Caribou gut and tongue for lunch. Geo. thought I would not eat them but I did and found it very very good."

George Elson set the rules of travel. The men did the heavy

work—paddled, carried loads that weighed up to eighty kilograms (Leonidas Hubbard was only ever able to manage thirty-four) over portages of sixteen kilometers, and set up camp. Mina strode across the landscape relatively unencumbered, carrying her mapmaking equipment, her knife, and sometimes a rifle. When the river was rough, Job, Joe, and young Gilbert ran the rapids while Mina and Elson walked the shore.

"Men have such a happy time together," Mina wrote, "and seem just in their element. Job loves to cut a trail and pole up a rapid just as an artist loves to paint. I think they would all rather be here taking this trip than anywhere else in the world." And on July 11, she noted, "They are gentle, considerate and polite always not only of me either but of each other as well and have such good times together.... Geo gentle sunny tempered, fun loving devoted. How easy I feel in the midst of them all. Could not feel more so as if they were my brothers."

Very quickly they became their own sort of family. The men sang; what a pity, one said, that no one had thought to bring a pack of cards; they played pranks on each other, and George teased Mina relentlessly.

> July 12.... Cleaning up my revolver this morning. It got a little rusty. Was putting some grease on it and in barrel. Geo said "don't put too much grease on it. If you put too much on the bullet will just slip out and...might kill something." Then followed one of George's rare laughs.... I love to hear it.

Gilbert, Joe, and Job
on the river

George and Joe cooked the game, Mina made bannock, and when they reached the halfway point, she made a campfire rice pudding with brandy chocolate sauce and "dressed" for dinner in celebration. "August 10....We had our rice pudding and I put on my Sunday waist [blouse] and took a clean handkerchief and put on my red tuque Laddie got me in Quebec. The men were greatly pleased."

When the weather was bad, they stopped for a day, did their washing and mending, rested, and reflected.

(Mina) "June 23...tonight sat on bridge sewing on tent front and watching sunset...very very beautiful."

(George) "July 18...rain Most all day and stayed in camp all day did some mending. and patching our Mocasins. dont like to travell in rainny weather on account of Mrs Hubbard as it would be very uncomfortable for her camping at night and things wet and no stove."

(Mina) "July 12.... So sorry men have so much packing to do. Wish I could be more like my husband and could express my appreciation and admiration for their work.... Who could believe Labrador could be so beautiful."

Pierre Berton, writing about the Hubbards seventy-five years later, described Mina's 1905 expedition as "a walk in the park" compared to her husband's doomsday voyage in 1903. The territory was every bit as treacherous, and they were longer on the river, but they were on the right river. They were never lost and never had to deal with blizzards and they had food. They were in control. Which is not to say that there weren't terrifying moments. The canoe overturned more than once, Job was nearly swept away, and they lost cargo to the river—crucially, the axe was lost. Without an axe, they could not cut their own path. George Elson wrote, more than once, that the portage route was very steep and "dangersome," every step blocked by bush and trees. "July 6.... Glad to see Mrs Hubbard...having good courage.... Tho she has to walk in such a rough country as we cannot even make a trail."

That same night, sitting in the other tent, Mina wrote, "George thinks I am getting on fine. Says there are lots of men who would... have jumped out of the canoe some places they have taken me.... Have done altogether a good deal of walking in bush and over loose rocks. Very tired...."

Mina's photographs of Naskapi man and Naskapi women and children

The George River was something else again. In some places, it was a kilometer and a half wide, in others more narrow, deeper, and always frigid. They could see the rocks below the surface, feel the whirl of the eddies, and hear the roar of falls as they drew closer. Elson was apprehensive. Their canoes were new and untested. "Those canoes surprises me what heavey swell they can stand," he wrote. Mina, in turn, began to understand and appreciate the skill it took to ride those rivers. "July 1.... Banks high on either side dark wooded and coming down between them a gale of warm wind almost as from a furnace. Had to... cross rapids to opposite side. All paddled as if for life.... Would have been awfully frightened had I not had such implicit confidence in my men."

The rapids became longer and the water colder as they went north. "Have been coming down falls and rapids all day yet tonight it registers 950 ft," Mina wrote. "One rapid alone where I look at it at head and foot was 50 ft. Made 5 portages this A.M. and climbed one hill 630 ft from the water.... The river has been magnificent but it has been most of the way like going down a toboggan slide. We have come down over 20 m [miles] of rapid altogether."

The land, she learned from George was not there to be conquered but rather to be understood. "July 1.... Sun setting over pt. Geo. stood for some time perfectly still, looking up the river. Wondered what he was thinking. Asked him. 'I was just thinking how proud I am of this river.'"

"June 29.... I find myself feeling astonished that Labrador can be so kind and so beautiful...."

She took pleasure in what she saw. "July 9.... Sun shining big heavy fleecy silver cloud, sky—deep beautiful blue, water.... Almost purple hills deep rich green and blue and purple"

What she smelled. "July 25.... As I walked along the bank, thinking not at all about anything about me, I became conscious of the most delightful fragrance.... I stopped and looking down saw a little vine with beautiful little pink bell-like flowers. It is the sweetest most fragrant thing I have found yet."

What she heard. "August 3.... This afternoon 4 loons calling to each other from long distance apart.... Never thought before that there was any beauty in loon music but did today...."

And, always, what she tasted. "Aug. 7...young wild geese for supper. Think I never ate anything more delicious."

When they set out from North West River, George Elson must have been asking himself how this white woman would manage in the bush, handle hours in a canoe. How would she behave with four "Indian" men? As the weeks went on, she proved herself, and almost despite himself, George began to like her a great deal.

July 28.... Mrs Hubbard she is really So good and a really kind hearted woman she is, she is more then good to me. My Sister could not be any kinder to me as she is. how glad and proud My Sisters would be if they knew how kind and what a good friend I have. Still I dont only want to say she is only a friend to me but that she is my Sister. God will help her and bring her again to her good friends home to where she came from. She is so bright and smart...and I am glad that she dose trust me.

A year later, George Elson guided two Americans, Frances Tasker and her husband, through much of the same territory. Frances Tasker admired "plucky Mrs. Hubbard," but she found no pleasure in "the murderous insects," the weary going with "no sport or comfort." She saw no beauty and wrote that the First Nations and Inuit they met were filthy, and she "swore a mighty oath to never cross those boundaries again." Mina found joy in it all, and her expedition diary is one of the most evocative pieces of early Canadian travel writing. The storied white men who explored Canada a century earlier—Simon Fraser, Alexander Mackenzie, David Thompson—left diaries that are often more instructive than descriptive. Fraser and Mackenzie and, to a lesser extent, Thompson, rather than reflecting on the land, were intent on claiming the West for Great Britain and the fur-trading companies.

Mina doing her laundry on the trail

Mina Benson Hubbard was not in Labrador to lay claim, nor was she like the "gentlemen adventurers" of her day who paddled a river or climbed a mountain to flex their muscles.

There were other Canadian women voyaging through the North, several of them also, coincidentally, disillusioned schoolteachers. Kate Rice, a 1909 graduate of the University of Toronto, who was, as far as anyone knows, the first woman prospector in Canada, lived and worked alone in Northern Manitoba. After years in the bush, Rice checked herself into a mental asylum, convinced that solitude had driven her mad, but was told by an enlightened psychiatrist, "No, you are not mad, merely unconventional." Then there was Agnes Deans Cameron, born in 1863 before the colony joined Confederation. She was equally as clever, curious, and audacious as Benson Hubbard and was not only a teacher but also the first woman in British Columbia to run a co-ed school, the brand-new red-brick South Park high school round the corner from Emily Carr's family home in Victoria. Outspoken and well-read, she advocated a more liberal approach to education and spoke out about women's rights until she ran afoul of the Victoria school board and, in 1905, found herself unemployed and looking for a new job.

Like Mina Benson Hubbard, Deans Cameron reinvented herself. She began to write and joined the Canadian Women's Press Club founded by Kit Coleman in 1904. Taking a commission from the Western Immigration Association, she and her niece Jessie Brown set off from Chicago in 1908 and went north via the Athabasca and Mackenzie Rivers to the Arctic Ocean. It was a seventeen-thousand-kilometer trip, and, like Mina, she carried her Kodak camera plus a typewriter with her all the way. Her articles went out to every publication she knew, including *Outing* magazine. *Outing* had somewhat ghoulishly published their backlog of Leonidas Hubbard material after his death. Agnes and Mina were quite different—Mina was feminine and attractive in the mode of the times; Agnes cut her hair short, wore a Stetson, had her photograph taken with the head of a moose, and was out to show that she was every bit as capable as a man. Yet Agnes Deans Cameron, bold as she was, followed an established route north, taking

Agnes Deans Cameron with a moose head, Peace River, 1908

stagecoaches and river steamers to the Arctic Ocean while Mina charted new territory. Agnes Deans Cameron was an early example of a PR woman selling the West. Mina cloaked her trip as an homage to her husband.

+++

*Two years ago last night Laddie asked "Will you miss me sweetheart...?"*
*Sometimes seems too much to bear.*

There he is, her Laddie, again and again in her diary. "June 21.... None so beautiful as my Laddie, none so loved as he; July 7.... So often seems as if he must be standing just near and that if I turn I must see him; July 16.... Oh what this trip would be if he were here; July 26.... Very

very lonely and hungry for my Laddie."

As they drew closer to the area near Seal Lake, the area where Hubbard had died, George Elson's memories of Leonidas Hubbard began to haunt him. "Aug 1.... Looking at this barren hill at last struck me that it looked like the Mountain Mr Hubbard and I had climed then not far south east from that Mountain.... It makes me just shiver and almost afread to look in that direction. To look at the Lake makes me feel how dreadful it was when we were wind bound. and could not do any fishing. and storms and cold winds that we had. and Makes Me think so Much about the [time] we were up there and how hungry and weak we were."

Mina and George together piled stones and built a monument on top of the hill. "Geo. Placed three smaller rocks and I put one on top of all." It was still standing ninety years later.

It was the mapmaking that saved her from her memories. "This work keeps me from being utterly desperate," she wrote. And it was the work that distinguished her and set her apart from Dillon Wallace and others like Frances Tasker journeying north. Mina Benson Hubbard was no tourist. She was there to take observations with her sextant and to determine, literally, where they were in the world. She knew what she was doing. During the year after Hubbard's death, she had taken lessons in cartography, and when she showed her instruments to the captain of the steamer that took them to North West River, he assured her that they were good and her readings would be accurate. It was the assurance that she both wanted and needed. "July 10.... Halted and I tried to get observation. Partly cloudy and don't think I got it just right. Puts us a little more than two miles farther north than we should be; August 10.... I have felt my lack of trainings and preparation very deeply and keenly and not until we reach Michikamau could I feel that my observations for latitude were correct. Yet even so we have opened the way and have led in it, and I can bring a tribute to the memory of my husband...."

The only tension came from the control that the men felt they had to exert over their Mrs. Hubbard to keep her safe. "June 30.... Today stepped on a big rock close to rapids. G. said 'Mrs. Hubbard you must not do that.' 'Why?' 'You will get dizzy and fall in.' Protested I did not get dizzy. 'Maybe you think you won't. It is alright when you are looking at the rapid but it is when you turn around that you will fall. It is very dangerous. If you are gong to do that then we will just turn around and go back to Northwest River.'"

They kept her on a tight leash. George was carrying a heavy burden. He didn't tell Leonidas Hubbard what to do in 1903, but now he had the life of his widow in his hands. Before they set foot in Labrador, Mina wrote that other passengers on the boat were "trying to scare the other men a little as to what may happen if they do not bring me safely back." Had anything happened, George Elson, a Métis man, would have had no future. "Wish I didn't have to be watched so close," Mina wrote, "but realizing their responsibility can't very well protest."

She might not have protested, but by the end of July, halfway through the trip, she was beginning to balk. "…Much disappointed. Such an ignominious sort of feeling to be an explorer and have one of your party tell you can't do something that he has done and is just going to do again for the mere pleasure of doing it."

A week later, George loosened the ties a little. One day when she was walking on shore, Mina was annoyed at herself for leaving her camera with the men, and George agreed that she could come back in the afternoon with her camera. "July 28…. How delighted I was to be allowed just once to go someplace and [do] something alone…. After lunch armed with kodaks and notebooks, revolver, bowie knife and compass I started for the hill…. I feel a good deal as I used to when a child and started out to do something I knew I ought not to. it seemed so fine to think of spending an hour or two up on top of that mountain alone with a glorious sky above and beautiful hills lakes and streams in all directions."

She walked along a high mountain ridge watching the men below. They lost track of her and began frantically searching.

Then they caught sight of me. Job waved his hat and I waved mine. When we met their faces were covered with perspiration and wore expressions which were a funny mixture of anger, distress, relief and much more. They had been thoroughly frightened. I smiled at them but there was no answering smile and Ge began to remonstrate with me.... "Well I guess you have very near done it this time.... How could any of us go back without you. We can't ever let you go any place after this...." I was really sorry for them...but I could not help laughing too at the wholly unexpected success of my little plan.... The brandy bottle does not often come out but when my bags were brought in I gave it to Geo. That they might have something to steady their nerves and be able to eat some supper for they looked really sick and their hands trembled visibly.... I need no bracer, for I was very very hungry and I had had "one good time."

+++

*August 25.... Was thinking today how strange it is. I have not wanted to see any one, I have been lonely for no one, we have come these 2 months through this deserted wilderness and I have never felt as I were far from home.... But I meant to try to face the other life as bravely as I can....*
*Only what am I going to do? I don't know.*

Triumphantly, they reached Ungava Bay, Kangiqsualujjuaq, on August 27. They had done it, destination reached. Suddenly, it was all over. From the minute George Elson rummaged through the bag and found Mina's sealskin boots and she squelched across the mudflats, her relationship with the men changed. The Hudson's Bay agent came down to meet them, and she followed him back up the hill, then she stopped, turned, and realized that she had forgotten to thank the men for what they had done. Mina was given a room at the Hudson's Bay post on the hill; the men slept in the tents down below. She wrote, "The sight of the two tents made the thought that I was no more to be a member of the little company seem rather a lonely one."

They were so comfortable in each other's company and so in

control of their voyage that at times they had almost ambled through Labrador. Yet they never took their eyes off the calendar, knowing full well that their voyage home was dependent on the Hudson's Bay's coastal ship, the *Pelican*, due at the Hudson's Bay Ungava post in late August. They could not afford to miss the boat; no one wanted to be marooned in Labrador for the winter. To everyone's relief, the *Pelican* was eight weeks late, and the panic they felt not knowing if they would reach the post in time turned into weeks of boredom and reflection. Mina made a slow start on "the book," looked over her maps, and made notes. She was busy. George was not busy enough. Sitting in his tent, his fingers numb from the cold, he did his mending. Mina took him a hot water bottle. Another day, she walked from the house with some books. The social distance between them lengthened. At the age of thirty-three, sitting at the edge of the Arctic, George Elson contemplated his future.

> I have thought a great deal of what I aught to do. This winter I would like to go to school…and May be or I am very sure could write a nice little Story. I am sure some one would be good enough to healp me in doing so. an other thing is in my mind, I would like now to get Married this fall. if I was luckly enough. What if I could strik luck and could get a white Girl that would marry me. and especially if she was well learnt we then could write some nice stories. because she would know lots more then I would. but not likely I will be so lucky. I think some way My chances are small in that way…. So many nice Girls in the world and yet None for me. as it looks very much like it.

Was George in love with Mina, and she with him? Did that "love" give way to lust? Were this a movie, it would have been tempting to turn it into a love story, but this was Canada in 1905 when the racial and class divide made a "relationship" between a white woman and a Métis man all but impossible. Nowhere in his diary does George Elson allow himself to refer to Mina as anything other than "Mrs. Hubbard," nothing more intimate than "his sister." And so there they sat day after day on the shore of Ungava Bay—George in his tent, Mina in her room; George with his mending, Mina with her maps, both asking themselves, "What shall I do next?" and Mina still wishing that she were not a woman. "Wish I were a man," she writes. "Would try for a place in H.BC [Hudson's Bay Company] service for a while in some of these out of the world places. Dread going back to face the crowd."

And what of Dillon Wallace? Seven weeks after Mina and her crew arrived at Ungava Bay, Dillon Wallace and his men were still out there somewhere in the Labrador wilderness. It looked like Wallace and his crew might miss the boat south and Mina was not so secretly pleased. She wrote in her diary, "If we should...get out soon. I might possibly get back and get my story and some of my pictures in print before Wallace is even heard from and that would be the thing for me. If I am to be successful that would make it complete. Oh, if it might only come that way. How grateful I should be and how complete would be my victory."

She was denied that victory. On October 16, Wallace and his crew arrived at the Ungava Bay post. It was dark, the tide was out, he was stranded on the mudflats, and, much to his embarrassment, had to be rescued in the morning. Once she had him in her sights, Mina confided to her diary, "Wallace a little more coarse and common than ordinary. Looks positively repulsive to me. Feel a little nervous about their coming and now it is an end to peace of mind for me."

Three days later, the *Pelican* docked at the George River Hudson's Bay post, and Wallace, much to Mina's relief, chose to go south overland while the others boarded the boat and sailed down the Labrador coast. George recorded, "All seasick...except Job. All feeling happy to think we are on our way home again."

The men shaved their bush beards, dug out their town clothes, and gradually the outside world began to intrude. Mrs. Hubbard received a telegram from the New York newspaper *The World* asking her to send five hundred words about the trip. News had reached New York that "the plucky little widow" had succeeded where her husband had failed. A few days later and another paper wanted three hundred words. There she was with one foot in the wilderness and one foot back at home. They rounded the southern corner of Labrador and headed west along the north shore of the Gulf of St. Lawrence. At Sept-Îles, there was talk of taking Mrs. Hubbard on a whale hunt if she came back next year—"would like to if I could," she wrote. Heading north, she had been a woman on a mission to complete her husband's work. Now she was a bold woman ready for her own adventures.

◆◆◆

*There has recently arrived in London a woman who, when her remarkable story is told, will, without doubt be accorded by a nation of explorers a place almost with out equal in the annals of travel. The new heroine is Mrs. Leonidas Hubbard. Her youth, her slender and graceful figure and the delicacy of her features are in striking contrast to the arduous and daring nature of her accomplishment.*

—London, 1907

Her Labrador photographs were delivered to her at home in New York state on Christmas Day, 1905. "There are none in existence can equal some of them," she wrote. Mina was riding high, and by January she was on the lecture circuit with stops up and down the Eastern seaboard, culminating in a triumphant appearance at the men-only Explorers Club in New York City. When she wasn't lecturing, she was working on the book. She made the strategic decision to find an English rather than an American publisher, settling on John Murray of London, the company that had published the work of other "lady explorers and travellers," including Isabella Bird, the first woman admitted, in 1892, to the Royal Geographical Society. Choosing Murray effectively served notice that her book, *A Woman's Way Through Unknown Labrador*, was a book to be taken seriously and so was its author. At the same time, her publisher adroitly highlighted her un-explorer-like appearance. The first edition featured a sketch of "the Author" in a flowing dress, a rose at her waist, and a single strand of pearls round her neck. Always a well-dressed woman, Mina Benson Hubbard had arrived in England with a fine selection of furs, and she cut a fine figure in London, looking and sounding—she had taken elocution lessons to get rid of her North American accent—like a young duchess.

Mina Benson Hubbard had checked into a quiet country hotel to finish her book, and one afternoon she struck up a conversation with another guest, Maria Rowntree Ellis, daughter of one of England's most prominent Quaker families and now matriarch of another. Mina, an attractive woman with an exciting story, was invited back to Wrea Head in Yorkshire in the north of England, the Ellis home, where she met the patriarch, John Edward Ellis, Liberal member of Parliament and supporter of the vote for women and other progressive causes. John Ellis took a shine to Mina and became an important influence in her life. Harold Ellis, his son, took to her with even more fervor. He was thirty-three, the handsome and wealthy son of a distinguished family. Mina was thirty-eight and a celebrity. It seemed like a good match.

When she was in London seeing her publisher, she mingled with Florence Nightingale, Rudyard Kipling, and Winston Churchill and made a place for herself among the liberal intelligentsia. This was a time when women who were stepping into new territory, whether geographic or social, had social cache. Supporting women's suffrage, if not necessarily their tactics, became fashionable. One London jeweler sold a line of elegant and expensive purple, green, and white jewelry in the suffragette colors.

1908 was a good year for Mina Benson Hubbard. In the spring, her book came out to positive reviews; she was praised for her descriptive passages, and her maps were considered superior to those of Dillon Wallace. How that must have pleased her. By the summer, she was engaged to Harold Ellis, clearly enamored and "theeing" and "thouing" him in the Quaker tradition. "Dearest Loved One, I want you so much tonight…," she wrote from the ship as she sailed back to Canada. "Oh I want you so much. It seems as if I could not wait for thou to come.… I love thee I love thee." In the autumn, the Ellis family sailed across the Atlantic on the *Lusitania*, and on September 14,

Mina Benson Hubbard married Harold Ellis in Toronto. In her wedding photographs, she had that same disdainful expression she had as a child. Harold Ellis would have done well to have taken note.

Their first daughter, Muriel Jane, was born the following year, then came John, their son. The youngest, Margaret, was born when Mina was forty-three. Mina's second marriage was once again blazing but short. Rural Yorkshire rapidly lost its charm, and the Harold Ellises purchased a London home, 66 Redington Road, huge and eccentric. With its musicians' gallery and a ballroom that could seat seventy-five, it was more Mina's house than Harold's. Mina presented recitals and performances by the dancer Isadora Duncan. George Bernard Shaw and H.G. Wells dropped by, as did a growing number of strong-minded women. Meetings of the Hampstead chapter of the Women's Suffrage Federation were held in that big ballroom. This was not what Harold Ellis had expected of his marriage. When World

Mina Benson Hubbard
Ellis and Harold Ellis
on their wedding day,
September 14, 1908,
Prince Arthur Avenue,
Toronto

War I was declared, he, true to his Quaker pacifist principles, went to Europe to help war refugees, but contrary to his upbringing, he met and fell in love with a Hungarian woman and then moved in with her and her daughter. His family was shocked, and Mina was livid. This betrayal was to Mina every bit as unforgivable as Dillon Wallace's betrayal of Leonidas Hubbard. Never mind that she and Harold Ellis did not see the world in the same way and that, in many ways, she was glad to see the back of him; Harold Ellis had betrayed her. Mina

Mina with Muriel Jane ('Mahlo'), her eldest daughter, and baby John

Benson Hubbard was a woman who did not forgive. Ten furious years went by before she agreed to a divorce. She received a handsome settlement, and Harold Ellis forfeited his claim to the family home in Yorkshire.

From the time Mina Benson Hubbard arrived in England, there had been no more talk of "if only I was a man." Now it was about being a strong woman. She was never a leader, but she became a suffragette. Her eldest daughter remembered at least one photograph of Mina leading a parade carrying a placard, and she contributed money to the cause. The Pankhursts; Margaret Bondfield, the first woman to hold a cabinet position in the UK; Ellen Wilkinson, labor politician and advocate of the unemployed—all knew their way to Redington Road. When Britain's involvement in World War I split the suffragette movement, with Emmeline and her daughter Christabel Pankhurst supporting the war effort and Sylvia Pankhurst remaining a pacifist and a committed socialist, Mina, influenced in part by her Quaker in-laws, weighed in with Sylvia Pankhurst and briefly became honorary treasurer of the International Women's Congress in the Hague.

Her lectures on Labrador continued in England and in North America. In 1936, she became the first woman to give the very prestigious annual Ontario Agricultural College lecture. Posters showed Mina in profile, an elegant woman with a feather in her hat, and the words "A Lecture by Mrs. Hubbard Ellis, F.R.G.S.—Fellow of the Royal Geographical Society." In 1927, she had applied and been elected to the society, not the first but one of the few women members. (The New York Explorers Club did not admit women until 1982.) She came back to Canada often, bringing her children to visit her family and more than once talked about moving back permanently. But she had been too long in England. She never went back to Labrador.

And what of George Elson? He returned to James Bay, worked in the fur trade, married but had no children, and sadly wrote no stories. He and Mina saw each other several times. Mina sent him a new boat one year. In the 1930s, when they were both in their sixties, they paddled up the Moose River in Northern Ontario together. George, like Mina, never forgot Leonidas Hubbard. He, it's said, would go down to the local railway station every year and tell the station master the story of Hubbard's death. There were tears at every telling.

+++

The Yorkshire afternoon was drawing to a close. The visitor had a train to catch in the morning, but Betty Ellis had more to say.

"Yes, she was close to me as she got older," Betty Ellis said a little hesitantly, "but always her own woman. Fearless, she was."

Redington Road, empty of servants, the garden turned into a vegetable patch, remained her home right through the Blitz and World War II. "She never slept in the air raid shelter." Betty Ellis was with her. She had come down from Yorkshire as a paying guest. "Washed the floors herself and kept everything very nicely. After the war she lived in hotels." Redington Road was sold.

Mina's son John left Betty soon after their daughter Judith was born. As Mina never forgave Dillon Wallace or Harold Ellis, she never forgave her son. They never met again. All three of her children found their mother "difficult." As Betty Ellis put it, the qualities that took her to the Arctic were "not easy to live with," and Mina valued her independence; she did not for a moment want to live with her children. By the mid-1950s, she was becoming increasingly absentminded and perhaps a little deaf. On May 8, 1956, as well-dressed and upright as ever and flourishing her stick, she set out for her daily walk. One of her shortcuts took her across the railway tracks near the station. She did not hear the train whistle. "The train brushed her, lifted her up, and threw her," said Betty. "There was just a bruise on her head."

It was a small family funeral; no one else was much interested. And that was the end of Mina Benson Hubbard. Forty years after she died, a plaque went up in a field on the country road where the family farmhouse once stood. It describes her as "An Early Twentieth century Canadian female explorer of Labrador and Writer." Accurate but woefully inadequate. A great-niece drives out from Cobourg every so often to cut away the bushes. A lonely plaque on a country road. It's hard to find. Very few people stop to read it.

+++

One summer day in the early 1930s, when she was at the height of her notoriety and Redington Road was its most splendid, Mina Benson Hubbard held a garden party. A few of her women friends wanted to help three teenage musicians from Canada who were studying in London and living hand-to-mouth. "Of course," said Mina and invited a hundred friends to Redington Road. The musicians were three neatly dressed young girls, a pianist, a violinist, and a cellist, and they behaved well and played beautifully, particularly the youngest, the cellist. The applause was loud, the contributions generous, and Mina was happy.

Their father thanked her profusely and mentioned suggestively that he was desperately searching for a good cello for fourteen-year-old Sara. Mina waved her magic wand and said, "My sister-in-law has a decent cello. She doesn't play anymore. I will speak to her." And within days the cello was handed over. Mina Benson Hubbard didn't realize quite what she had done.

Young Sara launched her career with that cello, a career that lasted for seven decades. She grew up to become Zara Nelsova, the Queen of Cellists.

# 2. ZARA

She tips her head back, thrusts her chin up even higher, and keeps her eyes closed, taking care not to wrinkle her brow. Her bow arm is fully extended away from her body, the tip of the bow delicately balanced on the strings of the cello. She holds the moment, holds the pose, and two thousand people hold their breath as the sound of the cello reverberates in the hall and fades to nothing. The audience waits for her to lower her arm, open her eyes, and let them know that she has said all she had to say, that the music is complete. Then they explode.

Younger, flashier cellists might have flourished their bow high in the air. Not Zara Nelsova. Every gesture has been measured and well-rehearsed in the mirror at home. Her chin comes down. She stands, sweeps her vast lavender skirts away from her chair, and smiles as the Berlin audience calls "Brava!" Reaching first left for the hand of the conductor, then right to shake the hand of the concertmaster, she turns back to her audience. Her gown flows out around her, the light catches the sparkling, dark-red paisley pattern dotted over the fabric, bounces off the faux diamond necklace, and makes her blonde hair—which, even after a performance remains perfectly in place—shine.

Seiji Ozawa steps down from the conductor's podium, lifts her hand, and they bow together; Nelsova, her cello in one hand, lifting

Zara Nelsova, 1970

her skirts with the other, threads her way through the orchestra and into the wings. Only then, out of sight, she looks down quickly at the swollen, callused fingers of her left hand. Someone hands her a handkerchief, and she checks for blood oozing from her cracked calluses, calluses built up from years of sliding her fingers over the steel-wound strings of the cello. In an hour, her fingers will throb and her arms will ache, and she knows it, but now hearing the applause mount, there is no pain. One last quick wipe of her fingertips and she sweeps back onstage, regal and composed; the music, her manner, it all appears effortless. As it should.

In the 1960s, when she was performing in Berlin, in New York, in London, being ushered onstage by the musical aristocracy of conductors, accepting yet another bouquet of roses as if it were her first, she was known as "queen of the cellists." Writers, fans, colleagues talked about her "sound," described her music as dramatic but never sentimental. They praised her "grand verve, consummate skill and unflagging strength." This woman who came from the north end of Winnipeg, who came from nothing, had become the first North American–born classical soloist with an international career. But what had it taken? Forty years of swollen, bloodied fingers, aching arms, a surgically repaired back, cosmetic surgery, concentration that could shut out a freight train, wigs, and the dresses, always the dresses.

+++

Zara Nelsova—Sara Katznelson in the beginning—was a scrawny little Jewish girl born in 1918. She was the last of three daughters of a Russian Jewish father—looking at a map today, a Belorussian Jewish father—one man in a wave of Eastern European Jews who arrived in Canada before World War I. Winnipeg was exploding; in 1886, there were only three Jews in the North End; by 1901, there were 1,100, and by the time Gregor Katznelson arrived, there were 9,000.

Canada was intent on filling up the Prairies. Clifford Sifton, a Manitoban and Prime Minister Wilfrid Laurier's minister of the interior, wanted farmers, hardworking peasants who wouldn't flinch in the face of a Prairie winter or wither under a hot Manitoba summer. Sifton was looking for men and women who would dig in, literally, to the West. And much to the dismay of white-bread Ontario, he went after Eastern Europeans. His ideal immigrant was "a stalwart peasant in a sheep-skin coat, born on the soil, whose forefathers have been farmers for ten generations, with a stout wife and a half-dozen children…." A shovel and a hoe, that was what a man needed to get to Canada. Gregor Katznelson was a classically trained musician, but he had felt the hot breath of the Russian pogroms on the back of his neck. If Canada wanted farmers, he would call himself a farmer. He was also an ambitious man and, it would turn out, somewhat ruthless.

He came from Babruysk, 1,500 kilometers southwest of St. Petersburg. By the late 1800s, when Gregor was born, Babruysk was 60 per cent Jewish. The early waves of pogroms—a uniquely Russian word meaning to wreak havoc or to massacre, usually Jews—had started, and Jews were leaving. "Katznelsons" were big in the Babruysk Zionist community. Berl Katznelson was a labor activist; Avraham Katznelson, born around the same time as Gregor, was a signatory to Israel's Declaration of Independence; his sister Rachel, a leading Zionist in her own right, became the wife of the third president of Israel. Quite how or where Gregor fit in the Katznelson family tree is unclear, but like the better-known Katznelsons, he knew enough to leave Russia.

Gregor had been rigorously trained and educated at the still relatively new St. Petersburg Conservatory. In Czarist Russia, there was a strict 7 per cent quota for Jewish students in all public universities. At the St. Petersburg Conservatory, the best private music school in the country, the joke was that there was a quota on non-Jewish students; Jews made up at least half the student body. Half the music teachers throughout Eastern Europe were Jewish. European Christians looked down on musicians; for Jews, music was a respectable profession, a way to climb the social ladder. Training at the St. Petersburg Conservatory was tough. Teachers were omnipotent and tyrannical. They demeaned students, heaved books across the room, whacked boys across the head.

The first Canadian Trio: Ida, violin;
Gregor Katznelson; Anna, piano;
and Sara (Zara), cello, c. 1928

It was literally the school of hard knocks. Gregor learned well, and having chosen the flute, it was easy to tuck his instrument into his knapsack when, as a self-proclaimed farmer, he got on the boat for Canada.

If the details of Gregor Katznelson's life are vague, those of his wife are all but nonexistent. Her name on the registration of Sara's birth is Bessie Erne—or Earn. Her background was probably German or Swiss, but neither Gregor nor his daughters ever mentioned her publicly. Not once. There is nothing to say if she was a loving or a mean mother, kind or shrewish, begrudging or lavish in her praise—nothing. She would have been hardworking. With four young children and little money, she had no choice. The only other reference to Bessie Erne comes from Sara's schoolfriend Eleanor Warren, who became an influential BBC music producer. "Their mother could only speak Yiddish," Warren said and then went on, as everyone did, to talk about Gregor. "Their father conversed in broken English." Added Warren, "[he] was a tyrant, ambitious for his children and would lock them in their rooms to practice for hours on end." Sara was shaped by her father.

Born at the end of World War I, Sara lived through the 1918 flu epidemic and the Winnipeg General Strike before she was eighteen months old. These were not easy times for immigrants. Gregor, who had immediately dropped the "Katz" and was now Gregor Nelson, played in the orchestra of Winnipeg's newly built Orpheum Theatre, a vaudeville house. He played for the likes of Fanny Brice, W.C. Fields, the Marx brothers, and Jack Benny. Eight times a week it was "Second-Hand Rose" and "I'm Forever Blowing Bubbles." He might throw in an extra trill or some ornamentation to prove that he could still do it, but he could never clear his mind of Mozart or Mussorgsky and what might have been. Every night when the curtain came down, he would put his flute back in its velvet-lined case and head home to the little house on Redwood Street in the North End. Even today, it is still a "little" house, the most meager on the block, just a front door, flanked by two plain windows, sitting nearly on top of the sidewalk.

Gregor had given up any hope of a music career of his own. Instead, he transferred his ambition to his children. He would, he decided, train them as he had been trained, and they would bring him the fame he never found and lift the family out of poverty to boot. That was the dream. He had seen it done back in Russia; he remembered the Cherniavskys, the three little boys who played for the czar and made a career for themselves and their papa. Gregor had three little girls, but he didn't see that as a problem. He had studied with a great many girls at the conservatory in St. Petersburg, where, reportedly, girls—most of them piano students—outnumbered boys almost two to one.

He started Anna, the eldest, on the piano; Ida, the middle daughter, became the violinist; and, by the time she was four, Sara had been handed her first cello. That little house on Redwood Avenue was cold, very cold in the winters. "Nobody had heating, there was a furnace and it would go out in the night," she said years later. On her fourth birthday, Christmas Eve, the temperature did not go above minus thirty-two degrees Celsius.

> My father awakened me one morning very early, about 5:00 am in our bitterly cold home. He shook me by the shoulder and said to me, "I have your cello." I sat on the edge of the bed...the bed clothes had become displaced, and I remember to this day the cold springs of the bed on my poor little bare bottom—and he handed me a viola...that he had turned into a baby cello.

Gregor started her off and then handed her over to the man who sat in front of him in the pit at the Orpheum, another East European refugee, Deszo Mihalek. Back in Hungary, Mihalek had studied with

David Popper, a performer, composer, and the man who, in the nineteenth century, had written the book on teaching young cellists. Before she could read or write, thanks to Clifford Sifton and his push to open up the Prairies with immigrants, Sara Nelson was getting a very solid technical grounding in the cello.

✦✦✦

> He would make me sit with him with his flute and we would start to practice long bows and he would practice his long tones and we would see who could hold the note the longest. This would go on every single morning for about fifteen or twenty minutes until I was about twelve.

Long bow exercises were long, drawn out torture, equivalent to a slow bicycle race. It took every ounce of strength to hold her position. Her arm would tremble as she drew the bow as slowly as she could across the strings. "And that was how I developed the control of my sound. He taught me discipline," she said. Then she paused and, in the cold light of the twenty-first century, added, "Today you would call it child abuse."

The girls were two years apart: four, six, and eight. Very quickly their father had them playing together and turned them into the "Canadian Trio." He put them on the road, and this Canadian Trio appeared all over Canada, at least as "all over" Canada as they could reach in the 1920s. Not often, but Sara did push back and pushed back hard. One winter's day, her schoolfriends asked her to go skating with them. When her father said no, she attacked her sheet music with a safety pin, stabbing it with such savagery that it became unreadable. Little Sara had a temper.

In 1926, when she was eight, he entered the girls in the Manitoba Music Festival. They tripped onstage in their patent leather Mary Janes. Someone in the community—Winnipeg had a huge garment trade—had run up three little dresses carefully designed with lots of room in the shoulders. The girls were prodigies, musically impressive, and undoubtedly "cute," and they knew right from the beginning that looking good was a big part of making a career. Child stars were big in the twenties and thirties. There was a particular appetite for fluffy little girls. Shirley Temple, the epitome of cute and precocious, was about to burst onto the silver screen. In 1934, the Dionne quintuplets were born in Northern Ontario, and thousands bought tickets just to look at them. Nearly 10 per cent of American children were out working, supporting their families in one way or another. There was nothing unique about Gregor Nelson's exploitation of his daughters.

The adjudicators of the Manitoba Music Festival, specially imported from England, were enraptured. The Canadian Trio was judged "best group" and Sara "best soloist." "Send them to London," said the chief adjudicator. "They will find the teachers they need and be exposed to the good music. Winnipeg is the wrong place for these girls." The Manitoba Department of Education gave them all music scholarships, and the people of Winnipeg raised the equivalent of $50,000, enough to send all six of them—by now, they had a baby brother—to England. Sara Nelson would more or less live out of a suitcase for the next twenty years. That little Winnipeg house on Redwood Avenue was the closest she came to a home for a very long time.

Sara Nelson,
aka Zara Nelsova, 1928

The trio was good, but the spotlight was on Sara. She was the most precocious, the real prodigy. The concertgoing public has always been enthralled by the six-year-old in a bow tie who can toss off a sonata or the little girl in a pink dress, waist-high to the

Ida Haendel, aged 9? Her age was always disputed

conductor, fearlessly blazing through virtuosic violin works. Prodigies carry a heavy burden. Ida Haendel, a contemporary of Nelsova and, like Nelsova, another Eastern European, also had both talent and a pushy father. Haendel's father was denied a chance to be a violinist by his rabbi father, and he, like Gregor Nelson, invested all his disappointment in his daughter. Ida Haendel was five when she won her first international violin competition, seven when she blew towering virtuosos out of the water. Decades later, when she was an angry old lady, Haendel said with some wistfulness, "I was never a child."

Yes, there was regret, but both Haendel and Nelsova knew they could never have done what they did, had the careers that they did, found reward in music, if they had not started early and skipped over childhood. There is no way around it. Malcolm Gladwell, the pop culture philosopher, said that "ten thousand hours is the magic number of greatness": it takes ten thousand hours of practice in any discipline to be one of the elite, to be "great." Prodigies like Haendel and Nelsova had put in close to twenty thousand hours before they were ten years old.

To be shut up in a room with only an instrument for company for hours every day goes with the territory for musical prodigies. It is not a recipe for "normalcy." More often than not, there is also a pushy parent or a pushy teacher. But a prodigious talent and thousands of hours of practice does not guarantee musical insight or vision, and even when there is talent, discipline, *and* vision, it can all go very wrong. Not many child prodigies transition safely to adulthood. All too often, there is despair and disappointment, bitterness, breakdowns. More than one child prodigy has taken their own life.

The child who became Zara Nelsova was nine when she and her family sailed for England in 1927. She fared remarkably well.

✦✦✦

*When we first arrived [in London] we were terribly poor…there were four children and we lived together in two rooms, no carpets, no electricity. I didn't go to school. My father was so determined that practicing should not stop. I practiced with my violinist sister in one corner and I in another for six hours a day with five-minute breaks at the end of each hour. As you might guess…I developed intense powers of concentration. It was…very, very difficult for a small child.*

The little girls put in their hours day after day. The intertwined sounds of violin and cello floated out of the open windows and across the London street. Their neighbor, Alfred Kalisch, could set his clock by them. Kalisch was a musician, a critic, and a librettist; he had good ears. He could hear that they played very well and could see that they were living very badly.

He turned to his sister. Constance Hoster ran "Mrs. Hoster's Secretarial Training for Gentlewomen." She was also secretary for the Society for Promoting the Employment of Women and vice president of the Society of Women Journalists, and this was the key, she sat on an ad hoc committee of powerful women intent on helping needy musicians. There was Lady Battersea, born Constance de Rothschild, founder of the Jewish Association for the Protection of Girls and Women that was credited with bridging the gap between the very Christian English women's movement and Jewish women. Then there was Edith Debenham, a painter who had the Debenhams department store family fortune behind her; Audrey Melville, a wealthy amateur cellist; and another Canadian, Mina Benson Hubbard Ellis, "the woman who mapped Labrador," who by now had married into money and was very much a woman about town. "The committee" moved fast—they set up a stipend for the Nelsons, found them a house and music teachers, and enrolled the girls in a "good" school, although how often the Nelsons showed up is another question. The Canadian Trio was invited to play at Mina Benson Hubbard Ellis's house more than once, and it was Mina's cello-playing sister-in-law (and noted activist) Edith Ellis who gave Sara a long-term loan of her cello.

It was the beginning of decades of women's networks, often informal, that helped first the child Sara Nelson, then the woman Zara Nelsova, stay afloat. Time and time again, there was unstated recognition that here was a woman of exceptional ability with something to give to the world, and one woman to another, they would get behind her.

Her father, whose reach always seemed to exceed his grasp, wanted to get Sara into the Royal Academy of Music. But the Royal Academy did not take anyone under ten. Ida Haendel said her father would lie about her age to the child-protection police, adding a year or two in order to get his daughter onstage in front of the public and then immediately subtracting a year or two to hype the publicity. Instead of the Royal Academy, nine-year-old Sara Nelson was taken by the London Cello School, where she met another little girl, Eleanor Warren. Warren said seventy years later that right from the start, the little Canadian had a sense of humor and friendliness that stood her in good stead for the rest of her life. "If she hadn't been a great cellist, she would have been a great clown," she said. Another student, Milly Stanfield, told the story of the day when a girl who, coincidentally, had been on the same ship as the Nelsons from Canada, rushed into the room as Sara was playing and cried out, "She's a genius." Clearly, Papa Katznelson had continued to put the girls through their paces onboard ship.

Even at that age, according to Warren, Sara had "fingers of steel that were flexible and able to stretch," fingers that could hammer nails, a huge advantage for a cellist. The Trio debuted at Wigmore Hall, the most prestigious London venue in the 1928–29 season, and in 1930, when she was twelve, Sara appeared as a soloist with the London Symphony Orchestra under English conductor Malcolm Sargent. It was a well-engineered beginning. Sargent, not a big fan of prodigies, was impressed. The other sisters contented themselves with the Trio while Sara was paraded around town and "made" to play for any visiting musician of influence, including Pablo Casals, the "greatest man to draw bow across strings" and reigning God of the cello. From the day she arrived in London, Sara understood that she was in

London to learn about music. But what no one had anticipated was that as she became a teenager, she also began to learn what it meant to be a woman and play the cello in public; to be a performer. The cello, the instrument, brought its own set of problems for a woman.

Singers were the stars. Divas were goddesses worshipped by audiences, by poets, even by royalty. Emma Albani, born Marie-Louise-Cécile-Emma Lajeunesse in Chambly, Quebec, Canada's first international star, was a favorite of Queen Victoria, who from time to time would ask Albani to sing for her at Windsor Castle. Singers were also among the wealthiest women in the world. A woman who played an instrument was a different story, and a woman who played the cello, squeezed it to her chest and opened her thighs and straddled her instrument, was almost beyond the pale. The mere sight would, wrote one German commentator, "give people immoral ideas." The only thing more provocative was the sight of a woman's mouth around a clarinet.

+++

*Madam, you have between your legs an instrument capable of giving pleasure to thousands and all you can do is scratch it.*

—Thomas Beecham, 1932

Sir Thomas Beecham
in rehearsal, 1948

Conductor Thomas Beecham, the story goes, was dissatisfied with his soloist, Beatrice Harrison, a well-respected and wellborn English cellist. He spat out that one-liner during a rehearsal in the hearing of the full orchestra. She was devastated and never lived it down; he dined out on it.

The piano, according to nineteenth-century composer (and pastor) Carl Ludwig Junker was "the best suited instrument for a woman's body. They may sit in graceful and feminine positions with their legs together and show off in fashionable clothing." Well into the twentieth century, women of any social position were expected to be musical, to play the piano. It was a social grace. And if they did not choose the piano, young women were directed to instruments with a gentler, higher sound, a sound best suited to a woman's mild and prudent temperament. The lute or the harp, instruments played by angels, were appropriate. But Sara had drawn the cello in the family's musical lottery. Its "masculine" sound, its depth, its sonorous quality, its strength were what she loved best. There were next to no women, apart from Beatrice Harrison, with anything close to a career as a cellist—with one notable exception.

In 1923, English artist Augustus John unveiled what was considered one of his finest paintings, nearly two meters high and more than a meter and a half wide, his portrait of the flamboyant Portuguese cellist Guilhermina Suggia. The painting hangs in London's Tate gallery today, and it is every bit as big and bold as the woman herself. When the Nelsons arrived in England, "La Suggia" was not just at the height of a brilliant career; she was infamous. Like Nelsova, Suggia began playing in her hometown—Suggia was from Porto—when she was a child. At thirteen, she was studying with Pablo Casals, who at that time was living in Spain. Still a young girl, she would go to Spain for weeks at a time, and he came to Portugal. Eyebrows were raised, although Casals was notoriously straightlaced. Casals moved to Paris, and in 1906, she followed him. This was Paris at the height of la Belle Époque, Paris, the world capital of art, dazzling Paris. Suggia continued to study with him, and now—she was almost twenty—they did become lovers. Soon they were performing together and regarded almost as musical

Pablo Casals, reigning God of the cello, 1917

equals. Suggia was independent, unconventional, and unapologetically focused on her career. "I study every day," she wrote, "and I will study to learn all that remains to learn." She and Casals were both strong and controlling. As a partnership, it was doomed. Six years after she moved in, Suggia moved out—her decision—crossed the Channel, and settled in England. Neither she nor Casals spoke publicly about their relationship.

Suggia, despite the liaison, was accepted in every drawing room in the country. She performed regularly in London throughout the twenties and thirties—at exactly the same time that the newly arrived Sara was soaking up every bit of music that she could find. There was teenage Sara, breathless with admiration, in the front row at every Suggia concert, listening intently, and most importantly, watching the way this woman cellist presented herself: with dignity, hauteur, and panache. The Augustus John painting shows Suggia in a blood-red satin dress. The neckline is low, her skin pale against her black hair. But what is important are the skirts of that dress. They billow and flow around

Zara in one of her
trademark dresses, 1960s

her, cushioning the cello that seems to float in space, independent of her thighs. Big skirts hid the provocation of her body, an artful solution for a woman cellist.

Suggia's stage dresses both served a purpose and made a statement, and so, when she grew up, did Zara's. Nelsova's big-skirted stage dresses of organza, brocade, velvet—rich fabrics that, like Suggia's red satin portrait dress, shone and moved as she moved. Those costumes became her trademark.

Augustus John was a man with many mistresses. He fathered thirteen or fourteen children by at least five women, one of whom was socialite Eve Fleming. In 1925, she had a daughter, Amaryllis, by John, a little sister to her four sons from her marriage. Amaryllis Fleming grew up to be a well-known English cellist. Her big brother Ian became an even better-known writer. In the early 1960s, when Zara was stepping onstage in Berlin, Ian Fleming published one of his last James Bond stories, *The Living Daylights*. The Bond girl this time is a KGB sniper, threatening, deadly, and beautiful. She is also a leg-spreading, instrument-straddling cellist. He had created a Bond girl who, as he wrote, was almost too outrageous, too exciting.

> There was something almost indecent in the idea of that bulbous, ungainly instrument between her splayed thighs. Of course, Suggia had managed to look elegant, and so did that girl Amaryllis somebody. But they should invent a way for women to play the damned thing sidesaddle.

"They" had invented a way for women to play sidesaddle. There were instruction manuals, and for decades, women had twisted themselves in knots to avoid straddling the cello. The unfortunate Beatrice Harrison, object of Thomas Beecham's scorn, was photographed playing sidesaddle, as Fleming must have known in a recording session as late as 1936. Young Sara Nelson escaped cello sidesaddle by only a few years. As a teenager growing into womanhood in London, she must have felt the penetrating male stares when she sat onstage with that "bulbous, ungainly instrument between her splayed thighs."

Gregor Nelson continued to stake his future on his daughters success. He booked the Trio all over England throughout the early 1930s. There he was, a small dapper man in his little round glasses, neatly turned out in his well-pressed suit, with them at every concert. Then, in 1935, at the height of the Depression, he went too far. Against the advice of all their teachers, he booked the Canadian Trio on an international tour that took them to North Africa, South Africa, and, it felt like, every small town in Australia. Anna was twenty, Ida eighteen, and Sara sixteen. Bessie and their little brother stayed in London, and the three girls and Gregor Nelson set sail from Southampton. They would be on the road for the next eighteen months. It would be a year and a half of stuffing concert dresses into steamer trunks, eating when they could, sleeping where they could, dealing with instruments that rebelled against the climate, with concert promoters who didn't pay, with illness. Three very young women in the care of one physically unprepossessing man. When they arrived back in England, they were exhausted, demoralized, and sick. Anna, the oldest, had contracted

Beatrice Harrison playing her cello sidesaddle, 1936

tuberculosis and recovered only to succumb a second time; Ida, always the most fragile, came back with, in Zara's words, "mental problems." Eleanor Warren, who spent time with them when they returned, simply said, "They all suffered from the experience." Suffered severely.

That was the moment that Gregor Nelson, ever more manager than father, announced that he was disbanding the Canadian Trio and moving on. *He* was moving on. Their father, who had managed their every move, was taking his wife and son and moving to Australia, leaving the girls to make a living as best they could. The girls were slack-jawed. All they could do was watch as their father packed up his wife and his son and got back on the boat. Anna, Ida, and Sara never saw their parents again. "They were sure we would be alright," Zara said weakly.

Anna had had enough of a musician's life. She regained her health, met a young American man named Gold, and married him. Mr. and Mrs. Gold left for California, where they joined the cult of the Russian mystic Gurdjieff. That left Sara, barely out of her teens, and Ida, the mentally ill middle sister, alone in London. Once again, friends saw them through. Constance Hoster, who had helped the family when they arrived in London in the 1920s, died not long after the senior Katznelsons left England, but her help stretched from beyond the grave. She left Sara enough money to pay for the transatlantic passage for both sisters back to Canada. Sara moved fast. Constance Hoster died in June; they left for Canada by September.

It was 1939. Although never an observant Jew, Sara had Jewish friends in the music world. They, in turn, had family and friends in Europe who wrote to them about growing anti-Semitism. Kindertransports, bringing thousands of Jewish children from Germany, were arriving in Britain. Oswald Mosley's Blackshirts were marching in London. In 1938, the year of Kristallnacht in Germany and Austria, Milly Stanfield, who had been at the cello school with Sara, wrote a letter to her cousin Otto Frank in the Netherlands, offering to take his daughters Margot and Anne Frank if he could get them to London. As history showed, Otto Frank never took up his cousin's offer. Zara knew that this was not a good time to be a young Jewish woman in Britain.

It was August of 1939, and she wanted to get back to Canada as quickly as she could. Much to her annoyance, she found out that the SS *Athenia*, the next ship leaving for Halifax, was fully booked, and had to settle for the RMS *Duchess of Atholl* leaving two weeks later. On September 3, 1939, Britain declared war on Germany. That same day, the *Athenia* was torpedoed by German U-boats and went down with a loss of all onboard. With a combination relief that there had been no room for them on the *Athenia* and apprehension over what was coming next, Sara and her sister boarded the *Duchess of Atholl* and set sail for Canada.

♦♦♦

*I had no experience of handling anything on my own. I knew we had to get back to Canada. I felt I wanted to get back. I had to find what it was like to stand on my own two feet. I had no career, I had nothing.*

The crossing had been rough, and now "Zara Nelsova," a new name for a new beginning as Sara Nelson had been ditched mid-Atlantic, held her coat tight against the cold and stood on the Halifax dock, listening to the seagulls and smelling the Atlantic. Her sister Ida was with her, her cello was beside her, their luggage stacked behind them. Rain had teemed down in Halifax the day before, and the two young women picked their way between the deep puddles. As she stood shivering and waiting for the train for Winnipeg, she knew this was the beginning of a very different life. For her first nineteen years, her father had driven her hard, but at the same time, she was feted and celebrated by everyone who met her. Her father pushed her and protected her. Gregor Katznelson had scarcely let his daughters out of his sight. He looked after the bookings, he looked after the money, and now he was God knows where, but he was not with her on the dock in Halifax.

All Zara really knew was music. She did not have much idea of the ways of the world and there was not much money in her purse. The only way she knew to make money was with her cello. The new name "Zara Nelsova," she thought, might help. It had an exotic ring to it, and a young performer needed all the attention she could get.

The train pulled up to the Halifax dock, their luggage, everything they owned in the world, was loaded on, and they were off on the four-day trip to Winnipeg. Their new life had begun. There is a photograph of Gregor and Zara taken on that ill-fated international tour, walking together along a seaside promenade. He, in his three-piece double-breasted suit and a Panama hat, has a half-smile and looks tired. Zara is wearing a pair of striped dungarees, grinning straight into the camera. She never had any problem facing the world.

When they got off the train at Union Station in Winnipeg, old friends and some of her mother's family were waiting for them under the rotunda. They were warm and welcoming, exactly what both young women wanted and needed, but Winnipeg in 1939 was not the place to launch a classical music career. They stayed six weeks. Zara had just enough of Constance Hoster's money left for the train fare to Toronto. They arrived on December 23, 1939, the day before her twenty-first birthday.

✦✦✦

*I didn't know where to go so I went to YWCA on Elm Street. I'll never forget those lovely people who, if I had a little concert, they would advance the fare for the train in that Y…so I could go and do it.*

There were small concerts with small fees in small towns, and she and her sister got by. They lived at the Y, an age-old refuge for young women on their own in a new city. They were there through the winter of 1940 and the spring of 1941 while Zara got herself back into shape musically. She practiced her long bows as her father had taught her, practiced scales, practiced exercises, kept up her technique. The staff at the Y had rules: "They said to me. You know it's not possible for you to practice in your bedroom. You could go and practice in the boiler room, and every morning I would go downstairs. It was warm, April or May, and I would practice with the window open."

Exactly as she had done in London as a child, she opened the window and let the sound float free. One day, she felt that she was being watched. "Suddenly I saw five pairs of eyes looking down at me from the boiler room window. They were musicians from the CBC orchestra, and they began introducing me to people." As Venus had arisen from the sea, Zara Nelsova arose from the boiler room of the Elm Street Y.

It was the beginning of what she called her second career. Sir Ernest MacMillan, conductor of the Toronto Symphony, made her principal cello of the orchestra. She had never played in an orchestra before. Perhaps with the wisdom of hindsight, Nelsova declared, "No soloist is ready to take his or her place as a soloist until they know what it is like to play in the orchestra." And she was enjoying herself. "I remember going out to Max Yeats' place [Yeats was a friend of the symphony], he was such a lovely man. We all went there, me, Ida, Sir Ernest and his wife, and we stayed overnight and ate fresh asparagus from his garden. It was a lovely time." The orchestra gave her two things she had never known: a regular, if small, income (in 1925–26, the honorarium for orchestra members was $14 a concert, and it had not gone up much if at all in the 1930s) and a boyfriend. Philip Spivak was her stand partner, the man who sat next to her in the orchestra, and she married him. She was twenty-two and perhaps looking for a little male protection, which she rapidly decided she did not need. "It was a disaster." When she told Sir Ernest, "I'm leaving Philip," he said, "I can't say I'm surprised." No one could imagine Zara settling down.

For the first time, she played chamber music with musicians other than her sisters, and she played new repertoire, including Canadian music. In 1942, she made her recital debut in New York; it was the concert that launched her in North America. European conductors, escaping Nazi Germany and relocating to the United States, were looking for new performers. They noticed Zara Nelsova. On the strength of a radio broadcast of a concert with the Toronto Symphony, she was hired by conductor Leopold Stokowski, who had come from England to North America earlier, for a summer tour. Solo dates were coming thick and fast; she left the Toronto Symphony after two seasons, a fully fledged soloist. There she was in her red or green or royal blue gown with those big skirts—the dresses were proliferating—the only woman in front of a sea of men in black suits.

In the forties, there were already a few women in the Toronto Symphony. Canadian orchestras were ahead of the Americans in hiring women, but then Canadian orchestras paid less, and the men were at war; they had to settle for women. The New York Philharmonic, a better-paying orchestra, did not hire its first woman until 1966. In London, the Queen's Hall Orchestra in London raised eyebrows when its conductor Sir Henry Wood hired six violinists in 1913. "I do not like ladies playing the trombone or the double bass," said Wood, "but they can play the violin...." It was often about the instrument. The BBC orchestra explicitly forbade women cellists. The older the orchestra, the longer it took to include women.

Many of the European orchestras could not, would not, break with tradition. When Zara took her bows in her sparkly lavender gown in front of the Berlin Philharmonic in 1962, there were only men behind her onstage. It was two more *decades* before Berlin admitted a woman. One Vienna Philharmonic violinist said with conviction that "ethnic and gender uniformity gave the orchestra a better sound." The Vienna Philharmonic admitted its first woman into the orchestra in 1997. She had been playing with the orchestra for twenty years, but her name had never been included in the program. Symphony orchestras were fiercely misogynistic, and so were many of their conductors. When he was conductor of the Los Angeles Symphony in the 1970s, Zubin Mehta was unequivocal. "I just don't think women should be in an orchestra. They become men. Men treat them as equals; they even change their pants in front of them. I think it's terrible."

There were women's orchestras going back to 1898—Montreal had a Women's Symphony led by Ethel Stark. Nelsova was supportive, and she appeared with them as a soloist, but women's orchestras by definition were segregated institutions, second-best, and Nelsova wanted to play in the big leagues.

In the 1940s and still in her twenties, it didn't occur to her that being a woman was a barrier to her career—at least a barrier that she couldn't vault. "No, in fact never in my entire life have I ever felt that being female stood in my way," she said forty years later. Not that she didn't notice that it was "different" for a woman. She gave audience talks—very funny talks—about the problems of the female cellist, but Nelsova was never intimidated.

♦♦♦

In the stories Zara Nelsova told about her career, good fortune always seemed to magically shine upon her. All she had to do was open a window, let the music float across the street in London or up from the boiler room in Toronto, and opportunity materialized. It was magic. There was nothing magical about it. Nothing would have happened without her talent and the hours of practice, but it took more. Zara was never backward about coming forward.

When she was still living in Toronto, she realized that she needed to learn from the masters. One of those masters was Gregor Piatigorsky, a great bear of a man and another Russian, known for his dramatic intensity. Piatigorsky had escaped Europe and was teaching in Philadelphia. When he visited Toronto, Nelsova "got up the nerve" and asked him if he would listen to her play. "I'm sorry," he said, "but I'm leaving first thing in the morning." She ambushed her quarry. "I got myself up around five in the morning…and I went to his hotel room and knocked at the door. He opened the door, absolutely astonished to see me. I said, 'Oh, Mr. Piatigorsky, I just happened to be passing by, and I hoped that you might be able to hear me.'" She could be remarkably disingenuous. "He invited me in and I played for him…. It worked. I studied three summers with him, going through the repertoire, concerto after concerto."

She did it again with conductor William Steinberg. Steinberg was co-founder of the Palestine Symphony Orchestra, what became the Israel Philharmonic, and in the early forties was living in New York. Nelsova went backstage after a rehearsal, plunked her cello down in front of him, and just started to play. He hired her as a soloist year after year when he took over the Pittsburgh Symphony. Zara Nelsova made her own luck. She was charming and forthright, and, not to put too fine a point on it, she hustled her way forward. Along the way, she formed fast friendships and gave back to those friends.

In the early years of World War II, when Nelsova was principal cello with the Toronto Symphony, a young German cellist, Charlotte

Lotte Brott
(Charlotte Goetzel),
1940s

Goetzel, was finding her way in Montreal. Charlotte grew up in Mannheim, where her father, Walter Goetzel, ran an import-export spice business. One day, when she was a young teenager feeling happy and confident in a brand-new dress, she stepped onstage for her school recital. Her way was blocked, and she was told, "Go back. There are people in the hall who do not want any Jews onstage." That was how Charlotte Goetzel discovered that she was a Jew, that she was different. Walter Goetzel sent his wife and his daughters to Switzerland not long after, for the girls to "continue their music studies," then he went north to Hamburg, got on a ship, and embarked on a "business trip." He never went back. Once the Goetzels reunited in Montreal, they began looking for a teacher for Charlotte. There was Zara Nelsova, another Jewish woman just three years older than their daughter, playing in the Toronto Symphony. Charlotte moved to Toronto, worked in Eaton's bargain basement, and forged a fast friendship with her new teacher. Two years later she went back to Montreal, married a young composer-conductor named Alex, and became Lotte Brott, a force of nature in Canadian music. More than twenty years after they met, Lotte Brott phoned Zara and asked her to help her son Denis, then a good twelve-year-old cellist, get to the Aspen Music Festival and School in Colorado, where Zara was teaching. Of course she would help, but there would be no special treatment. Denis, his heart in his mouth (he says today that twelve was far too young), flew to Colorado with Zara. At the airport in Denver, she said hello to her driver and climbed into the very comfortable car the Festival had sent for the six-hour drive through the mountains to Aspen. At the same time, she very firmly pointed twelve-year-old Denis toward the bus. No student got an easy ride with Zara. "They have to be so strong. They can't take every little discouragement or setback as something that destroys them," she would say. "I could never have gone through my career if I wasn't aware of that. I would have folded a long time ago." She had, however, quietly arranged for another woman to "keep an eye on" young Denis Brott.

Sixty years later, Brott remembers Nelsova arriving for lessons at Aspen, impeccably dressed with her tan purse and matching Ferragamo shoes. And he remembers the heavy calluses on her fingers that in the dry air of the mountains would split and bleed.

✦✦✦

In the early fifties, her performing career really took off. She did a monthlong tour of Israel, appeared in Norway, played chamber music with Glenn Gould in Stratford—Gould was difficult. She played up to a staggering eighty concerts a year. Composers sought her out. Ernest Bloch called her "Madame Schelomo." His "Schelomo" became her signature piece. When he came to America, Bloch, who was Swiss, settled in Agate Beach, Oregon, a very small town on the Pacific coast. Nelsova wanted to work through the music with him before a performance, and in the summer of 1949, she and her cello got on the bus in Portland. It was late at night when the driver called out "Agate Beach." The rain was coming down hard as she got off the bus, peered into the

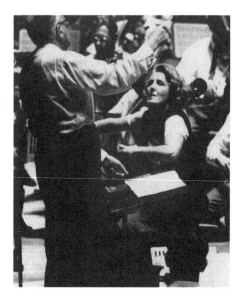

Zara Nelsova performing
Sir William Walton's Cello Concerto
with Walton conducting, 1958

dark, and saw a little man standing by himself in the dark, holding an umbrella. Bloch and his wife put her up in a flat over his garage. She would practice upstairs, and he would put on his hip waders and go down to the beach to search for agates. After a couple of hours, she would hear him come back and start to polish his stones downstairs in the garage, listening all the while. When something he didn't like caught his ear, he would stomp up the stairs, sit at the piano, still in his hip waders, and show her what he wanted. Nelsova convinced Bloch to write three pieces on Hebraic themes for solo cello, which he dedicated to her.

Throughout the fifties, she regularly debuted music—always more work for a performer than playing familiar repertoire; gave solo cello recitals—rare at the time; and became known as not only a top performer but also an intelligent, serious musician, a combination almost unheard of, or acknowledged in, a woman. But what she did not have was the instrument that she wanted—a Strad. There are more than five hundred Stradivarius violins in the world, but only sixty Strad cellos.

After World War II, she moved back to England and picked up

old friendships. One of her best friends was Audrey Mainville, another of the women who had subsidized the Nelson family in the 1920s. Mainville was an amateur cellist, and she understood instruments. She owned a Stradivarius. Years earlier, Guilhermina Suggia had been given a Strad as an engagement present. She broke off the engagement but she kept the instrument. Suggia, who had returned to Portugal for the war, was back in London. Mainville invited both women to tea.

A sharp-eyed maid bringing in hot water to refresh the pot that day—tea was still rationed in postwar England—would have seen something out of the ordinary. There were three fashionably dressed women holding translucent cups and spreading jam on their scones. Their shoes were of soft leather, their tea party dresses in all likelihood were trimmed with lace, their jewelry was delicate, but their fingers.... As she poured the hot water into the teapot, had the young maid looked closely at Mrs. Mainville's guests their fingers would have caught her eye, the fingers on their left hands. For each of them, those fingers were gnarled and callused—those calluses that were as thick and hard as if they were on the pickaxe-wielding workmen repairing the streets of bomb-damaged London.

Audrey Mainville, Suggia, and Zara talked cello, and they got on well. Suggia invited Nelsova to come to Portugal and play in Porto and Lisbon. But during that London visit, Suggia was diagnosed with cancer, and Nelsova arrived in Portugal a few days after she died. The memorial concert for La Suggia took place in London in 1950. The Augustus John portrait hung in the entrance to the concert hall. Onstage, the soloist's chair sat empty. The cello solos came from within the orchestra. They were played by the young Zara Nelsova.

Not long after, Suggia's Strad was sold for £8,000, and the proceeds funded a scholarship in her name. Nelsova still did not have her Strad, and the more her career grew, the more Nelsova wanted a Stradivarius. Years earlier, Audrey Mainville had willed her Stradivarius to the Royal Academy of Music to be lent to promising young students. Unbeknownst to Zara, on April 15, 1953, Mainville wrote a letter that was not to be opened until after her death. It was seven years later when her executors opened the letter and gave it to Zara:

Dear Zara,

I have for some time been thinking a great deal about what is to happen to my cello after my death. Ever since we made friends I have felt I would like you to have it. I know if you get to know it you would love it as much as I do, so Zara I HAVE DECIDED TO LEAVE IT TO YOU for your life or as long as you are able to play.

Goodbye, Audrey.

Zara Nelsova had that cello for forty-two years. In the final weeks of her life, she would get up in the night, say, "I'm going on tour," and, still in her nightgown, pick up her Strad.

✦✦✦

Nelsova unconsciously modeled herself on Suggia in many ways, but not every way. Suggia had legions of lovers. Zara did not. Or if she did, she was remarkably discreet. There were stories that she told—like the night the German conductor Wilhelm Furtwängler, then leading the Berlin Philharmonic, looked her up and down, figuratively twirling his mustachios, and said she looked very "healthy"—"I was wearing a tight sweater at the time," she said—and invited her to cook him dinner. "It was moving a little too fast." She had been up to her old tricks and put herself in his way, musically speaking, and taken her cello to a dinner party. Before the plates were cleared, she had set herself up at the end of the dining room and started playing. What she wanted was an invitation to play with the Berlin Philharmonic, and she got it. She debuted with the Berlin Philharmonic in 1958, four years after Furtwängler died.

In 1963, when she was forty-four, Zara Nelsova married again, this time to Grant Johannesen, a highly respected American pianist well known for his finesse. They were both teaching at Aspen when he proposed, and within four weeks, they were married. They were

Pianist Grant Johannesen

well-matched musically, but for Johannesen it was a marriage of convenience. Rumors were thick on the ground that he was gay. His wife had been killed in a car accident and he had a son by his first marriage, but his closest companion in those years was Steinway piano executive David Rubin. Rubin had also married quickly. Homosexuality was not decriminalized federally in America until 2003, the year that Rubin died. Marriage deflected curiosity.

Somehow, Nelsova missed all the signals, or she chose to ignore them. Their shared musical sensibilities were important; at the same time, they were competitive. When they appeared together, Zara, in her gowns, was glamorous. He was just a man in a suit. Cellists often play on a low podium to add resonance to the sound. That meant she sat taller than him onstage and Johannesen felt that he came across as an accompanist, not a partner. He was not happy. Grant Johannesen has been described as a "deeply cultured individual who happened to play the piano." He and Rubin would talk poetry and literature for hours. Zara, who did not go to school past the age of twelve, had great gaps in her education. Music she knew, but she couldn't tell you what Goethe meant to Schubert or which poets were favored by Faure. "They ridiculed her," her former daughter-in-law Julia Bedford said, "particularly Rubin." (Julia Bedford had been married to Johannesen's son, David, and remained close to Zara.) In his obituary, the *New York Times* wrote about Rubin's elitism. He was known as an intellectual snob and blamed Zara for any downturn in Johannesen's career. The most unconventional marriages work when there is honesty and mutual respect. Nelsova and Johannesen made recordings together, they toured South Africa together, played at the White House. But things were best between them when they were

Jacqueline du Pré

each on tour alone, thousands of kilometers away from each other for three or four months at a time. After ten years, the marriage didn't just end; it blew up. She came home from tour in 1973 and found Johannesen calmly moving furniture out of their New York apartment; she countered by not so calmly moving furniture out of their farmhouse in the Berkshires.

A lifetime later, Julia Bedford, reflecting on her former mother-in-law, said there were two Zaras. There was the public Zara—restrained, well-spoken, good with the press—and then there was the less public, earthy Zara, who bonded with Ernest Bloch over dirty Jewish stories, had long raucous conversations with Raya Garbousova, another Russian cellist, and, still in her concert gown, piled into her Vancouver friend Judy Fraser's Volkswagen Beetle after a concert with her skirts trailing out the door, laughing all the while. The ascetic, refined Johannesen was no match for this Nelsova. He had duped her, made a fool of her, and she was furious. After the marriage ended, unbeknownst to concert audiences, she would wear a pair of Johannesen's black socks under her concert gowns, "so I can walk all over him."

Christmas Eve, 1966, London. The young Argentinian Israeli pianist Daniel Barenboim went to a party and met a girl. They laughed, talked, fooled around at the piano, and stayed up very late. Her name was Jacqueline du Pré. She was twenty-one, blonde, willowy, romantic, always smiling, and she played the cello. It was love at first sight. Within six months, Barenboim and du Pré flew to Israel and gave concerts during the Six-Day War. The war ended, the relationship intensified, and du Pré converted to Judaism overnight. They were married at the Western Wall. One of the witnesses was the conductor Zubin Mehta, renamed Moshe for the occasion.

That same year, Zara Nelsova became the first American cellist to tour the Soviet Union. (She had taken out American citizenship a few years earlier.) The Soviets praised her "nobility and temperament…the beautiful and expressive sound." That Soviet tour should have been a career-boosting triumph, but no one was watching Zara; everyone was watching Jacqueline du Pré. The concertgoing public respected Zara Nelsova; they adored du Pré. She was in the first flush of youth, and by then Nelsova was middle-aged. Where Nelsova was passionate but studied, du Pré was instinctive and emotive; where du Pré threw her head back and moved like a wild ballerina, Nelsova's every gesture was restrained. Du Pré's hair flowed loosely and moved across her shoulders; Nelsova's was sprayed in place. Nelsova's dresses were a shield against lustful gazes; du Pré's clung to her body. Nelsova was experience; du Pré was innocence.

Jacqueline du Pré rocketed to fame and a place in twentieth-century music history. It did not hurt that she had married into the world's most powerful classical music "syndicate." Daniel Barenboim was a protégé of American violinist Isaac Stern, who controlled classical music–making in North America. He could and did make or break careers with a nod. Stern's protégés were stellar musicians—Itzhak Perlman, Pinchas Zukerman, Mehta. Jacqueline du Pré was the first women to become part of that charmed circle. Zara Nelsova was invited to the

Zara Nelsova in concert

parties, greeted as a friend, but she was never part of the club. Nelsova never disputed du Pré's talent, and she was never rancorous. Rather, she cast herself as the wise elder and told anyone who asked that she had been invited to listen to du Pré play when she was still a child. And when du Pré became ill, Nelsova went to see her in England and, always a health food enthusiast, took her a big bag of papayas. Because suddenly, in the early seventies, Jacqueline du Pré was diagnosed with multiple sclerosis and went from blazing star to tragic heroine. Her body began to fail, and very quickly she could no longer pick up her bow, let alone play. But when she had to cancel a concert in Tel Aviv, it was the ever-dependable Zara Nelsova who stepped in. Jacqueline du Pré's career ended when she was twenty-eight. She died fourteen years later. Daniel Barenboim remained married to du Pré but had moved on to a new relationship.

Nelsova continued giving concerts all over the globe into the 1980s, traveling with as many as ten concert dresses and now big-skirted rehearsal dresses in the same style but made out drab brown or gray. The luggage, and there was a lot of it, was part of the image. In 1984, when she had been performing for sixty years, the *Los Angeles Times* talked about the "freshness" of her music-making. But the big recording labels were not asking for her anymore. A brilliant young violinist in a strapless gown was better box office, and Nelsova was not getting the main stage concerts. Men as they aged were talked about as "seasoned," their trembling fingers and creviced faces seen to hold the musical secrets of the ages. The great Polish pianist Mieczysław Horszowski was playing concerts and selling out at ninety-nine. Most women soloists were long retired—English cellist Beatrice Harrison stopped performing publicly at forty-two; Zara's friend Raya Garbousova had married a doctor in DeKalb, Illinois, and restricted herself to teaching. Not Zara. When Ida Haendel discovered in her "old age" that another violinist was being offered the big concerto at an international festival and she was given the dribs and drabs, she let them know what she thought and pulled out of the festival. Not Zara.

In the summers, she taught at Aspen, and in the winters, she gave master classes at the Banff School in Alberta, all the while teaching at the Juilliard School in New York, the top music school in the United States. Juilliard was a couple of kilometers from her apartment at 200 Central Park West, described as one of the finest Art Deco buildings in New York City. No one called her one of the "great teachers." There is no list of famous young cellists who were taught by Nelsova. Her teaching methods became old-fashioned. Nelsova demanded the same

Zara at the Banff school, 1980

long bow exercises that her father had demanded of her, the same exercises. When a student arrived at a lesson, as one did wearing jeans with holes in the knees and untied high-top sneakers, she tore a strip off him and talked about stage deportment. Inevitably, there was some eye-rolling, particularly from young women.

At the same time, Nelsova grew in public estimation for her integrity and her compassion. She sat on a panel of internationally known cellists at a music festival in England and was asked, "When do you tell a student that they are not good enough?" A difficult question. Zara was clear. "It's not the responsibility of the teacher to say this. Their job is to teach, support, and help the student as much as possible. In the end, life will tell them."

✦✦✦

*She was a gutsy player. She played with the force of six men....*

*...the way she attacked the music, it was...masculine.*

Nelsova's colleagues and music writers struggled to find words to describe how she played, what she was as a musician. Olga Samaroff, an American pianist, said that in at least 80 per cent of her reviews, they said that she played like a man. "When they said I played like a woman, it meant that they didn't like me."

In 1930, it was said of Suggia, "She was known for the nobility of her phrasing and 'tone of masculine power seldom heard from a lady cellist.'" It was the same for Nelsova. Feminine language implied weakness, and Nelsova was never weak. Throughout her career, she was praised for her strength, for her tone, for her seamless playing. She played on four continents, built a career that was more varied and lasted as long as any cellist—seventy years—and when she was praised by Mstislav Rostropovich as one of the greatest of women cellists, she pushed the words away. "I hate that 'woman cellist'—a performer is a performer."

It was mid-October 2002. Julia Bedford rattled the hangers along the rail of the cedar closet where Nelsova kept her concert dresses in her New York apartment. Zara had died a few days earlier. Breast cancer. Her scent floated heavily in the room. Had these dresses ever been cleaned? Bedford fingered the dressmaker's double-stitching, the reinforced seams under the arms, and she could hear Zara say once more that she was going shopping for dress fabric on West 37th. Julia had gone with Zara to every chemo and radiation appointment, been in and out of that apartment every day for the past two years. What was Zara to her—her "ex-stepmother-in-law?" No, Zara was her friend. She had helped at the musicians' parties, sat at the dining room table for birthdays and the batches of beet borscht Zara made in the old galley kitchen.

The remnants of the Katznelson family had surfaced when Zara was dying: a nephew, son of the eldest piano-playing sister, and a niece, daughter of the little brother who had washed up in Atlanta. Zara's friend cellist Bernie Greenhouse had called a few days before she died. She told him that she had just gotten off the phone with her dressmaker, making an appointment for the next concert dress. Always the dresses.

The nephew asked, "Would Julia like a dress to remember her by?" She chose three: an old deep-red silk, a gold dress, and something in white, one of her summer dresses. She took them home and stuffed them in the back of her closet, where they stayed for the next twenty years. Now, in her seventies, Julia Bedford started to think about Zara and what to do with those dresses. In 2021, the Manitoba Museum accepted the gift of three concert dresses worn by Zara Nelsova, the woman who grew from the little girl born in the North End of Winnipeg in the cold winter of 1918.

# 3. TRIXIE

*Turbulent Currents in the presence of Waves.*

—Helge Lundgren

Beatrice (Trixie) Helen Worsley was always quiet and solitary. She never in her lifetime lit up a room, but in the fifty years since her death, Trixie Worsley has become all but invisible. She was there at the birth of modern computers almost despite herself—she became the first *person* in the world to earn a PhD from Cambridge in what became computer science, and she knew as much about the development of computers as anyone, but for most of her life she was not interested in putting herself forward, and neither, until very recently was anyone else. Invisible Trixie Worsley.

Right from the beginning, her life was full of contradictions, contrasts, and question marks. She was born in the midst of great drama. Her English father, Joel Worsley, was a working-class man from Manchester, the nineteenth-century hub of the textile industry. He married well, his wife's family owned a textile mill in Mexico, and in 1908, Joel Worsley and his wife were sent across the Atlantic to keep an eye on the family business. And it did need watching. At the time, Mexico was dealing with drought—not good for the cotton harvest—financial crises, and, to put it mildly, political instability: the Mexican

Revolution had just begun. Legendary revolutionary leaders Pancho Villa and Emiliano Zapata, each commanding their own factions, were creating havoc, and the rebel cry of "land and liberty" rang loud. By 1913, Mexico City had become a battle zone. Joel Worsley must have been watching with a worried eye, as well he might, and four years later, rebels destroyed the family textile mill. Joel Worsley changed employers, and the Worsleys moved north to Atemajac, where, in 1920, their son, Charles, was born. They moved again. Beatrice was born the following year in Querétaro, the city known as the birthplace of Mexican independence. Violence continued all around them, and the children were kept close. They were homeschooled and seldom met or played with other children. They had so little contact with Mexicans that they barely spoke Spanish.

Zapata was killed in 1919, Pancho Villa in 1923, and when, five years later, it looked as though calm might finally be restored, the President-Elect General Álvaro Obregón, known as the "peacemaker," was assassinated. The Worsleys had had enough, and in 1929, when Charles was nine and Beatrice seven, Joel Worsley packed up his family and moved north to Toronto—no one knows why he chose Toronto—just in time for the Depression.

Depression or not, there was enough family money to send the children to fee-paying private schools. Charles went to Upper Canada College. Beatrice went to Bishop Strachan School for girls (BSS). By the 1930s, BSS was a well-established school catering to the social elite and intent on training girls for a new kind of future. Anne Thompson, principal in the 1870s, told her "girls," "Remember, you are not going home to be selfish butterflies of fashion. The Bishop Strachan School has been endeavoring to fit you to become useful and courageous women. I believe you will yet see our universities open to women. Work out your freedom, girls! Knowledge is now no more a fountain sealed; drink deep!" (The University of Toronto admitted women in 1884.)

No one had to push Beatrice Worsley to "drink deep" from the fountain of knowledge, and she had no interest in becoming a "selfish butterfly of fashion." Intellectually, she could not be contained. Her

Pancho Villa
and company

headmistress, Margaret Lowe, described Beatrice as "one of the most brilliant pupils at the school ever." She swept the field academically and, in 1939, graduated from BSS and moved on to the University of Toronto (U of T); by second year, she was firmly committed to mathematics and physics.

In the late 1930s, *The Varsity*, the U of T student newspaper, was running articles about football games and golf tournaments, and as a concession to the growing number of young women on campus, a column headed "The Sportswoman." One week, it was all about "preppy coeds at Western who demanded instruction in the science of watching a football game." None of that worked for Trixie. In her first year, she was a wide-eyed eighteen-year-old, curious but never much of a sports fan, never really a joiner of any sort. When she read *The Varsity*, she paid a little more attention to advertisements for Bert Niosi, "Canada's King of Swing," and his band and for classical concerts. Zara Nelsova had arrived in Toronto that same year, and Trixie may well have gone to the occasional recital, but she was genuinely more interested in physics and mathematics, her subjects.

*The Varsity* did run a story in 1938 on thirty-five newly appointed professors, all of them men, the star being physicist Leopold Infeld, a Polish Jew who had collaborated with Einstein at Princeton. Einstein had presented his theory of relativity in 1915, and in the late 1930s, not only was physics, particularly relativity, an important discipline, but people were interested in physics. Infeld made headlines. He was certainly a star in Trixie's world. But she was far more likely to have met and talked to Cecilia Krieger, a Polish woman who taught both physics and math to undergraduates. Krieger, in 1930, became the first woman in Canada to earn a PhD in mathematics. Her dissertation was dauntingly titled "On the Summability of Trigonometric Series with Localized Properties—On Fourier Constant and Convergence Factors of Double Fourier Series." Trixie would have known what that meant, even in her early university years. Cecilia Krieger, with her accent and broad smile, gave Sunday afternoon teas for students. There were cakes, good conversation, and even a little matchmaking. Did Trixie bite into one of Cecilia Krieger's pastries and lick the whipped cream from her fingers? They would have been good pastries in the Central European tradition. Did she plunge into the conversation bubbling around her? Probably not. As a young woman, Beatrice Worsley was shy, self-contained, and took pleasure in her own company. It does not seem that she had much of a social life. Hobbies, piano and photography. Nothing that involved other people.

Philosopher's Walk is a lovely, heavily treed, quiet pathway that runs north through the university alongside Trinity College, Trixie's college. She must have wandered down Philosopher's Walk sometimes in the company of another young math student, Cathleen Synge, later Cathleen Morawetz. Synge was a year younger than Trixie, and she came from a family of mathematicians. Her father, John Synge, nephew of the great Irish playwright John Millington Synge, was internationally respected. Cathleen Morawetz went on to become a full professor at New York University, president of the American Mathematical Society, and the first woman mathematician to be awarded the American National Medal of Science. In 1997, more than half a century after she and Trixie were undergraduates together, Cathleen Morawetz came back to Canada to receive the Krieger-Nelson Prize for women in mathematics. In her acceptance speech, first she credited Cecilia Krieger with giving her the encouragement she needed to stay in mathematics, and then she took the University of Toronto to task, pointing out that Cecilia Krieger had remained a "lecturer" for twenty years before she was promoted to "assistant professor," and that was as far up the academic ladder as she climbed. Trixie, long dead by 1997, could have looked back on her own academic career and told much the same story.

But in the early forties for Trixie, it was all just beginning. She took courses in classical physics, in thermodynamics, and in relativity, finishing near the top of the class in nearly every subject and winning scholarships as she went. Her professors, when they talked about her, used words like "gifted" and—what every employer likes to hear—"dependable, conscientious, and painstaking." In 1944, her graduation year, everyone in the class was asked how they saw their future. "Delightfully indefinite," said one young man. "Want to find a good cook, preferably congenial," said another. "Ambition is a job shoveling snow in California," wrote a third. It was all in the yearbook. By 1944, Canada had been at war for five years, hundreds of thousands of young men and women were in the army and the navy, serving overseas, too many of them already among the war dead. Yet both the young men and young women graduating that year sounded optimistic and lighthearted. "Likes Toscanini, Artie Shaw," said one young woman and, from another, "Interests are numerous, prospects vague." One of the more ambitious wrote, "Plans to be in who's who in five years." Beatrice Helen Worsley stands out. There was nothing frivolous in what she wrote: "Future War Service and advanced study." She knew where she wanted to go even if she wasn't entirely clear how she was going to get there.

+++

Charles, her brother, had graduated in 1943 and signed up immediately with the Royal Canadian Engineers. Trixie, like more than six thousand other Canadian women, enlisted in the Women's Royal Canadian Naval Service (WRCNS), the Wrens. She was a slim, dark-haired twenty-three-year-old, not particularly strong or sturdy, but confident. The Wren recruiting officer wrote on the intake form that "Miss Worsley was quiet, pleasant and composed." Quiet, again. The recruits were put through four weeks of basic training, physical drills, and lectures about the navy then, those with a university degree, like Trixie, were given four weeks of officer training. By the end of 1944, probationary sub-lieutenant Beatrice Worsley graduated from HMCS Conestoga in southwestern Ontario. There she stood in her navy uniform—white shirt, dark tie, heavy double-breasted wool coat, and her naval officer's cap with the gold anchor—ready for service.

Most women in the Wrens were assigned to administration and intelligence. Trixie asked for research and lab work, and that's what she got, becoming one of six women in the Naval Research Establishment at HMCS Stadacona in Halifax, the Nova Scotia shore base for harbor defense research. Since 1940, one of the NRE's essential tasks had been "degaussing" ships, diffusing the magnetic strength of the hulls of ships to deflect German torpedoes. By the time Trixie arrived in Halifax, degaussing techniques were down to a routine, and there was little new or challenging that came her way. Yet there was something about the inevitably austere working environment of the NRE that must have appealed to her because, when the war ended and everyone turned in their uniforms, Beatrice Worsley, alone among the handful of Wrens, stayed on. The research was new and, to her, much more interesting. She was assigned to the minesweeper HMCS *Quinte* to investigate hull corrosion. (Minesweepers are among the smaller of navy ships, fifty meters long, compared to destroyers, which were double the length.) There she was, out on the deck of the *Quinte* in the middle of the North Atlantic, cold, wet, peering out from under her oilskin hood taking readings and measurements, conducting experiments, and rolling with the waves. Lieutenant Worsley spent one hundred and fifty days, five months, aboard ship—longer at sea than any other WRCNS officer, a record that still stands. Computer science historian Scott M. Campbell wrote that her endurance in what she called "a man's job" "earned her much respect from crews," and the onshore specialists had "no argument with her expertise." As a Wren, she did her job well and, as far as anyone knew, she was happy in the middle of the North Atlantic.

*+++*

*Consider a future device…in which an individual stores all his books, records, and communications and which is mechanized so that it may be consulted with exceeding speed and flexibility.*

—Vannevar Bush

These were the opening words of "As We May Think," an article by Vannevar Bush that appeared in the July 1945 issue of *The Atlantic* magazine. Bush was an engineer, an academic, and the man who headed the US Office of Scientific Research and Development throughout World War II. His article in *The Atlantic*, a mass circulation magazine and not a scientific journal, is credited with forecasting the Internet and planting the idea of the computer in the public imagination. In the war years, the US OSRD generated 40,000 reports and thousands of concrete results, ranging from advances in the mass production of penicillin and, research on cholesterol to the development of the atomic bomb. Thousands of senior scientists in the US and Europe had been deployed in war work. What were they to do next? In 1945, *The Atlantic's* editor at the time, Edward Weeks, told his readers that "the perfection of these pacific instruments [computers] should be the first objective of our scientists as they emerge from their war work." Bush was suggesting that perfecting this new machine—what would become the computer—was the answer to the question, "What are scientists to do next?"

It is difficult to imagine that Trixie, holed up in her harbor defense laboratory in Halifax, let alone out at sea, ever laid hands on that issue of *The Atlantic*, but she did not need to read the article. The ideas that Vannevar Bush was writing about had begun swirling round the halls of academe for more than a decade. In the late 1930s, when he was at the Massachusetts Institute of Technology (MIT), Vannevar Bush had invented a differential analyzer, essentially an analog computer, a mass of spinning discs and rotating rods. Computer ideas were uppermost in the minds of theoretical physicists at MIT, where she was headed next.

The navy demobilized Beatrice Worsley in August 1946 when the Wrens disbanded. A month later, she moved to Cambridge, Massachusetts, and enrolled at MIT to do a master's degree in mathematics and physics. MIT was overflowing with more enthusiastic young physicists, engineers, and mathematicians in the making than anyone had seen in years, many of them demobbed GIs and newly freed-up foreign students like Trixie. The place was busy, buzzing, and alive. MIT was so consumed with the joy of mathematics that there was even an a cappella singing group called the Logarhythms.

Trixie's field was applied mathematics, theoretical math applied to practical problems, and the practical problem that attracted her was this new "instrument of knowledge," the computer. Ideas, developments, and disagreements were fomenting not only at MIT but all over the world. Creating the machine—building the hardware—was the big job, and those builders and creators were not from any one discipline. There were physicists, engineers, sometimes philosophers, and mathematicians working together. The breadth of the discussion across disciplines and countries was vital, and thinking encompassed all dimensions—the physics, the mathematics, and the ethics of these new knowledge machines. For her master's thesis, Beatrice Worsley pulled prototypes and theories together and compared plans, characteristics, and results where there were results, of all these "computers," both completed and planned. She wrote about the Harvard computers, what was going on at Princeton and at MIT, what IBM was doing, what was going on at the National Physical Laboratory in England, where between 1945 and 1947, Alan Turing, the "father of computer science," was working, and she looked at what was going on in Manchester in the north of England.

Manchester, the city where her parents were born, over the last century had developed extensive and sophisticated manufacturing facilities. It was a Manchester plant that had manufactured the cathode ray tubes essential for radar detection in World War II, and would, in 1948, make the Williams tube, a cathode-ray-tube memory system, the first fully electronic memory system. Manchester University was the birthplace of nuclear physics and now boasted a remarkable community of thinkers. At the same time, mathematician Maurice Wilkes and a large team were working on a computer at Cambridge University in England.

As Beatrice Worsley was writing her thesis at MIT in Massachusetts across the Atlantic, the Electronic Delay Storage Automatic Calculator (EDSAC), the computer that captured her heart four years later, was beginning to come together. Beatrice Worsley's MA thesis was a series of mathematical comparisons, with pages of tables of, as far as was known, every computer in the world in 1946, a master's thesis for the record. She earned her master's degree, impressed her thesis advisers with her—again that word—"painstaking" work, and, most importantly, had sold herself on the subject. When she came back to Canada in the summer of 1947, Trixie told her brother and sister-in-law that computers were her future. Charles Worsley was surprised, not that his little sister was thinking about computers but that she had spoken about herself and her future at all. Alva Worsley, Charles's wife, said of Trixie, "She was so very quiet and did not talk about her work too much. I guess she realized that it was beyond our comprehension."

It didn't really matter what her tiny family thought; computers were what she wanted to do, and that was that. Intellectual curiosity has a will of its own. So it was with Trixie.

+++

Back in Toronto in January 1948, Beatrice Worsley signed on with the newly created Computation Centre at the University of Toronto. There were only five people on staff. This was a "computation centre;" no one was ready to think of computer science as an academic discipline. U of T in those early years was ahead of every other university in Canada in computer research, and the men who were doing the work had good relationships with leaders in the field, particularly those working in England. What this little Toronto center did not have was resources: money. The Canadian government needed convincing before it would do anything more. Over that first summer, perhaps to make what money the Computation Centre had go further and to supplement its operating equipment, Trixie built a differential analyzer out of Meccano, the precursor to Lego, with its small metal pieces that could be screwed and bolted together. Raw materials—$75. Two or three other mathematicians and physicists—including Vannevar Bush—had built Meccano analyzers earlier, but Beatrice tinkered, as did almost everyone, and she felt she had improved the design. The Toronto group put Trixie's machine to use. The Meccano differential analyzer worked, but it was limited. What U of T, and everyone else in the world working on computer research, wanted was its own electronic computer. In the late 1940s, that was what it was all about: building the hardware, the machine. Programming, telling the machine what to do and how to do it, came later.

In England, the Cambridge engineers and mathematicians continued to work on the EDSAC, which they were confident would be the world's first electronic computer. Within months of her return to Canada from MIT, Trixie and the other project assistant, a young man she knew from her undergraduate days, were sent over to join the Cambridge group to learn, to bring back information, and to contribute what they could. While she was there, the plan was that Trixie would also work on her PhD. There had been women at Cambridge since the nineteenth century but the university had only begun granting women degrees in 1948. Trixie was in the first wave of women whose work at Cambridge would be supervised by Douglas Hartree, the Cambridge mathematician leading the EDSAC project, and the notorious and eccentric Alan Turing. It would not be easy.

Arriving in Cambridge with its narrow streets, its colleges, some of them dating back to the thirteenth century, and their "backs," those green pastures stretching down to the River Cam—there were cows still grazing on some—she must have felt transported and, at the same time, overwhelmed. This was her fourth country, fifth if you count those five months onboard ship in the Atlantic, and she was only twenty-six. Then too, 1948 Cambridge was not all history and bucolic delight. This was postwar England with food rationing and

Alan Turing at work

bombed-out ruins; the English were only beginning to recover from six years of air raids and destruction, and now, with demobilized troops, there was massive unemployment. Everything was makeshift and catch-as-catch-can—including the Cambridge Mathematical Laboratory, where the EDSAC was being created. The Math Lab, Trixie discovered, was housed in what had been the anatomy building. One young man working on the project reported that in the summer, gases left over from the formalin used to preserve bodies vaporized in the heat. The smell, he said with British understatement, was "penetrating."

A Cambridge "computing laboratory" had been established in the late thirties and almost immediately taken over by the war effort. However, it was the war effort—specifically the need to break German military codes at Bletchley Park—that pushed things forward and eventually made Alan Turing a recognized name.

He was a classic British academic eccentric—a tortured soul, off-kilter, and brilliant. His father, a civil servant in India, had remote connections to royalty. On the memorial plaque on the house in Manchester where he died, he is described as "father of computer science, mathematician, logician, wartime code breaker and victim of persecution." In 1952, following his arrest and conviction for "homosexual acts," Turing chose chemical castration over prison, and two years later died of cyanide poisoning. Whether it was suicide or accidental is still unclear.

Trixie found the Math Lab in the old anatomy building and she found Turing and the EDSAC still under development. It was philosophers, and physicists—men including Turing and Hartree—who conceptualized then debated, argued, and experimented. The machines were built by engineers, men of a different stripe and often of a different class. Tommy Flowers, the engineer who built the Colossus, the WWII Enigma code-breaking computers, was the son of a bricklayer from the east end of London. When it came to pulling things together and problem-solving, anyone in the room, even visiting Canadian graduate students, could chime in. Programming was almost an afterthought.

By 1949, the Cambridge computing laboratory had a staff of fourteen—including two "boys" and a cleaning lady—who had together spent the past two years building the EDSAC. It was a huge task, and they created a huge machine; this was the era of computers big enough to fill a room, and now, in the spring of 1949, it was complete and ready for its first test run. The logbook reads: May 6, 1949 "Machine in operation for first time. Printed table of squares (0–99), time for programme 2 min 35 sec."

What the logbook did not note was that the test program they ran, simple though it was, was written by Beatrice Worsley.

There is a 1949 photograph of the mathematics lab staff. Trixie is sitting at the end of the first row, her hands clasped demurely in her lap, an Alice band holding her hair back. She is smiling just a little. What is a bit surprising, perhaps, is that there are seven other women in the photograph.

1949 staff of Cambridge Computing Laboratory; Trixie Worsley, bottom right; detail

+++

The world's first computer programmer was a woman. On December 10, 1815, Anne Isabella Milbanke gave birth to a baby daughter she named Augusta Ada, better known as Ada Lovelace. The little girl's father was the romantic poet and notorious rake Lord Byron. Isabella could see this relationship was not going to work. Byron's heart was not in the marriage, and Isabella was gone within five weeks, taking Ada with her. Byron left England days later, never to return. For years, Isabella loudly decried her husband's immorality and, as she saw it, his poetic madness. In an effort to offset whatever insanity this genetic poetic propensity might have created in little Ada, she had the child tutored relentlessly in mathematics. Fortunately, Ada liked math.

When she was a teenager, she met philosopher and visionary mathematician Charles Babbage. They corresponded and discussed the "analytic machine" that he had designed but never built and never would build. What Babbage envisaged was an all-purpose analog computer. It gave Ada a lot to ponder. Three years after she met Babbage, Ada married the future Earl of Lovelace, but much to the distress of her mother, her intellectual relationship with Babbage continued, and her mathematical mind was infected with imagination. Ada Lovelace thought about Babbage's analytic machine more and more and wrote an article with a detailed mathematical explanation of how it would work—a program. Ada Lovelace programmed an imaginary machine more than a hundred years before the first computer became a reality. It's a good story, but like as not, Trixie Worsley never heard of Ada Lovelace. There were no computer heroines for Trixie.

Women had, however, been the embodiment of the word "computer" for decades. They *were* computers. From the late-nineteenth century into the early twentieth century, ranks of young women were hired to add, subtract, and calculate endless columns of numbers—tedious tasks that demanded skill and dedication rather than innovative thinking. The best known were the "Harvard computers," a team of half a dozen young women hired by the Harvard Observatory to make sense of the patterns of the stars. They could be paid less than men and

The Harvard "computers," including astronomer
Henrietta Swan Leavitt

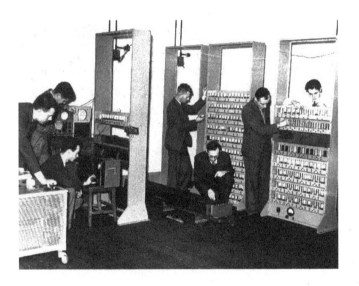

The computer boys building the EDSAC at Cambridge University

they did consistently "good" work. In the UK, as late as 1945, Maurice Wilkes at Cambridge complained that he had funds for six "computers," but he could only find three.

The gender division continued as the early computers were developed. The expectation was that women mathematicians—and there were a surprising number—would write the instructions and program the machines to do what the women "computers" had done manually.

As the commercial potential of these new computing machines grew, marketing became important. The key was to convince potential purchasers that these new computers were simple to operate, so simple that even a woman could do it. Advertising campaigns featured lovely young women sitting like typists at a seemingly simple console. The early idea was to make computers seem sexy. One company hired young women from the Windmill Theatre, London's rather staid version of the Folies Bergère to sell its computers. In reality, "running" computers in the early days was no mean feat. Women with graduate degrees in mathematics were hired to go round the world and "demonstrate" how they worked.

Two of these computer demonstrators were Audrey Bates and Cicely Popplewell. As Alan Turing's assistants, they shared an office with him, although everyone was much happier when Turing chose to work at home. Audrey Bates had graduated in mathematics from Manchester, Cicely Popplewell from Cambridge. In talking about Turing years later, Cicely Popplewell did not mince words. She said, as she and Audrey Bates saw it, Turing went through the day "not really recognizing their right to exist." Remarkably, Alan Turing considered Trixie Worsley, almost alone among the women working in Manchester and at Cambridge, worth his time. There are letters and notes in the Manchester University archives showing that Turing and Worsley had what is described as an intellectually productive relationship both in person and in letters. Her principal PhD supervisor, Douglas Hartree, was a man with more generosity of spirit who collaborated well with women. Hartree was one of the few prominent figures in the development of computers in the UK who had not been to an all-boys school. He had exchanged ideas with women all his life.

Trixie Worsley's conceptual thinking and her by-now encyclopedic knowledge of computer development put her in a unique position. By the time she left Cambridge in 1951, "she was one of the most computer literate people in the world."

+++

Beatrice Worsley was expected to stay in Cambridge for up to three years to finish work on her PhD, yet she left Cambridge and got on the boat back to Canada two years early. Why? That is one of the question marks in her life. Might her money have run out? Unlikely, since she had a good grant from the Canadian Federation of University Women. Or, as some have speculated, did she leave Cambridge early for "health reasons"—either physical or mental? Life in Cambridge may have become too much. She was alone in England, a colonial among the upper-class Brits, a crowd never known for its welcoming nature. She kept her head down, and years later, no one at Cambridge could remember Beatrice Worsley. Or did she go back to Canada early because this constant moving between countries had finally worn her down? She kept her reasons to herself but she left England. There were touchstones for her in Toronto.

Ada Lovelace, 1852

What is clear is that she was not running away from her academic work. Once she was back in Canada, she completed her dissertation quickly. Douglas Hartree came over from Cambridge to Toronto, approved her work, and in 1952, Beatrice Worsley received a PhD in mathematics from Cambridge. She was the first person in the world to write a dissertation on modern computers, but no one noticed.

Dr. Worsley was back at the University of Toronto's Computation Centre as a staff mathematician. While she had been away, the men at the center continued to develop what they hoped would be Canada's first electronic computer. In the fall of 1951, the Canadian government finally pulled the plug on the funding. The argument was that it was too expensive and taking too long. Computers then were handcrafted, almost one-of-a-kind machines. Similarly, the UK government had canceled its contract to purchase Manchester's Ferranti Mark 1 computer and now, with no computer of its own in sight, U of T bought the UK's Ferranti Mark 1. Once installed—and that took some time—the Ferranti was handed over to Beatrice. It was like bringing home a very large puppy that no one knew how to train. The first thing Trixie did was rename it, and it became the FERUT (Ferranti-U of T). This still very large machine was the only computer in the country, and it was expected to serve the nation. Trixie's FERUT was to be *the* computer for major government projects and for academic research, available to anyone who wanted to run data. The importance of accurate, straightforward—if not easy—programming suddenly became clear.

The FERUT didn't come with a user-friendly manual. When it arrived, it took six weeks and someone with a PhD to program the thing and get anything done. Worsley and her boss, Calvin Gotlieb, gave programming courses for actuaries, scientists, and graduate students, sophisticated thinkers who wanted to use the machine. Less than a third of the class completed the course. The FERUT was too complicated for its own good. It was doing nothing to increase public acceptance of computers. Trixie and Pat Hume from the physics department were told to find a shortcut, and together they developed what became known as Transcode, a shorter, simpler approach to programming. Courses in Transcode took two hours compared to the weeklong course that defeated most people. The FERUT, slow and cumbersome as it was, became usable. Years later, when she discovered that the FERUT had been more or less junked, Trixie wrote to the National Research Council in Ottawa, "This is a great disappointment," she said, "…as we had set our hearts on founding a little computer museum…I am deploring the lack of Canadian pride in her heritage which has resulted in this state of affairs."

In the next few years at the U of T Computation Centre, Beatrice Worsley wrote seventeen technical papers for publication; she taught first extension courses, then courses for graduate students and under-graduates. Eight years later she was still only a "staff" mathematician, not considered good enough to be "on" faculty. At least one of her col-leagues agreed, looking back, that had Beatrice Worsley been a man, it would have been different.

Trixie remained as ever quiet and composed, and solitary. A bit of a loner, but after a few years back in Toronto, she made one lasting friend. She never knew how deep the friendship ran. Charlotte Froese was from the University of British Columbia and in the 1950s, she was in Toronto visiting the Computation Centre and the FERUT comput-er. She and Trixie had more in common than either of them realized.

When they were little girls, both women had been lifted out of violence and suddenly landed in Canada. Trixie had grown up during the Mexican revolution; Charlotte Froese and her family were Mennonites and, in 1929, were passengers on the last train out of Donetsk in Ukraine. Stalin had just announced his first five-year plan and the collectivization of farms. With it would come the Holodomor, the famine that killed millions of Ukrainians and the deportation of

Trixie Worsley with the FERUT computer, 1950s

many Mennonites to gulags in the north. The train took the Froese family to a refugee camp in Germany, then Canada took them in, and they landed in Chilliwack, British Columbia.

Both women were mathematicians and earned their doctoral degrees under Douglas Hartree at Cambridge. Trixie had been the first programmer of the EDSAC computer at Cambridge, and Charlotte, a few years later, programmed the same computer for atomic-structure calculations.

What did they talk about during that brief time they worked together in Toronto? Did they share thoughts about life as women in the world of mathematics and physics? Or did Trixie tell Charlotte where to get nylons on sale as they washed their hands in the women's washroom? Whatever they talked about, a lot was left unsaid. Years later Charlotte Froese said with some regret, "You spend time with a person and you think you know them but there are so many things about them you don't know." Her time at U of T over, Charlotte Froese went back to her faculty position at UBC. They never met again, but Charlotte Froese did not forget Beatrice Worsley.

In 1960, Trixie was made an assistant professor at the University of Toronto. After nine years, she was finally on faculty. In the sixties, she taught more and helped groups on campus that were looking for better access to computerization. She got a grant from the National Research Council to work on computer automation for libraries. But her career wasn't going anywhere. Her PhD had the imprimatur of Alan Turing and Douglas Hartree; she had published more papers than anyone else in the Computer Centre; she knew as much about computers, if not more, than anyone in Canada. Others rose in the ranks, but, like Cecilia Krieger thirty years earlier and other women in academe, Beatrice Worsley's career stalled.

Enough was enough, and in 1964, much to her colleagues astonishment, she announced that she was leaving U of T, and going to Queen's University in Kingston, Ontario. The mouse had roared.

+++

As a career move, it was surprising. Queen's did not have a computer department. Trixie Worsley went to Queen's as a "computing adviser." Her job description said that she was to advise local high schools, get a system together for the new library, and schedule computer time for users. No more research; her work was now administration and basic teaching. The 1965 Queen's calendar added that Trixie was to make "arrangements…for undergraduates experienced in programming, to learn to operate the computer." Beatrice Worsley was something akin to a driving instructor when she could have been redesigning the engine.

What had attracted her to the university was the promise of being part of the development and shaping of a new computer science department. She was put on faculty within a year or so and did some teaching, but a computer science department was slow in coming. The university slowly, far too slowly for Trixie's liking, was moving in that direction; other universities were well ahead. In 1967, the university senate struck a committee to consider the question. The director of the computing center, Mers Kutt, a businessman and inventor, was put on the committee. Trixie was not. When the senate issued its report, she let it be known, diplomatically, that Queen's was out of touch, there were more computer science positions opening up across the country than people to fill them; and that the university had better make up its mind and get on with it. Promises were not good enough to attract good people. She added that "few of them would be prepared to display such faith and patience in Queen's as the undersigned." She was beginning to lose patience.

Computer science became an academic department at Queen's two years later. The new head was recruited from the National Research Council and appointed a full professor. There was an opening for another full professor. That job went to another man with experience in the private sector, a zoology graduate. Trixie remained an associate professor. By now, she was a director in two national computer organizations, she was organizing conferences, writing instruction manuals. Beatrice Worsley was getting to be known.

And by now, she was not merely losing patience with her

university, she was getting angry. Her first sabbatical was coming up and she was looking forward to the break. It was April, the year was winding down, when she received an interdepartmental memo asking her to help the department "state its case [for funding] to the administration." Specifically, she was asked to describe her teaching and research work. This time she did not even take the time to put a piece of paper in her typewriter. She scrawled her answer in her big, loose handwriting across the memo and let them have it.

When it came to research, she said, "The administration knows I haven't been given time to do any in the past 3 years."

With regard to teaching, she wrote, "The Admin knows that *you big bullies* got together last fall and scrapped all the courses I'd been teaching for the past 5 years. No one can now give me any idea of what I'll be expected to teach after my sabbatical. No one has even done me the courtesy of telling me who is likely to teach what, in 71/72. In the past, however, I have taught all the high-enrollment courses (or were they high-enrollment *because* I taught them?)."

She signed off, "B. H. Worsley Assoc Prof (with Tenure)." "With Tenure" was underlined twice.

There is no record of any answer to her note. Beatrice Worsley's archival files provide slim pickings. She seemed to be a woman who did not keep things—anything she did not need went in the garbage. It was pure luck that memo made its way into her archival files, as did another very short note. A colleague had written looking for "historic documents." She wrote back and offered some material related to the "Computing Centre of years gone by." Then she went on, "My really old things (20 to 25 years old) are going into the Smithsonian Institute in Washington at the invitation of…Cmmdr Grace Hopper."

Grace Murray Hopper was a rear admiral in the US navy and another woman who was in on the ground floor of computer science. Both women were in Cambridge, Massachusetts, at around the same time—Trixie at MIT, Hopper at Harvard. Grace Hopper, among other things, developed a "compiler" that would translate English into computer code. She turned more to the private sector while Beatrice Worsley went to the academic world. They were both women who had been in the navy, both computer pioneers, but Grace Hopper put her work and herself forward in the best American tradition. She was recognized with forty honorary degrees from universities around the world, a guided-missile destroyer named the USS *Hopper*, and the Presidential Medal of Freedom, the highest US honor.

It is a testament to Beatrice Worsley that in 1971 Grace Hopper thought Beatrice Worsley's work sufficiently important to invite her to send her papers to the Smithsonian in Washington. It was a colleague-to-colleague mark of recognition. True to form, Trixie seems not to have mentioned it beyond one line in a memo.

When she closed the door to her office before she went on sabbatical, she must have heaved a sigh of relief. She was going to spend her year at Waterloo University, a university in the Canadian vanguard of computer science research. Was she looking for a new job? Perhaps, and perhaps there was something in the offing.

But it never came to that, and Queen's never had to have that discussion about what she would be teaching when she came back or ever have to listen to Beatrice Worsley complain again. As she was winding up her year at Waterloo, in May of 1972, Beatrice Worsley had a massive heart attack and died. She was fifty.

♦♦♦

Realization slowly dawned on the computer science community that she had been shortchanged. Trixie Worsley had been dead for more than forty years when the Canadian Association of Computer Science gave her a posthumous lifetime achievement award in 2014.

A year earlier, her friend from the 1950s, Charlotte Froese, proved her friendship in a very big way. She created a Beatrice Worsley Scholarship at the University of Toronto. Memories of Trixie stayed with her, and seven years later Charlotte Froese, now a woman in her nineties, added another $100,000 to the scholarship fund. "U of T has done very well with the scholarship I created," she said. "I figured I should give a little more."

Charlotte Froese Fischer receiving an honorary degree
from Western University, 2018

After she died, her executors went through her well-ordered files and found her will. Beatrice Worsley had no family. She bequeathed her entire estate, more than $150,000—the equivalent of over a million dollars today—to Cambridge University in England with the direction that Cambridge was to establish a "hardship" award for foreign students, preference to be given to computer students. It was, she had written, to be called the Lundgren Research Award. Who was Helge Lundgren?

No one knew. If Trixie had ever mentioned Helge Lundgren, no one remembered. Lundgren was a Dane a little older than Trixie and the "son of a servant," a young man who must have known hard times. Following World War II, he came to America, to Harvard, as part of that wave of postwar foreign students, to do a master's degree and then a PhD. Lundgren was at Harvard, and Trixie was at MIT, ten minutes away. Lundgren's passions were boats, harbors, and mathematics. She was fresh off the HMS *Quinte*, a mathematics student discovering computers. He was a young man alone in a new country.

Helge Lundgren, 1987

Did they meet? Did they construct mathematical models together? No one knows.

Helge Lundgren was ninety-seven when he died. He had a big career in Denmark and was much respected in the world of harbor research and construction. When he was still alive, Denmark even named a harbor after him.

A few years ago, the city of Toronto put up a small, blue "Beatrice Worsley lived here" plaque near the St. George subway station. It was vandalized and disappeared recently. Now there's nothing.

# 4. ALLIE

*A sweet and fitting thing it is to toil for truth.*

If Trixie Worsley had arrived at Queen's University in Kingston a few years earlier, she would have met a woman who knew her frustrations firsthand and understood her real but dimming hope that this university might offer a new beginning. That woman was Allie Vibert Douglas, she was twenty-eight years older than Beatrice Worsley, and she was a professor of physics and dean of women. There would have been a cup of tea—loose tea leaves, no tea bags, and china cups and saucers—a piece of cake, and most importantly, some unsentimental, practical advice firmly given. Something along the lines of "never abandon your principles, work hard, and do not lose your temper." Allie Douglas was a strong, no-nonsense woman who believed in doing rather than complaining. She understood the realities that confronted a woman in science in the 1950s, attitudes that were even more pronounced in the 1920s, when she had been making her way. Allie Douglas remembered quite clearly the day she had been told, "There are *no* women of excellence in science. Marie Curie? Bah. The wife of a chemist."

They might have had a good conversation.

Allie Vibert Douglas

But when Trixie Worsley came to Queen's, Allie Vibert Douglas was gone; she had retired as dean of women six years earlier. And, if truth be told, they probably would not have got on very well. Dean Douglas did not have much time for computers or the people who muddled with them.

"Aunt Allie could talk to Einstein about relativity, but she could never wrap her mind around computers. I tried to teach her," said her great-nephew Stephen Douglas, and he laughs. "She still did her income tax with her slide rule."

✦✦✦

Allie Vibert Douglas was an astronomer, and in 1926, she became the first person in this country to earn a PhD in astrophysics; there wasn't another for nearly fifty years. It had taken her time to land on the branch of science that she wanted to pursue—in her youth, the lines between physics, astronomy, and mathematics were fuzzy, to say the least, then came nuclear physics and astrophysics. This was the time of big thinkers—Einstein and the theory of relativity, Rutherford, the "father of nuclear physics." What a time to be a young woman trying to find your place in the scientific world. When she did find her calling, she became not merely an astronomer but an internationally respected astronomer. But like Trixie, she had very few women in her field to talk to.

Right from the beginning, she was a joiner, the antithesis of Trixie Worsley, and when she joined an organization, as often as not, she ended up running it. In her very disciplined fashion, she championed the scholarship of young women. She was the first Canadian president of the International Federation of University Women. Allie Douglas was also a "spinster," as were the majority of academic women in her era. Intellectual women were considered "unnatural," drawn—the thinking was—to matters of the mind rather than the heart, let alone to motherhood. She had no children, but she had nieces and nephews and, later on, great-nieces and great-nephews, whom she loved and mentored. Above everyone was her brother, George. They had been everything to each other going back to their earliest days in Montreal.

The Douglases were a Westmount family in every way. Writing in *Maclean's* magazine in 1962, Peter Gzowski called Westmount "still the highest and mightiest small town in Canada." Stephen Leacock, humorist and, often forgotten, an economist on faculty at McGill, said that Westmount was betwixt and between, "neither urban nor rural, neither straight nor crooked, too rich for the poor, but too poor for the very rich." It was Anglo and it was affluent. There were prominent Jewish families who lived in Westmount, but first and foremost, Westmount was the Protestant bastion in Quebec—the right place for the Douglas family.

Allie Vibert Douglas's father was John Vibert, an accountant; Grandfather Vibert had been a sea captain, an adventurous man who settled down and became the port warden of Montreal. Allie and her brother were born Viberts; it was her mother, Alice, who was a Douglas, the youngest of three daughters born to George and Maria Douglas. They were not the richest family in Westmount, far from it, but the Douglases were moral leaders. George Douglas had immigrated from Scotland as a child—his father, like most immigrants, was looking for opportunity. Originally Presbyterian, the Douglas family was "drawn" to the Methodist Church, and George felt the call. In 1848, a year of revolution and redefinition in Europe and before Canada was a country, he made the sea voyage to England to attend the Wesleyan theological college and, an eloquent speaker and a natural leader, he was given a church before he even started his training. He ministered in Bermuda, then came back to Canada, first to Kingston, then Toronto and Hamilton, and finally to Westmount. The Wesleyan college had been right—George Douglas was a natural leader. He filled his church every Sunday, was invited to speak throughout Ontario and the United States and then, as his reputation grew, at international Wesleyan Methodist events. In Westmount, his church became known as the "Douglas" Church, and it was George Douglas who became head of the Wesleyan theological college affiliated with McGill University. As Allie later wrote, the college operated "within the environment with the special problems of the Province of Quebec," that is, a large francophone population and the politically influential Catholic Church. Lord Dufferin, the governor general at the time, referred to Douglas as the "Bismarck of Canadian Methodism," a unifier. George Douglas ran his church, ran the college, and, by the time he died in 1894, had made his, and his family's, place in the community. His daughters had his sermons bound, and years later Allie would read them, like it or not, to the great-nephews and great-nieces. It was not that she was a true believer, although she searched for her connection to the universe all her life; rather, she admired her grandfather and she learned from him through those sermons.

In 1892, Alice Douglas and John Vibert had a son. Grandfather Douglas died in 1894, and later that year, Allie was born. But Alice Douglas died of Bright's disease (acute nephritis) a week after her daughter was born. John Vibert and his tiny children went to live on University Street with their Grandmother Douglas and the aunts, Mina and Mary. Allie and George were motherless children, yet, as Allie Douglas describes it, it was an idyllic childhood. They explored the "mountain," Mount Royal, then full of woods, fields, and creeks, and from their grandmother's house, they watched their neighbors. Every morning, Henry Birks, already a successful jeweler, and his three sons would leave their house up the street and walk down to their store. Birks and Sons, with their trademark blue boxes, was expanding across the country. In 1897, they watched the fireworks display that marked Queen Victoria's diamond jubilee and waved their Union Jacks. There were electric lights and a telephone in their grandmother's house and a nursemaid who would take them out in the mornings. In the winter, they took sleigh rides, warm under buffalo robes, the sleigh driven by fur-cloaked coachmen. It was all a little too good to be true and couldn't last forever—and it didn't. It was beginning to become clear that their father, John Vibert, was not well, and in 1899, when Allie was five, he was diagnosed with tuberculosis. Treatment for TB then was rest, fresh air, and time. John Vibert was bundled off, first to Saranac Lake in upstate New York, where ten years earlier Scottish poet Robert Louis Stevenson had been treated, and then to Colorado with its clear mountain air. Letters regularly came back to University Street, and John Vibert reported that he was doing well, and it wouldn't be long before he came home. He had even found a little accounting work. In the fall of 1902, Grandma Douglas decided that they—grandmother, the aunts, and the children—would all go to England and John Vibert would join them there. They packed up the Montreal house, put the furniture in storage, and boarded the *Lake Erie* for Southampton. The Douglas family was never short of conveniently placed friends. In London, they moved in with the McArthurs, a "typical English professional family with two or three servants and a Nanny," as Allie described them. The comfortable if somewhat eccentric life continued, when the entire entourage moved to the country where they were boarders on a chicken farm owned by a Mr. Wilson, a former schoolmaster. Mr. Wilson, after he finished feeding the chickens, became both George and Allie's first teacher. Her life as one of the boys had begun.

> …he began to teach the "sons of the gentry" in day classes and agreed to include me as well as George…. The class of about a dozen included the sons of the local doctor, of a retired engineer, and an Admiral. I was included in everything and played goalkeeper on the football team. I remember nothing of what I learned but recall the weekly sessions in the barn where Mr. Wilson had fixed up a small chemistry laboratory…. One day Mr. Wilson took us with him to buy more rabbits and he gave us each one to carry home. I can still feel that warm furry throbbing little body in my hands and my apprehension lest he slip out of my grasp.

She was eight. They did their lessons, paddled in the sea, and took long walks on the Sussex Downs.

> We looked over the low wall at the home of Rudyard Kipling. We visited the picturesque town of Lewes where greatly to the amusement of our Aunts, Grandma insisted on finding and pointing out to us the home of Tom Paine, the free thinker [philosopher and activist in the American Revolution]. To Grandma he was a godless unbeliever, with her heritage of fifty years of Grandfather's nineteenth century Methodist orthodoxy.

This very pleasant experiential learning continued, and when they went back to London, it was supplemented with a little formal instruction in mathematics and Latin in the mornings. In the afternoons, "we went to historic places, to parks, museums, art galleries, the zoo…. One day in the south Kensington Museum we stood in a long queue awaiting our turn to enter a dark cubicle, move a lever and see a faint glow of light…the first public showing of the mysterious substance Radium."

And that is how Allie Douglas was introduced to radioactivity and all that it brought to twentieth-century science. Pierre and Marie Curie won the Nobel Prize in physics for their research in radiation the next year, 1903. The Douglas clan was still in London and "rented a window" to watch the funeral procession of the king's uncle, and when Parliament opened, they rented another window and watched "the six grey horses with outriders, the gold coach with King Edward VII and Queen Alexandra." Pomp and circumstance. Allie Douglas had a soft spot for royalty for much of her life.

The family had been in England for more than a year when in June 1904, a "disquieting" letter arrived from Colorado. John Vibert had recovered from tuberculosis but had been diagnosed with Bright's disease, the same kidney condition that had killed his wife, and was seriously ill. They sailed for Canada immediately, and Aunt Mina and the two children got on the train in Montreal for Denver. John Vibert died on July 11, within days of their arrival.

Allie and George Vibert Douglas were orphans. He was twelve, she was not quite ten.

+++

John Vibert's long illness had eaten up his savings, and now the Douglas family was living on Grandma Douglas's modest widow's pension from the Methodist Church and her investments. They lived carefully and did not own their home but rented, always in Westmount. The family's position in the community flowed from their grandfather, but when it came to their schooling, their friends, how their lives would be shaped, Maria Douglas made the decisions. Her father had been "a stern Plymouth Brother." The Plymouth Brethren were Protestants from Northern Ireland who preached a life in accordance with the teaching of the New Testament including a subordinate role for women. Women—if they were allowed to learn at all—should learn in silence. Not surprisingly, permission to marry George Douglas, the young Wesleyan Methodist, was refused. But young Maria had the gumption to disobey her father, a decision that must have taken considerable strength knowing, as she did, that she would be cast out of her family.

George Douglas was a progressive Methodist and placed great faith in the "ever ascendant power of women for good." He was in favor of higher education for women in order that they "might gain equality of independence." And he went further:

> Give her but time, give her the ballot, give her the recognition that is coming on apace and women…will regenerate and cleanse political life and put the impress of her purity, her elevation and all that pertains to the recovery of this world for God.

It was women who would reform political life, according to George Douglas, quite a responsibility. One Wesleyan woman, Emma Whittemore, campaigned for a living wage for the working woman and called on women to "band together and earnestly wait upon God to see what could be done regarding the starvation prices paid for the labor of so many of our dear young girls." The Reverend Douglas would have probably agreed with her. Both he and his wife encouraged their daughters' education and their independence. In 1877, before it became a degree-granting university, Mina Douglas, the children's younger aunt, became the first woman to receive a diploma from McGill. It was Mina who, unaccompanied, took the children to Denver to see their dying father. The elder aunt, Mary, with a woman friend, went to New York City for a weekend to see the Metropolitan Opera. All the Douglas women had minds of their own.

When Grandmother Douglas became a widow in 1894, she could legally own property and even vote in municipal elections. Almost immediately, she bought a very small island (one-third of an acre) in the St. Lawrence River from the federal government. White Calf Island and other islands in the St. Lawrence had been carved out of a reserve allocated to the Mississauga First Nation. Maria Douglas paid $350 for her island, and the Douglas clan immediately renamed it Ashkirk after the village in Scotland where Grandfather Douglas was born.

That island became a constant for five generations of the Douglas family. Allie Douglas remembered her uncle James, gray-haired, bearded, and nearly six feet tall, pulling into the front dock in 1901: "The aunts had come down to meet him," and he said in a slightly Scottish accent, "He's dead. President McKinley has been assassinated, shot in Buffalo by an anarchist."

The two children, George and Allie, less than two years apart in age and bound by the death of their parents, grew increasingly close. It was a women's household, but it was a given that George, because he was a boy, would have more options and opportunity. More doors would be open for George. Yet, perhaps because it was easy to follow her brother, more likely because she was pushy, Allie did everything that George did, and George *wanted* his sister with him. They were as one. Whatever George discovered, Allie discovered. Wherever George went, Allie went. When George climbed a wooden tower up on the mountain, Allie followed.

> One day when the view across city and river…was wonderfully clear, George urged me to attempt the ascent, about 35 feet. The first horizontal beam was well out of reach. Boys shinnied up one of the four main supports to reach it. George hoisted me up to it and then came the straightforward climb by cross beams and horizontals to the top where a group of rather surprised boys looked at me with astonishment. I felt the glow of achievement after my deliberately slow and cautious descent.

From the beginning, she would not be held back because she wore a skirt, and just in case, she invented her own winter uniform. "I did all my sliding, snowshoeing and skiing with moccasins over two pairs of long over-stockings, petticoat tucked into knitted bloomers, and a heavy skirt well below the knees."

When it came time for school, George was sent to the Westmount Academy for boys and Allie to the Queen's School for girls. Even then they were joined at the hip. Their grandmother liked to give them a long summer at Ashkirk, the island, and they were allowed to skip the first four weeks of school if they studied and made sure they were up to speed when they went back. So, brother and sister learned together while they were doing chores, cutting wood, or going out on the water. It became a game.

> I remember sailing with him…back and forth across the foot of the lake in 1911 when he taught me the formulae and proofs of the rules of combination of indices in multiplication, division and powers. "$x$ to the $m$ times $x$ to the $n$ equals $x$ to the $m$ plus $n$," we shouted to the southwest wind. Then would follow the proofs, all visualized without benefit of paper and pencil.

And when she showed up at school a month late, Allie was the only one to score 100 per cent on the math test. As they grew older, rather than drifting apart, they seemed to grow closer. She wrote a school essay on the "nebular hypothesis," and when her teachers shrugged and found it a little odd, George was as annoyed as Allie. Their minds worked in tandem. She idolized him and he her. Her brother did all that he could to include Allie, even where there was a "boys only" rule. She wrote about the club he and his friends had in high school.

> …the Society for the promotion of science and Literature, the SPSL. To it they invited a very few chosen friends, and they took turns presenting papers on topics of their choice, meeting in the homes of one or another. I was very envious, but it was for boys only. When they met in our dining room, George encouraged me to listen from the hall and he carefully left the door ajar.

Allie Douglas had a big brother who opened the door for her.

+++

*The introduction of the abstruser sciences into a course of studies for females is of the highest utility.*

—Mount Allison *Academic Gazette*, 1855

George took his matriculation exams and graduated from Westmount Academy in 1911. Allie would graduate from Queen's School for girls the following year. The results of the province-wide matriculation exams were published in the newspaper, resulting in a few heart-stopping moments in some families when the paper was delivered on results day. For George, it went well enough. It was there in the newspaper for everyone to read—George Vibert Douglas finished with, as Allie put it, "high standing in the province." Their friend Étienne Biéler, who later became an internationally respected geophysicist, had done better and come first in the province. Ever competitive, Allie wanted to do better than both of them.

> I was quite obsessed with this ambition, working single-mindedly all the 1911–12 school year. In late July 1912 we had a family picnic at Leek Island and towing one boat home I got the strong impression that the results of the examinations might be in that day's Montreal *Gazette*.... I insisted on going over to Gananoque to collect the...mail at the post office. There I hurried, opened the paper and found the list, hardly believing my eyes on seeing my name at the top of the list by a margin of 50 marks.

She had beaten the boys.

The Douglas children did not for a moment consider any other university; they were going to McGill. For one thing, they lived almost next door. The family had moved into a three-story, respectable but not opulent, rowhouse on Mount Pleasant, a half-hour walk down Sherbrooke Street. And McGill had moved on from Aunt Mina's day and was now granting degrees to women.

Mount Allison University in New Brunswick was the first in the British Empire to welcome women and let them learn (even the "abstruser sciences") and, in 1875, the first university in the British Empire to award a woman a degree. Mount A, as it's still known, had a graduating class of eight that year, seven men and Grace Annie Lockhart. McGill was not far behind. Women at McGill were given "permission" to earn degrees in the arts in 1888. Mind you, they had to sit in separate classrooms, and some subjects were off-limits, medicine for one.

By the time George and Allie started at McGill, they had legally renamed themselves and were no longer Viberts; now in deference to their grandmother and their aunts, they were Douglases.

George enrolled in applied science; Allie went into arts, which in 1912 meant courses in math and physics. For her, McGill was revelatory: her math professor, she wrote, "carried me into a marvelous new world of thought." A physics professor "opened up the great visible and invisible world of physics. I cannot recall any moment of doubt about my choice of honours mathematics and physics." Again, like Beatrice Worsley thirty years later at the University of Toronto, "I did not share the social life of students." She played basketball and did gymnastics but had no interest in what others would call "having fun"; frivolity was not in her nature. Rather, she and George went to natural history lectures; they were in the front row at the brand-new Art Association of Montreal museum for a series of lectures on Dante—"I never forgot a single sentence." She was eighteen, and she drank it all in. Certainly, she would not be stopped or slowed down because she was a woman. Allie Douglas had grown up under the care of two single, relatively independent aunts and their grandmother Douglas. When Allie entered McGill, Maria Douglas was in her eighties. In February of 1914, she died. Five months later, Archduke Ferdinand was assassinated in Sarajevo, and World War I began.

George signed up immediately. They were children of the Empire, this was their war, never mind what the francophone majority in Quebec might think. Thirty-three thousand Canadian volunteers sailed for England weeks after war was declared; two-thirds of them had been born in the British Isles. There were only 150 French-speaking men among those 33,000, and Sam Hughes, leader of the war effort and Canada's minister of defence, refused to allow them to speak their language.

There were drills at McGill. George was a lance corporal, marching and waving the flag and, in a matter of months, sailing for England. The entire family went to New York to see him off. When Allie got back to Montreal, she continued to walk to McGill in her ankle-length skirts and long coat and spent the winter attending classes and going to more lectures. That was the winter she first heard Sir Ernest Rutherford, father of nuclear physics, lecture. Rutherford had been a professor at McGill and announced his law of radioactive disintegration, the law of physics that won him a Nobel Prize and a knighthood, in a McGill classroom. "I had been studying radioactivity for two years," Allie Douglas wrote, "a subject which fascinated me and this lecture by the great Rutherford on his latest discoveries provided exciting new knowledge of the dis-integration sequences." Not many young women found joy in disintegration sequences, but for Allie Douglas, listening to Ernest Rutherford was as exciting as a rock concert would be to young women a century later.

George, by now in London, was having his uniforms tailored and showing himself to be of "officer class." He wrote to the aunts that he thanked them daily for his "careful training in table manners for manners in the Officers Mess were impeccable," and, he said, he never once felt "gauche." As good British subjects—Canadian citizenship did not exist until 1947—the aunts and Allie decided that they should be in England to support George and the war effort, and once again the Douglas women crossed the Atlantic. World War I marked huge social change, the dawning of the modern world, and they were swept along. When they came back to Canada five years later, they had, like the rest of the world, all seen too much. In one of his letters to Allie from the front, George included a handful of grass and lavender from the battlefield. It is still there today, in its own little envelope in her archives.

George was one of 37,000 men awarded the Military Cross for gallantry in World War I and he wore his medal proudly. (The first woman to be awarded a Military Cross, Private Michelle Norris, won it in 2006.) Allie Vibert Douglas had her own decoration tucked away in her small traveling case on their return voyage. She had been made a Commander of the British Empire—curtsying before the king, she looked into his pale blue eyes and whispered, "Thank you."

For Allie and tens of thousands of women, World War I was many things, most of them dreadful, but it also meant opportunity. Cataclysm causes change. With so many men called up and so much work to do, women were dragooned into nearly every job of work. The Women's Land Army started in 1917, and city girls found themselves digging potatoes and herding cows; bright young women ran their local post office and then were bitterly disappointed when the men came home and they were, once again, relegated to housework.

When the Douglas women arrived in London, Aunt Mina found volunteer work making surgical boots. Allie applied to the civil service and was hired by the Debenture Section of the Customs House, checking documents for signatures. Not exciting work. Allie Douglas wanted more—after all, she thought, I almost have a degree. Some months later, following the Battle of the Somme when George was home on leave, she asked him to pull some strings. It did not take long, and she found herself "head of women clerks" in the War Office. One day, as she was going to work, looking out the window of her bus, she saw Emmeline Pankhurst in Trafalgar Square. Pankhurst had put her campaign for the woman's vote on hold, having decided that supporting the war effort was more important. As Allie Douglas watched, Pankhurst climbed up on the base of Nelson's Column and harangued the crowd, drumming up more recruits to go and fight in the trenches. Allie did not listen for long. "I dislike women urging men to enlist," she said.

But recruitment was a big concern in the War Office. England was still operating with a volunteer army, and the women in the War Office had to track recruitment patterns. They copied the data on volunteers from every recruiting center in the country and added the columns horizontally, then vertically. It was tedious, slow work, and they were constantly falling behind. When conscription was introduced, there were even more numbers and more "clerks"—often they were injured soldiers:

> ...privates appeared in our office with instructions to make charts of percentages of some recruiting data, and there they sat all day doing simple percentages by long division.... I felt so sorry for them that when I had a free moment I would take my slide rule and chair over to one of them and run off percentages for him twenty times as fast as he could do them.

Allie, with the confidence of youth, took the bit between her teeth and "revolutionized" the system. It did not take much. She introduced graph paper and comparative charts in colored ink. The mid-management men of the British civil service, in their shabby suits with their wing collars and detachable cuffs and their owlish round glasses, were shocked as this young Canadian woman took over. She created mathematical models that projected army growth. Allie Vibert Douglas with her slide rule and graph paper had a good deal to do with keeping British army recruitment records in some sort of order in World War I. She and George were on the same honors list on January 1, 1918, and went to Buckingham Palace together to be given their war decorations.

When they got back to Canada, brother and sister returned to McGill to finish their respective degrees. Because of the war, there was a staff shortage, and—almost by necessity—Allie Douglas was asked to teach. Looking around, she was hard-pressed to find and learn from any other faculty women. There was Carrie Derick, the first woman to teach at a university in Canada. She had graduated from McGill in 1890 and became a "demonstrator" in botany. Then, as Allie Douglas would do, she went to Europe to study, in her case at the University of Bonn in Germany. She became a researcher, taught—for no pay—and finished the work for her PhD in Germany but came away without her doctorate. Bonn did not grant degrees to women. Back at McGill, after a lot of letter writing, Carrie Derick was promoted to assistant professor and paid a third as much as the men. All this was while Allie Douglas was still a girl at school. Carrie Derick became a full professor in 1912, founded McGill's department of genetics, and is trumpeted as a success story. Some success. She was told by the McGill president, in case she began to think too much of herself, that she was not really a professor—it was a courtesy title, and Carrie Derick was given work and paid at the level of a demonstrator. It looked like Allie Douglas might wait a long time before she became anything more than a demonstrator.

George and Allie Vibert Douglas both graduated with undergraduate degrees in 1920. George won the essay prize; Allie won the Anne Molson Gold Medal for achievement in mathematics and physics. She wasn't the first woman to take home the medal. In 1898, it went to Harriet Brooks, considered Canada's first female nuclear physicist and another object lesson. Brooks worked with Ernest Rutherford at McGill, and it was Brooks who discovered that one element could change into another through radioactive decay. Her work contributed to Rutherford's on radioactivity, for which he won the Nobel Prize in 1908. Brooks was not mentioned.

Now Allie had the same gold medal in her hands. She and George, still operating in tandem, both went back for their master's degrees, George in geology, Allie in physics, focusing on radiation. When they received their MAs in 1921, she was twenty-six and he twenty-eight. It was time for them to go their separate ways. George got a job with Northwestern Oil and headed west. Allie fell into a fellowship for graduate work from the Imperial Order Daughters of the Empire, and she and the ever-present aunts got on the boat for their third trans-atlantic crossing. This time she was heading for Cambridge University, and she had no idea what she was in for.

+++

*The lies, and truths, and pain?...oh! yet*
*Stands the Church clock at ten to three?*
*And is there honey still for tea?*

—Rupert Brooke, "The Old Vicarage, Grantchester"

The summer of 1921 was hot, very hot, and dry in England. The Conservatives were running the country, and unemployment reached two million. It was an uncomfortable summer for many. In Cambridge, life carried on essentially unchanged. There were solemn moments as the war dead were memorialized and plaques unveiled, but young men still punted down the Cam in their striped blazers, wandered along the tow path to Grantchester, and lounged in deck chairs and had their tea at The Orchard Tea Room, as they always had.

In 1918, 8.4 million women over thirty got the vote in Great Britain. Women were becoming more demanding. The old British universities were slow to change their ways. Women were allowed to attend classes and sit exams but were not awarded degrees. Cambridge was the slowest to change. Oxford granted women university degrees for the first time in 1920, and when Allie Douglas arrived in 1921, women were pressing at Cambridge.

She and her aunts moved into lodgings near the river and Allie began, like Harriet Brooks before her, working with Ernest Rutherford, going to his laboratory every day and tackling problems that he assigned. Women were "allowed" to do what Allie Douglas was doing—work with professors, take classes, and attend lectures but only with permission from the professor. That was how things had been since 1869, when Girton, the first of two women's colleges at Cambridge, opened. Allie was a nonresident research scholar at Newnham, the other women's college, but neither Girton nor Newnham were voting members of the university. Now there was a proposal to admit the women's colleges as voting members of the university community, and if passed, it would signal the beginning of academic equality at Cambridge.

A similar motion had been put to the vote twenty-four years earlier and been defeated by more than a thousand votes. The day ended in a riot. The vote on this, the second try, was scheduled for October 20. Every "fellow" of the men's colleges could vote, but they had to vote in person. Hundreds of men arrived at the old colleges throughout the day and milled about for hours waiting for the results. Once again, the women and their colleges were soundly defeated. When the result was announced, it was 8:30 at night and fourteen hundred young men celebrated their victory. They drove a hearse bearing the slogan "The Last Male Graduate," throughout the town while a battalion of men describing themselves as "Mere Males" walked behind. The fourteen hundred started chanting, "We don't want women!" then marched on Newnham College and stormed the iron gates. Windows were broken and doors were smashed. The proctors—the college's own security force—kept the men at bay but they could not prevent thousands of pounds of damage. In the days afterwards, the rioters were publicly rapped on the knuckles for "bad manners." They cried out that their masculinity was threatened. It would be twenty-seven years before Cambridge granted women degrees.

Allie Vibert Douglas had just finished her dinner at her lodgings in Cambridge when less than a mile away, these well-bred young Englishmen began their marching, chanting, and attacking

Arthur Quiller-Couch

Newnham—her—college. Had the windows been open she could have heard it all. And yet she does not say a word about any of it in her memoirs. Was it something she would rather not think about, a reminder that her time at Cambridge would be enlightening, but at the end there would be no degree, no mark of recognition? In fairness, that October, Allie was distracted and worried about her family. Aunt Mary had become seriously ill, and on October 19, the day before the storming of Newnham College, Mary Douglas died. She was sixty-five.

When the young men were shouting, "We don't want women!" Allie was arranging her aunt's funeral.

Allie Vibert Douglas knew that she, and every other woman at Cambridge, was there on sufferance. There were students and professors who treated Cambridge women more or less equally, but when she went to lectures, she sat with the other women at the back of the hall; she could listen and learn but it counted for nothing more. And how comfortable did she feel asking questions? For Allie Douglas, who had excelled in everything she tackled, things were suddenly different and difficult. It started with Ernest Rutherford. She arrived at Cambridge thinking that radiation, nuclear physics, might be her area of study.

> Rutherford was gracious, affable, and friendly at my first interview and set me a problem on the heat emission from a certain radium disintegration product. This was one side of Rutherford, bluff, genial, self-confident, and hearty. But he could not suffer fools gladly and when I talked with him about my work...he thought I very nearly fell into that category and was extremely, abruptly, gruff, and rude. This was his other side.... As the months passed...I became more aware of my own limitations....

Rutherford shook her confidence. As did Sir Arthur Quiller-Couch, professor of English literature, who unabashedly disapproved of the university policy of admitting women. Quiller-Couch gave public lectures on Dickens and Jane Austen that were well attended and always attracted a great many faculty wives and women students. He sat on his chair at the front of the room, looked out at his audience, and began, "Gentlemen...." Then there was F. Shillington Scales, a radiologist with whom Allie and the aunts had a distant connection, friends of friends. When the Scaleses invited the Douglas women to tea, Allie wrote,

> Like Quiller-Couch he deplored the presence of women in the academic life of the University and neither of his two talented daughters was encouraged to enter Newnham or

Girton. The first time I was at tea in their house he sat beside me on a sofa, inquired what I was doing and then proceeded to impress upon me that no woman had ever excelled in science or literature. Who were the great writers, poets, artists, composers? All men. Even in the field of the domestic arts, the great cooks and fashion designers were men. There was so much general truth in all this that I said I could only agree, but in the case of science he must make an exception, namely Mme Curie. Looking at me with the utmost scorn he replied "Mme Curie—the wife of a clever chemist."

By now she doubted her ability not only to master nuclear physics but to become a scientist of any kind. That winter, "when I finally realized that I was on the road to nowhere," she came dangerously close to giving up. Instead, she continued her academic "sampling." One cold day in January 1922, Allie sat, as usual, in the back of the lecture hall with a Newnham College friend, Cecilia Payne. Together they were trying to grab a little warmth from the fire that was toasting the toes of the young men in the front of the room. It was a day she remembered because that was the day when she stumbled on astronomy, the science that would occupy her for the rest of her life, and

Allie Douglas's friend and classmate astrophysicist Cecilia Payne-Gaposchkin

Allie Douglas, second row, left, Yerkes Observatory, Wisconsin, 1925

when she met astrophysicist Arthur Eddington. Eddington had developed major new theories of stellar energy that were directly related to Einstein's theory of relativity. He was no feminist but, she writes, he was "ever courteous" and was prepared to teach her. Cecilia Payne, like Allie Vibert Douglas, also became an astrophysicist and an astronomer. Payne decamped from Cambridge for Harvard and a major career in the United States.

As Allie was trying to find her feet in Cambridge, her brother George was in Antarctica. He was a geologist on Ernest Shackleton's final polar expedition, and when Shackleton died mid-voyage, he returned to England with literally tons of rock samples and was now at Cambridge doing his own work at the Polar Institute. As ever, he provided Allie with moral support. George, Allie, and Aunt Mina lived together in Cambridge for the next nine months. Happy months for Allie Douglas. Arthur Eddington invited her and Cecelia Payne to a special meeting of the Royal Astronomical Society, a mark of recognition and respect for both women. Douglas had found her subject, but she wanted the PhD that she could never get from Cambridge.

Back in Canada for the summer, brother and sister spent their time at Ashkirk, the island, always their solace and their joy, and they regrouped. George went on to geology at Harvard and worked on his PhD. She, with all she had learned at Cambridge, registered for the PhD program at McGill. Once again, she was hired as a demonstrator in physics. She taught the pharmacy students, led laboratories for arts students, and along the way wrote a paper that a senior man presented *for* her at the Royal Society meeting. Then, her fortune turned: she was invited to be a volunteer research assistant at the Yerkes Observatory in Wisconsin. Yerkes, run by the University of Chicago with its 40-inch refracting telescope—then the largest in the world—was known as the birthplace of astronomy. It was a glorious four-month assignment, learning and working with some fun thrown in.

Now she had both her subject and the research material for her dissertation. She took herself to Harvard to see both George and his new wife, medical student Olga Crichton, and to talk to women at the Harvard Observatory. Her Newnham College friend, Cecilia Payne, was there and flourishing, and so was the legendary Annie Jump Cannon. Cannon had been one of the six Harvard "computers," six haphazardly chosen women whose newest assignment was to establish a system to classify the stars. One of these women was a single mother and a former housemaid, Annie Jump Cannon and Henrietta Leavitt were deaf, another was the daughter of a previous observatory director. Only one woman had any formal training. Together they created what amounted to a catalog of the stars. It was Annie Jump Cannon, a suffragette and a member of the National Women's Party, who devised the classification system. Allie Douglas wanted to see that catalog and meet that woman.

Annie Jump Cannon

With her research under her arm and a spring in her step she returned to Montreal and wrote her dissertation. She said that there was no one at McGill who was particularly interested in her work, and McGill had trouble coming up with examiners for her oral presentation, but in 1926, she got her PhD. Finally.

◆◆◆

McGill didn't quite know what to do with their new "Dr." Vibert Douglas, so they did nothing. They kept her on as a lecturer and a demonstrator—helper jobs—and when she taught, it was often to students who *had* to take a science course. She liked teaching well enough, but she—as anyone would—wanted more prestige and the salary that went with it. Academe was a male domain, reverentially male. Professors were high priests, keepers of the flame of knowledge. At Cambridge, knowledge was so sacrosanct that for centuries "fellows" at the university, like monks, were celibate and not allowed to marry. It wasn't until 1860 and an act of Parliament that "fellows" were allowed to marry, and, remarkably, not many did. It somehow followed, therefore, that no woman could be a true scholar. Any woman making a bid for recognition in the twentieth century had to be undeniably and demonstrably more intelligent, insightful, and dedicated then her male colleagues, not to mention brimming over with confidence.

Allie Vibert Douglas had many but not all of the ingredients for success in the academic world. She *was* better and more dedicated than many of her male colleagues, and she was, in the context of Canada, thanks to her grandfather Douglas, from a "good" family with social position, and that certainly counted.

Her academic excellence was undeniable. She had placed first, was better than anyone else in the province as she left high school. She could brandish that Anne Molson Gold Medal from McGill, she had sat down and talked science with Ernest Rutherford and Arthur Eddington, two giants in the field at Cambridge, and the Harvard Observatory, one of the leading centers in astronomy, had welcomed

Allie Vibert Douglas, 1930s

her. But she was a woman. She remained a demonstrator—the bottom rung of the academic ladder at McGill.

It might have helped if she had had social connections in the university world. Wilhemina Gordon, one of the first women on faculty at Queen's, was the daughter of Daniel Gordon, principal of the university, and had become a handmaid to her father, keeping house for him when her mother died. Whatever her competence, she was the principal's daughter. Yet, according to Isabel McInnes, who taught at UBC and was at Queen's when Gordon was in charge, "Gordon did not want women appointed to staff." Wilhemina was lucky. Allie Douglas did not have those connections, nor had she been taken on as anyone's assistant, another way in for women in academe.

Carrie Derick managed to be made a full professor, even though the principal said it was just an honorary position. She pushed hard to the point of being considered almost vulgar in her assertiveness, certainly not quite "womanly." Allie Douglas was different. She was organized and thorough, but she was well-mannered—perhaps a little too well-mannered in the early days for her own good. In 1937, after seventeen years of laboring in the salt mines of the McGill physics department, she applied to be warden, head, of Royal Victoria College, the women's college at McGill. She submitted *eight* letters of reference with her application. One was a character reference from a High Court judge, another from a senior and respected mathematician, another from the director of the physics laboratory, A. Norman Shaw, the man to whom she reported. In his letter Shaw listed her academic qualifications and went on to say that "Dr. Douglas has been on the staff of the department of physics as a lecturer and a demonstrator since 1920 and she has been qualified long to hold a position of higher rank than her present post…[she] has published about ten papers on her work in astrophysics and twenty-five well-written popular articles on topics in Physics and astronomy…." Norman Shaw, judging by his letter, thought she deserved more, yet as director of the Macdonald Physics Laboratory, he had not promoted her. Did he not have the authority or was he wary of sticking his neck out? But Warden of Victoria College was a woman's job. Nothing—it seemed—blocked her path.

Despite her glowing references, Allie Douglas did not get the job. It went instead to Maude Parkin Grant, who could "organize an empire single-handedly," according to Eugene Forsey, later a Canadian senator and Allie's cousin. Maude Grant also had social connections. Her sister Alice was the wife of Vincent Massey, then high commissioner to the UK and later Canada's first native-born Governor General. She did not have academic qualifications to match Allie Douglas, but academic excellence did not tip the balance. Losing that competition was the final straw for Allie Douglas at McGill. She, like Trixie Worsley when she left the University of Toronto nearly thirty years later, had had enough. Years later, her nephew Patrick Douglas said that while she was at McGill, she had been paid next to nothing and never got the recognition that was her due. Teaching at McGill was a chapter in her life that she did not talk about. By the late 1930s, both her aunts were dead, and George was working for Rio Tinto mines, a job that took him first to Spain and then to Northern Rhodesia. There were friends, but she had nothing to tie her to Montreal and, something she was not comfortable with, the francophone majority in Quebec was beginning to assert its presence. Kingston was not that far away, and it was closer to Ashkirk, the family's island retreat, so when Queen's University offered her the job as dean of women, she took it. There would be academic compromises, and she knew it.

✦✦✦

*Dean of Women: Such a woman should be a scholar. She should be a woman of some age and experience, with good judgment and a knowledge of life; a lovable woman, dignified and reasonable; one who understands Canadian character and ideals and sympathizes with them. That the women students will respect her, she should be influential in the management of university affairs and hold a position of adequate authority.*

*—Ubyssey, 1921*

The new job at Queen's was a package deal—she would be appointed an associate professor in the department of physics, the academic position she had coveted, but only if she signed on as dean of women. She could not have had one without the other. It also meant that she all but gave up her research in astrophysics, gave up serious academic study. That was the compromise. Keeping up with old friends, she wrote to Ludwik Silberstein at the University of Chicago in 1942, "I have been at Queen's as Dean of Women since 1939. It is very all-absorbing and carries a good deal of responsibility, so that there is very little time left or energy for astrophysics." Allie Douglas must have written that letter with more than a little regret.

She was dean of women at Queen's from 1939 to 1959, longer than any other woman in the job, and for all that time she lived in a small apartment in Ban Righ Hall, the women's residence. Day and night she was surrounded by hundreds of young women who might be laughing wildly one minute and in tears over boyfriends and essay deadlines the next. They climbed out windows, forged permission slips, lost their towels, and got themselves in all manner of trouble all too often. It would have been enough to drive anyone mad; Allie Douglas put up with it for twenty years. What must have made it worse was that women students hated being under the thumb of the dean of women. It was a position that had been around since the end of World War I. No matter who was in the job, she threatened and hampered the students' freedom—which was what she was supposed to do. It wasn't so much that the university was concerned about the safety and virtue of these young women—no, the fear was that these brazen bluestockings would corrupt the young men and distract them from their studies. As the Queen's Encyclopedia says, "concerns grew about the morals and deportment of women students living in crowded boarding houses, often alongside men." The dean of women was there first and foremost to keep the women in check.

There were curfews and rules against male visitors. The dean of women made and enforced rules about off-campus living—women students could only live in "approved" boarding houses, never in boarding houses that housed men. Dean Douglas, right up to 1959, held fast to a no-slacks rule (except, strangely, at breakfast), and it was her job to keep track of furniture and supplies. She had to be part chatelaine and, as that job description in the University of British Columbia's student newspaper, the *Ubyssey*, said, a scholar and "a lovable woman." Allie Douglas loved her nieces and nephews, and they loved her, but she was a scholar; she did not aspire to be, did not want to be caretaker, let alone *lovable*, to two hundred young women who wished she wasn't there to begin with. It was ridiculous. "Lovable" was not in the job description of any of her male colleagues.

She was tough, unyielding, stern—not surprisingly, students called her an "old battle-axe." They had no idea that Dean Douglas was Canada's first astrophysicist known all over the world for her scholarly work. She might not have been interested in making herself lovable, but she was deeply interested in women's education. In 1920, when she was only twenty-six, Allie Douglas had joined the International Federation of University Women. In 1949, she become the IFUW's first Canadian president.

Allie Douglas, newly elected president of the International Federation of University Women being congratulated by the previous president, Stanislawa Adamowicz, from Poland, Toronto, 1946

Allie Douglas, back row, sixth from the left, Canadian Federation of
University Women, Edmonton, 1969

There is a group photograph of Allie Douglas with more than
thirty other Canadian university women taken in 1969. They face the
camera, all of them wearing summer dresses, legs crossed at the ankle,
their purses and gloves in their laps and nearly all of them smiling at
least a little. All of them, that is, except Allie who stands in the middle of the back row, her graying hair parted in the middle and pushed
straight back, almost glaring at the photographer.

When she died, her friend Shirley Brooks described Allie
Douglas: "Her hair was held back in a neat little bun, she wore comfortable tweeds and stout walking shoes." Brooks added that "she had a
strong handshake and a warm smile." Kind, firm, and constant, yes, but
there are no photographs of a smiling Allie Douglas.

Dean Douglas might not have been fashionable, fun, or loose with
the rules, but when it came to matters of principle, that was different.
At the beginning of her tenure in 1939 a young woman in her charge
became pregnant, something that must have happened nearly every
year; the administration wanted to expel her, no further discussion.
Allie Douglas faced them down and said, "If this is so, you have my
resignation." During World War II, she began a program of required
war service. Every woman had to put in her hours. Later, Allie Douglas
championed the cause of the father of one of her astronomy students,

a Latvian refugee, an agronomist by training stuck in an unskilled job. She wrote around until she found him a job that matched his qualifications. Something no one had done for her.

Her mailbox was almost always overflowing with letters from all over the world. She had kept up her contacts with the astronomers, mathematicians, and physicists whom she had come to know. And she was never shy about writing to "important" people. There was a note one day from the prime minister, Mackenzie King, thanking her for forwarding a copy of a paper she had written. She had met him a few years before, and he added, "I shall always retain a vivid recollection of the inspiring address I heard you give in the theatre of the National Museum of Canada...." She sent copies of her academic papers to scores of people. Her old colleagues at Newnham College in Cambridge wrote to congratulate her when she was elected president of the International Federation of University Women. They had archived all her scholarly papers and the "popular" pieces that she wrote for magazines and newspapers. In 1939, as she was leaving McGill, she wrote an op-ed congratulating Stephen Leacock on his essay "All Right, Mr. Roosevelt," saying that "it is the duty of every one of us—not of that gifted author alone—to fight against injustice and intolerance in *all* their forms with every means at our disposal." She had asked Leacock's permission to circulate her article and he responded, "God Bless my soul! Use it! Placard it on the college fence. I am deeply appreciative of the compliment."

In 1944, Arthur Eddington, the man who introduced her to astronomy and astrophysics, died. Eddington had never become a household name, yet the obituary that she wrote was widely noticed and praised. An American mathematician wrote saying, "You should write a biography in the form of a book." And slowly it came to pass. Eddington was one of a small circle of men and at least one woman (Cecilia Payne) who delved into general relativity. He made the link between energy, matter, and the stars, taking Einstein's theory a step further. Allie Douglas had studied relativity with Rutherford, talked it through with Eddington and with a good many other mathematicians and philosophers. Very few people anywhere could have had those conversations. She was supremely qualified to write his biography. Every day, she taught her classes, came back to Ban Righ Hall, made sure all was well in the dining room, checked that the laundry was back, dealt with whatever was going on with the students, and then sat down and wrote to Bertrand Russell or Albert Einstein or many others. "Dear Dr.... I studied under and worked with Eddington in 1921–23.... What is the value and where are the weaknesses in his Fundamental Theory?" It was clear in her letters to the "great men" that she understood relativity, that she understood astronomy, that she could keep up. And the great men answered her letters. The mathematical questions were answered, and the physics was dealt with, and then they added their stories. The German mathematician Hermann Weyl, considered one of the most influential mathematicians of the century, told of how in 1933, following a meeting of the International Astronomy Society in Göttingen, he had taken a train ride with Eddington and, as they sat alone together in a compartment, told him that he was preparing his escape from Nazi Germany. Weyl escaped almost the next day and got his Jewish wife and his child out. His letter to Allie Douglas ends, "I will never forget in those anxious days at this decisive turn of my life, I had for a brief moment the comfort of Eddington's company, quiet understanding and encouragement." Only someone of Allie Douglas's stature, with her intellectual capacity and humanity, could have coaxed stories from these men. Bertrand Russell wrote, as only Bertrand Russell would,

> I used to enjoy asking him [Eddington] questions to which nobody else would have given a definite answer. I would say, "Eddington, when was the world created?" and he would reply "In the year ninety thousand million BC".... He told me once, with evident pleasure that the expanding universe would shortly become too large for a dictator since messages sent out with the velocity of light would never reach its more distant portion. I naturally asked, "How about God?" but the answer to this question was not considered within the province of the physicist.

Then came her forty-five minutes with Albert Einstein. When she wrote to Einstein asking for his view of Eddington, he replied

Albert Einstein

self-effacingly, "His creative achievement in the field of relativity and the theory of matter did not carry conviction for me. But this may be my fault. The German physicist and philosopher, Lichtenberg once said, 'If a head and a book collide and it sounds hollow—this is not necessarily caused by the book.'"

Allie Douglas was invited to come to Princeton and meet Einstein. He would give her forty-five minutes. It was 1954; he would be dead less than a year later. Early in January, she took a taxi to the Kingston station and the train to New Jersey. When she arrived, Einstein had a bad cold and she found him at home. She was captivated. As she wrote later to her family: "Mes chères…. He has a massive head and a great sense of humor…. He sat in a large chair in a brown dressing gown with a brown silk muffler round his neck…." But she did not only sit and idolize Albert Einstein. She had the courage to disagree with him. Popularizing science, at least making it comprehensible was important to Allie Douglas.

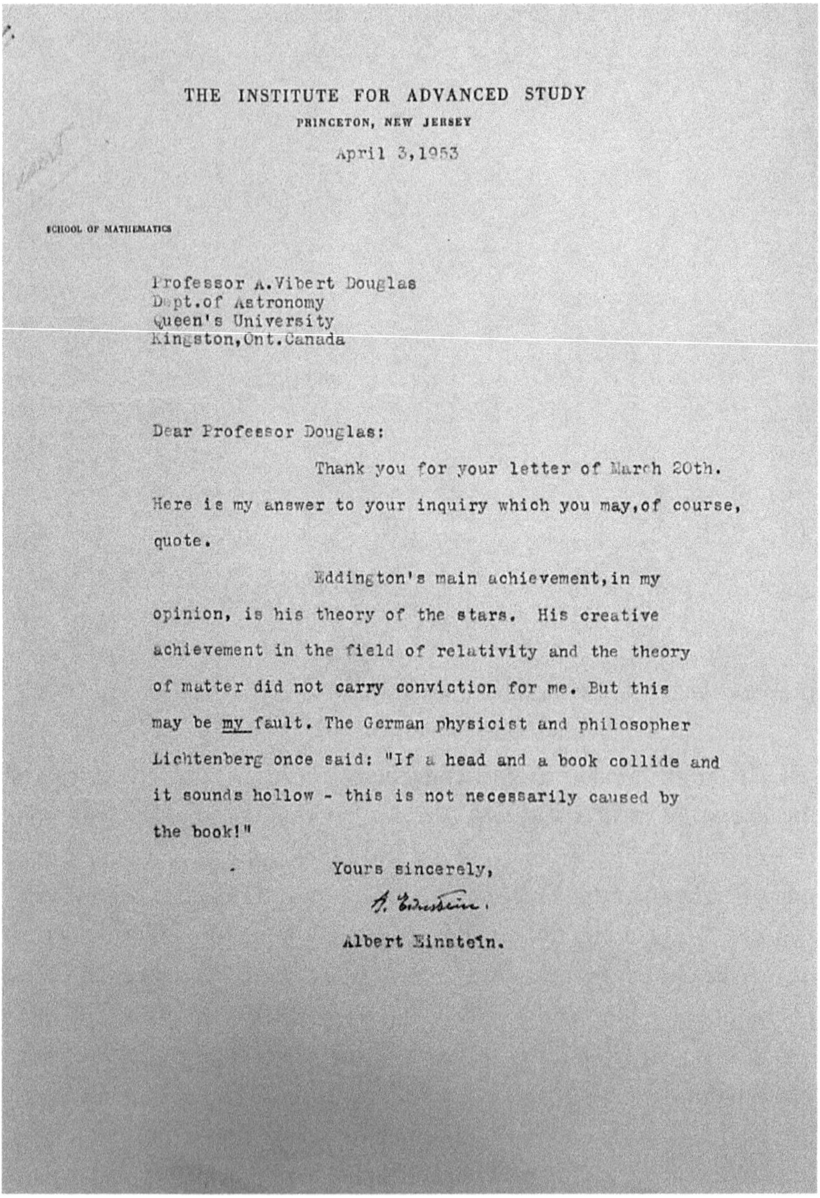

THE INSTITUTE FOR ADVANCED STUDY

PRINCETON, NEW JERSEY

April 3,1953

SCHOOL OF MATHEMATICS

Professor A.Vibert Douglas
Dept.of Astronomy
Queen's University
Kingston,Ont.Canada

Dear Professor Douglas:

Thank you for your letter of March 20th.
Here is my answer to your inquiry which you may,of course,
quote.

Eddington's main achievement,in my
opinion, is his theory of the stars.  His creative
achievement in the field of relativity and the theory
of matter did not carry conviction for me. But this
may be my fault. The German physicist and philosopher
Lichtenberg once said: "If a head and a book collide and
it sounds hollow - this is not necessarily caused by
the book!"

Yours sincerely,

*A. Einstein.*

Albert Einstein.

Letter from Albert Einstein

Allie Vibert Douglas's letter to her family after her visit with Albert Einstein

On Train - Princeton to N.Y.
1954 Jan 4

Mes chers

I have had a very wonderful 3/4 hour with Einstein. He has a massive head + a great sense of humour. I got to Princeton at 10:40 + walked on + on beyond the College Blog + whole hunks of residents + then the huge Grad School + on another ½ mile through fields + country side to the brick Inst of Adv. St. — to be told E was at home with a cold but would see me there. They kindly sent a girl in the Inst. bus to take me to his little white house in the town. A house keeper took me up to his study. a glass wall looking over fields + adjacent gardens — 2 walls of book cases, books + reprints. He in a large chair in his brown dressing gown with a brown silk muffler round his neck, his sec. a Miss Hoffman by him at a small low square table with math Mss on it + ashtrays + a little carved monk.

He gave me one instance when Edd. had the insight

Einstein praised what he called Eddington's ability to give "…the intelligent lay reader at least some understanding, some insight into the significance of new scientific ideas—but with a smile," then, as she told her family, "he added that a scientist is mistaken if he thinks he is making the layman understand; a scientist should not attempt to popularize his theories, if he does,'he is a fakir—it is the duty of a scientist to remain obscure.' I said I could not agree, a scientist had a duty to try to educate the public at least to an appreciation of what the scientist is attempting to do; but Dr. Einstein shook his head." To Allie Douglas, science was about ideas and belief as much as theory and fact.

Arthur Eddington had been a Quaker, and as she was leaving, Einstein quietly said to her, "If I wasn't a Jew, I would be a Quaker."

Allie Vibert Douglas's biography of Arthur Eddington came out in 1956 to much international acclaim and was reprinted in 2018. It was one of her crowning achievements.

Requests to speak and to publish her work continued to come in. In 1959, there was a letter from the Indian Astronomical and Sanskrit Institute: "Sir," it said—she always signed her professional correspondence A. Vibert Douglas—and the letter asked if their Institute could publish her newest research. She wrote back and said, no, she had not done any serious research, apart from her biography of Eddington, certainly not any research in astronomy, for a number of years.

That little letter drew a line under her scientific career.

+ + +

*Modern Science is the daughter of astronomy; it has come down from heaven to earth along the inclined plane of Galileo, for it is through Galileo that Newton and his successors are connected with the keeper.*

—Henri Bergson, *Creative Evolution*

In 1958, George Douglas, her brother, died. George, the boy who left the door open so she could eavesdrop on his science club, the young man who had got her the "more interesting" job in the War Office, and the man who had been her science sounding board all her life. He was sixty-five and had been teaching geology at Dalhousie in Halifax, Nova Scotia, for more than twenty-five years. They had remained close; it was reflected in their letters. Formal letters to Allie Douglas began, "Dear Dr. Douglas;" letters from friends started, "Dear Allie;" from the nieces or nephews, "Dear Aunt." When George wrote to his sister for her birthday in 1942, he began, "Allie my precious one," and ended, "God Bless you my darling." Her relationship with her brother had been the closest and most intimate of her life. The year after George's death she retired as dean of women.

Knowing that they were about to lose their dean of women, the university searched for a replacement. As columnist Doris Anderson reported in the *Toronto Star*, Queen's offered the job to Pauline Jewett, who was then teaching in the political science department at Carleton University in Ottawa. They proposed the same package deal that Allie Vibert Douglas had accepted twenty years earlier: an associate professorship and dean of women. Jewett had been an undergraduate at Queen's and she knew and respected Allie Douglas. "She was a brilliant Astro-physicist," she said, "but as a student I remember her doing all kinds of menial tasks such as counting towels in women's residences." Pauline Jewett insisted on sitting down with Allie Douglas and as good as asked her, should I take the job? She replied, "Pauline, why go through the back door when you can go through the front?" Pauline Jewett said no to Queen's and went on to be elected to the House of Commons and then became the first woman president of a Canadian university, Simon Fraser University in British Columbia. She would not make that academic compromise and take the package deal; twenty years earlier, Allie Vibert Douglas had had no choice.

For a few more years she taught astronomy and physics, then said, "That's enough of that," and began traveling with a vengeance, adding more stamps to her passport every year. She continued to work with the International Federation of University Women and with the Royal Astronomical Society. She was a delegate to a UNESCO conference and awarded honorary degrees around the world. In 1967,

Canada's National Council of Jewish Women named her one of the ten "Women of the Century." For fun, she chased solar eclipses. When she knew another was coming up, she would zero in on the optimum viewing location, lasso one of her great-nieces or -nephews, and, just as her aunts had taken her to see Halley's Comet in 1910, take them to see the next eclipse. Stephen Douglas had his turn with his great-aunt in Jaipur in India. There they were, a teenage boy, his elderly aunt, and a busload of white-haired astronomers, every one of whom had turned and greeted Allie Douglas like the legend she was as they got on the bus. At one point on the trip, he was asked if he would like a ride on an elephant. He was a polite young man and he turned to his Aunt Allie and asked, "Would you like to go?"

"No, no, no, dear," she replied. "I've had my ride on an elephant." Then she paused and added, "London, Hyde Park, 1903."

There were trips to Pakistan and Afghanistan, a conference in Karlsruhe, and a visit to Berlin with another group of astronomers. One morning, everyone except Allie piled on a bus for a visit to East Berlin via Checkpoint Charlie. At dinner, someone turned and said, "We missed you, Allie. Where did you go today?"

"East Berlin," she said. "I just walked through Checkpoint Charlie. Walking is always the best way to see a place."

Astronomy grew from the riddle of the ages—but as science defines the realities of the skies, must it destroy the mystery of the heavens? Growing up with the leatherbound sermons of her Grandfather Douglas on her bookshelf and the graves of her parents close at hand, in an age when science and philosophy were closely intertwined, she never divorced the spiritual from the scientific. Questions of the soul, of "creative evolution," were always with her. Allie Douglas searched for her place, not only in the world but in the universe, all her life. Every year she asked her students to create a book of literary quotations about the stars and the skies. Those little books with their scores of lines from Tennyson, Wordsworth, Shelley, Byron, Browning—the stalwarts of English literature—are still in her files. She never threw any of them away. As she aged, she became more spiritual. In one of the many tributes after her death someone said, "She was almost otherworldly."

Allie continued to row herself out to the island in the St. Lawrence River as long as she could. One of her great-nephews remembers learning to row as a teenager and suddenly realizing that his teacher, his great-aunt, was a woman in her seventies. The little house on the island with its small red table and chairs that she and George used as children, the mismatched coffee cups, old photographs, no electricity—it was all as it had been. There had been no move to modernize it. And every summer, first the nieces and nephews, George's children, then the great-nieces and great-nephews would come to stay, and they would look at the skies together. Several of those young men and women went to Queen's, and as she grew older still, they took turns staying with her, taking a daily glass of sherry with their aunt. Remembering.

"I remember coming back to the island with her in the boat one evening." Her nephew Patrick was a man in his nineties as he looked back. "I was trying to bring us in. She took over and so easily managed the boat. Slipped with the current one way then another, nothing else, just moving with the water and sliding into the dock. She knew where she was going."

+++

*Every spring and autumn we drove out to our lot in Mount Royal Cemetery. George and I were always rather oppressed by these pilgrimages to the burial place of our great-grand Parents, our Grandfather and our Mother. After trimming the shrubs, weeding or other little chores, Granma would produce candies and a biscuit before the drive home (1898).*

Allie Vibert Douglas was a very little girl when her family started those pilgrimages to the family plot in the Mount Royal Cemetery. Little girls wander off when the adults are busy, and Allie must have wandered down some of the many pathways that wind through the cemetery. She would not have gone far before she passed two much older and unmarked graves, burial sites of two paupers who could not afford a headstone. Did the little girl stop and wonder about these people?

Years later, when she came back from Cambridge and visited the family plot, Allie Douglas, by now a woman, would have seen the new, tall headstone erected in 1927 marking those anonymous graves. She must have stopped and read "to the memory of the greatest of Canada's geographers who for 34 years explored and mapped the main travel routes between the St. Lawrence & the Pacific. David Thompson." And she might well have looked down and seen the simple slab embedded in the grass at her feet and read, "Charlotte Small Thompson 1785–May 4 1857. Beloved wife of David Thompson."

Perhaps Allie Douglas read the names and wondered who was this woman, Charlotte Small, as she walked down the mountain and back to Westmount.

# 5. CHARLOTTE, LOUISA, AND NANCY

*See what it is to be without women.*

—Alexander Mackenzie

From the vantage point of the twenty-first century, no matter how many times stories of teenage brides have been told, there is hardly a woman who doesn't shudder at least a little as this one starts: "Charlotte Small married David Thompson, the great explorer, when she was thirteen," then shudders a little more, "and she had thirteen children." What is more difficult to comprehend is that, certainly by the standards of the day, it was a happy marriage. Louisa Mackenzie was sixteen when she married Angus Bethune; she had seven children. Her sister Nancy had twelve, and she was twenty when she and John McTavish got married. Thirty-two babies—more than half of the children of these Métis women, were born in fur-trading posts or on the trail. Only one died in infancy. These women kept their babies safe.

Charlotte, Louisa, and Nancy were Métis women born at the end of the eighteenth century, their European husbands were explorers and fur traders, partners in the North West Company. They all were part of the familial web of early Canada. Cousins of "great" explorers, aunts to members of the Family Compact, and wives to the monied men of the fur trade and, not incidentally, ancestors of some powerful modern men and women.

The story of David Thompson and Charlotte Small has been called one of the great romances of early Canada. Romantic or not, it was a successful, enduring, and affectionate marriage. The pair of them kept each other going for fifty-eight years, longer, it's said, than any other nineteenth century Canadian marriage. There were other such marriages that lasted, white husbands who loved their Métis wives and their families—John Macdonell and Magdeleine Poitras from Qu'Appelle, Saskatchewan, were together for fifty-four years. James Douglas, governor of the new province of British Columbia, was married to a Métis woman, Amelia Connelly, for nearly fifty years and spoke of "the many tender ties which find a way to the heart."

Inevitably, it did not always turn out that way. White fur traders—too many of them—left their Indigenous families and went back to Eastern Canada, England, or Scotland, deserting both the country and their families. That is what happened to Charlotte Small's Cree mother—no one knows her name. Her husband was Patrick Small, a North West Company partner in charge of the Île-à-la-Crosse fur-trading post in what is now Northern Saskatchewan. They had three children, Charlotte, Nancy, and a boy, Patrick, after his father. The senior Patrick Small had come west in 1784, and, as one account puts it, "felt the absence of help-mate and wife." He married Charlotte's mother in a *mariage à la façon du pays*—according to the customs of the country; clergy were few and far between—and Charlotte was born on September 1, 1785.

Small ran the post at Île-à-la-Crosse well. The fur trade was a highly competitive business that relied on a good working relationship between First Nations and the company. Traders and explorers from other companies, and in Small's time they were various, came through Île-à-la-Crosse trying to cut in on his territory. Twenty-two-year-old Alexander Mackenzie had been sent by one of those other companies to set up a rival trading post, but Small had cornered the market and established a working relationship with the Cree that could not be broken. The fur trade was not only about trapping and bringing in

Explorer Alexander Mackenzie

the furs, work usually done by men. It depended just as much on the work of the women. Alexander Mackenzie wrote to his twenty-five-year-old cousin, Roderick, "There are about ten Crees at the other [Small's] fort—all family connections—none of them come near us—I have no one that can make *raquettes* [snowshoes]. I do not know what to do without that article. See what it is to be without women."

It was First Nations women who made the snowshoes, and no one could go outside the fort to collect firewood, let alone trap, without snowshoes. They made moccasins, mitts, leggings—clothes that could withstand the weather—and the food. The women dried salmon, whitefish, and goose, and they collected berries and prepared pemmican, the portable nutritious food that kept everyone on the trail alive. It was the women who trapped and snared small game, the rabbits and martens that were also, David Thompson noted in his diary, the women's to trade. Charles McKenzie—there were many McKenzies in the fur trade—was a clerk with the Hudson's Bay Company. He wrote to his children about his Métis wife, a woman then in her seventies: "Your good mother is still as brisk as a Bee—She must take her hunting exercise—I believe she snared upwards of 600 Rabbits this winter—merely to give them to the people whose wives do not set a snare."

The women dressed the furs and harvested the roots used to sew the bark canoes. Some—particularly, it's said, Chipewyan women—were also paddlers. There were two women paddlers on Alexander Mackenzie's trip to the Arctic in 1789. (Feminist historian Sylvie van Kirk writes that one Chipewyan chief told explorer Samuel Hearne that "Women...were made for labor; one of them can carry or haul twice as much as two men can do.") Traders needed Indigenous women to survive and had done so since they arrived in North America. Marriages to Indigenous women were key in building alliances with First Nations, and marriages between First Nations women and white men brought economic advantages to those First Nations. What those marriages meant to the women themselves was something else again.

By the early 1790s, Patrick Small decided that his work in the West was done. He had established a professional relationship with the Cree that he could hand on to whoever replaced him and now, after seven years at Île-à-la-Crosse, it was time to retire and move back to England. He also had a personal relationship with a Cree woman, the mother of his children. What would happen to them? For Small it was not a difficult decision, "knowing the ridicule and ill treatment awaiting his wife and children in the land of the White men," he would go back to England alone. He set up a small pension for his wife and the three children, in all likelihood asked someone to keep an eye on his family, and with a clear conscience, Patrick Small left. Mrs. Small, and she would have been known as Mrs. Small, was on her own.

She was a Cree woman; her children were Métis and part of a bridge generation. The girls had learned Indigenous skills from their mother, they had grown up with white men, and, as children of a North West Company partner, they had social status in the white world. Métis women were also desirable wives for incoming traders. They understood the business and understood life in a fur-trading post better than any white woman ever would, and they were capable on the trail.

When Patrick Small went back to England, his son was a baby, Nancy was three, and Charlotte was five. Mrs. Small got them all into the fur trade, her son became a clerk, and both of her daughters married partners. She did well by her children.

David Thompson's mother, Anne, like the Cree mother in Île-à-la-Crosse, was also on her own. The Thompsons were from Wales, and not long after they arrived in London, her husband died. Now she too was an eighteenth-century single mother with two sons to launch. She got them into a charity school with connections to the Hudson's Bay Company, a desirable placement. At the age of fourteen, David Thompson was indentured to the company and left England bound for Churchill Factory on the west side of Hudson Bay. He never saw his mother again.

Churchill Factory, the story goes, would not have existed were it not for a Chipewyan woman named Thanadelthur. The Chipewyan were in constant conflict with the Cree and around 1713, having been held prisoner by the Cree for at least a year, Thanadelthur escaped. Starving and exhausted, she arrived at Churchill Factory—then the most important post on the Hudson Bay coast. Knowing enough to appeal to the commercial instincts of the fur traders, she told the traders that the Chipewyans would not trade with them unless there was peace with the Cree and she needed their help. Thanadelthur led a year-long "diplomatic peace mission" out on the tundra. Her tough, persuasive tactics deeply impressed the Hudson's Bay men:

> She made them all Stand in fear of her she Scolded at Some, and pushing of others…and forcd them to ye peace. Indeed she has a Divellish Spirit and I believe that if thare were but 50 of her Country Men of the same Carriages and Resolution they would drive all the Northern Indians in America out of there Country.

Thanadelthur got what she wanted. The Chipewyan traded with the Hudson's Bay Company unmolested by the Cree, and Fort Churchill was built.

Thompson served out his apprenticeship in Churchill and began to learn to survey, the trade that would make his reputation. He lived through winters in the Subarctic, learned to speak Cree, and began to understand the ways of the business. He also fractured his leg and survived—a broken leg was often fatal in the eighteenth century—and in 1797, it is not clear why, he literally walked away from the Hudson's Bay Company. He switched companies. At 2:30 in the morning, in the middle of a snowstorm, he snowshoed to the nearest North West Company post and signed on as a surveyor. He was twenty-seven.

As David Thompson was snowshoeing away from the Hudson's Bay Company, much farther west, eleven-year-old Charlotte Small, in Île-à-la-Crosse, was looking after her little brother and sister. At eleven, she was close to marriageable age.

Île-à-la-Crosse was, if not a hub, certainly a crossroads in the fur trade. Everyone passed through. Roderick Mackenzie had briefly been an assistant to Patrick Small in Île-à-la-Crosse and then in 1788 was sent to establish Fort Chipewyan on Lake Athabasca more than 600 kilometers north. Fort Chip under Roderick Mackenzie became known as the "Athens of the North"; he had imported more than two thousand books from Montreal and set up a library for anyone in the fort. He had also taken a Chipewyan wife, no one knows her name either, and they had two little girls. His girls were younger than Charlotte. In 1797, when David Thompson signed on with the North West Company, Nancy was seven and Louisa only four. 1797 was also the year that Roderick Mackenzie's cousin Alexander became the first white man to reach the Pacific by land, making him a fur trade celebrity. He had already "discovered" the river that bears his name and paddled to the Arctic. A year later, Alexander Mackenzie ran into David Thompson in Sault Ste. Marie. Thompson had not been idle either. He had surveyed the route along the forty-ninth parallel, the expected border between the United States and Canada, and vast amounts of the interior of Canada. Mackenzie gave the younger Thompson a slap on the back, in his Scottish brogue told him what a fine fellow he was, and raised a cup. Thompson, an abstemious Welshman, returned the compliment without the toast. The next morning, Mackenzie continued east to make his fortune; David Thompson went west heading for Île-à-la-Crosse to make his reputation.

*** 

*We know so little about Charlotte Small that it is tempting to invent. We imagine her a beauty. We attribute to her, wisdom and devotedness. We construct between Thompson and Small a patient and loving partnership.... The fur trader and the Cree woman together symbolize all that we imagine for a secret history of Canada.*

—Aritha van Herk

Long after her death, Charlotte Small's grandson William Scott described her as "about five feet tall active and wiry, with black eyes and skin almost copper colored." Thompson called her "my lovely wife," and that is about all that we really know. She obviously caught Thompson's eye early on. When he went through Île-à-la-Crosse on his way west from Sault Ste. Marie, with only ten Cree in the fort, he must have at least seen the young Charlotte. He would have known that she was the daughter of a company partner and that the Smalls were an abandoned family. A year later he was back. At twenty-nine David Thompson had decided it was time to marry. Why Charlotte? Was he rescuing her? Who knows. On June 10, 1799, Thompson wrote in his diary, "This day married Charlotte Small." Nothing more. It too was a *mariage à la façon du pays*; the closest clergy were half a continent away. As Thompson described it in his diary,

> Nothing is required but the consent of the parties and the parents.... When contrarity of disposition prevail, so that they cannot live peaceably together, both parties are free to attach themselves to who they will, without any stain on their characters.

No-fault divorce. It did not give the wife any financial security if the marriage failed, but then there was not much security for a wife in a Christian marriage in eighteenth-century Canada.

The thirteen-year-old Mrs. Thompson packed up what belongings she had, and they set out together, traveling wherever the North West Company sent them. David Thompson traveled incessantly throughout the first ten years of his marriage, and Charlotte was with him all the way. They paddled together, climbed together, walked together for days on end. When they went on horseback through the mountains, babies were strapped into cradleboards or carried in saddlebags. On the river, husband, wife, children, baggage, crew, and supplies were all packed into the canoes. Harriet Sinclair Cowan, a doctor's wife from Fort Garry, described a canoe trip north to Moose Factory:

> We went in a large canoe—a *canot du nord*, as it was called, about thirty feet long, light and wonderfully strong. It had a wooden grating on the bottom to protect the birchbark. We had buffalo robes and blankets for our bedding, and tarpaulins to shield us from the rain. In bad weather the tarpaulins were stretched over the tents at our camping places. Our luggage and supplies had to be as light as possible. We had a large kettle, a frying pan and a tea kettle all of iron, for ourselves; and the men had the same.

The North West Company's rival, the Hudson's Bay Company (HBC), did not want their men to take their families with them on these work trips, trips that could last for months. HBC Governor George Simpson, the most influential man in the fur trade in the nineteenth century, made every effort to stop family travel. It cost money and more.

> ...it is attended with much expense and inconvenience on the voyage, business itself must not yield to domestic consideration, the Gentlemen become drones and are not disposable, in short, the evil is more serious than I am well able to describe.

At the turn of the nineteenth century, the Hudson's Bay Company reported that it was supporting between twelve and fifteen hundred wives and children. Something that persisted until 1810, when a new accounting system was introduced, giving officers a share in the profits. Family expenses fell sharply.

The HBC never sanctioned "country marriages," a prohibition more honored in the breach than the observance. The North West Company, Thompson's company, were more of the mind that a happy man is a productive man and never forbade those unions. That first year of their marriage, Charlotte and David Thompson wintered on the North Saskatchewan River at Fort George. By the spring of 1801, Charlotte was pregnant with their first child. They kept moving further west and Fanny Thompson was born in Rocky Mountain House. Charlotte was fifteen

That same year the two little Mackenzie girls, Nancy and Louisa, were about to see their lives turned upside down. They had grown up in Fort Chipewyan, and although they were Métis children, they benefited from their father Roderick Mackenzie's position. After all, they were "Mackenzies," the children of a partner in the Company. By now they had a little brother and a baby sister but, the speculation is, their mother had died. Roderick Mackenzie had spent nearly fifteen years in the northwest, he was nearing forty, the cold was penetrating his bones, and he decided, like Patrick Small before him, that it was time to move back to a more comfortable life. He began to pack up and decided that he would take his two youngest children with him. He left his library behind, and he left Nancy and Louisa. He put them under the guardianship of twenty-one-year-old John Stuart, his second in command, whom he had known since he was a boy. In the late spring of 1801 when the ice had broken up, Roderick Mackenzie paddled off across Lake Athabasca and headed east. Stuart, presumably, with Louisa and Nancy in tow, would move from fort to fort all over the northwest over the next eight years.

Roderick Mackenzie was heading for the annual meeting of the Nor'Wester wintering partners who, with their load of furs, would

"Charlotte Small,"
as imagined by
Melissa Jayne

meet the eastern partners with trading goods. From there, he would continue to Montreal.

The Thompsons kept traveling, David trading and surveying in the west. Samuel, their second child who grew up to help his father with surveying, was born three years later on the trail. Ten days after her son was born, Charlotte packed up the baby, and they all set out east across the Prairies for Fort Kaministiquia, later to be renamed Fort William, at the head of Lake Superior, and that big annual meeting. The population would grow from twenty or so based at the fort to more than twelve hundred people camped outside the fort and across the river. They would be there for a month or so while the voyageurs, the paddlers, would rest up and make the exchange of fur for goods.

The trip from the west could take two months. David Thompson paddled into Fort William in 1804 with Charlotte and his two children.

It was a good year for him: he became a partner in the company. He was sent back west and told to continue charting western Canada, but the winter of 1805 was a bad one. They were north of Lake Winnipeg, and supplies had run very low. In those winter months, it was Charlotte who went out, again and again, in her moccasins and leggings, and snared rabbits as she had been taught by her mother. She kept them fed. She had two small children in tow and was seven months pregnant with Emma, her third.

+++

In 1806, now with three children, they paddled back to Fort William for the big meeting. The company's growing priority over the next few years was to find a viable route to the Pacific Ocean. David Thompson, Simon Fraser, and John Stuart, who was by now Simon Fraser's lieutenant, were all set the same task—find the river that could take them relatively easily through the mountains and down to the Pacific.

Charlotte, now with three children under four, continued to travel with her husband. There were great parts of the discovery of Canada's west that were a domestic undertaking, at least for the Thompsons. They crossed the Rockies through the Howse Pass north of Banff and made their way down the west side of the mountains. Thompson wrote in his diary,

> The water descending in innumerable Rills, soon swelled our Brook to a Rivulet, with a Current foaming white, the Horses with Difficulty crossed & recrossed at every 2 or 300 yards, & the Men crossed by clinging to the Tails & Manes of the Horses, & yet ran no small danger of being swept away & drowned.

If the men were clinging to the horses' manes and tails, how was Charlotte managing to hang on to her own horse and look out for her three small children, the youngest still a baby? In the spring of the next year, they returned by the same route but this time there was snow

on the ground. Suddenly, one of the horses began to "behave wildly."
Thompson was all too aware of the risk to his children.

> One of my horses nearly crushing my children to death with
> his load being badly put on, which I mistook for being vi-
> cious, I shot him on the spot and rescued my little ones.

A few days later, Fanny, his oldest daughter, went missing.

> ...at 3 P.M. we reloaded, but missing my little Daughter &
> nowhere finding her, we concluded she was drowned & all
> of us set about finding her—we searched all the Embarrass
> [log-jams] in the River but to no purpose. At length, Mr.
> McDonald found her track going upwards. We searched all
> about & at length thank God at 8 ½ P.M. found her about 1
> Mile off, against a Bank of Snow.

Charlotte climbed and searched frantically for her daughter, all
the while hauling her big belly up and down the mountain. Once
again, she was pregnant, seven months. John, their fourth child, was
born in August 1808. It was after his birth that they decided, perhaps
under pressure from the company, not to travel en masse. Charlotte
and the four children stayed put while Thompson carried on in the
west, establishing new trading posts in what became Montana and
surveying the Columbia River basin. Like Mina Benson Hubbard, he
traveled with his sextant and compass. David Thompson also carried
a telescope with him in his canoe—that would have appealed to Allie
Douglas.

◆◆◆

There are great blanks in many stories from the west, no records to
substantiate events but widely held supposition. In 1809 it is supposed
that John Stuart, the man from Fort Chip in loco parentis to the
Mackenzie girls, came to the Fort William meeting with Louisa and

David Thomson and Charlotte Small, by sculptor Rich Roenisch, Windermere BC

Nancy in tow. Stuart had just made the very dramatic trip with Simon Fraser down the Fraser River in BC and would have been well-received in Fort William. It was during that Fort William meeting that Louisa, the younger Mackenzie daughter, met the man she would marry, a match undoubtedly engineered by Stuart. Louisa's future husband was Angus Bethune, the oldest son of John Bethune, a United Empire Loyalist and the first Presbyterian minister in what is now Ontario. Angus was twenty-six and established in the fur trade, Louisa was sixteen. He called her "little green blanket."

Louisa Mackenzie, as the daughter of a company partner, grew up in European clothing but she, like many other Métis women, kept one remnant of her mother's Indigenous clothes—the blanket was always there. Alexander Ross, fur trader in the West then sheriff at the Red River Settlement, was firmly of the opinion that "the blanket" was a little too present.

The blanket as an overall is considered indispensable, it is used on all occasions not only here—throughout the continent.... If a stick is wanted for the fire, or a pleasure party is to be joined away from home the blanket is called for. This invariable habit gives them a stooping gait while walking and the constant use of the same blanket day and night, wet and dry, is supposed to give rise to consumptive complaints which they are all more or less subject to.

Louisa had her green blanket, her sister Nancy a blue blanket, and in the only statue of Charlotte Small that exists, a conjured up image, she too has a blanket around her shoulders. Always the blanket.

But "little green blanket" was not with her husband long. In 1810, the company sent Angus Bethune to Rocky Mountain House to help David Thompson prepare for what became his epic journey down the Columbia River.

✦✦✦

Now with four children, Fanny, Samuel, Emma, and John, Charlotte and David began to show signs of settling down. This time when David set out to go down the Columbia River, Charlotte stayed put at Rocky Mountain House and reinforced family ties. Her sister, Nancy Small, had married John MacDonald of Garth, another trader, and the two sisters and their children were together for the next two years. There was one more Thompson baby, Joshua, born in 1810, and that same year David decided to send their eldest daughter to boarding school back east. It cost David Thompson £62 10s—a huge sum of money in 1810. "It is my wish to give all my children an equal and good education," he wrote to his friend. "My conscience obliges me to it, and it is for this I am now working in this country." There's nothing to show whether Charlotte wanted an exclusively European education for her daughter.

After more than twenty years, Thompson had finished, as he saw it, his work in the West. He arrived at the mouth of the Columbia River, only to discover that the Americans had got there first and built Fort Astoria, and then he doubled back and finished mapping the Columbia River saying, "Thus I have fully completed the survey of this part of north America from sea to sea, and by almost innumerable astronomical observations determined the positions of the Mountains Lakes and Rivers and other remarkable places on the Northern part of this Continent."

David Thompson was proud but very tired. He wrote to an old friend and told him that like Roderick Mackenzie and Patrick Small, he too had had enough. "I am getting tired of such constant hard journeys; in the last twenty months I have spent barely two under the shelter of a hut, all the rest has been in my tent."

In 1812, Thompson headed back upriver, met Charlotte and her sister and the children somewhere near Winnipeg, and they all headed east to Fort William for one last partners meeting. When he announced that he was retiring, the room must have fallen silent. Who else could have done what he did? Who would replace David Thompson? The company treated him well, giving him an unusually large retirement bonus. It was something positive to tell Charlotte as she contemplated with some trepidation this new life she was facing—Thompson had decided that they were going to live in Montreal.

They were all there at that 1812 meeting—Thompson and Charlotte and their five children; Angus Bethune and his wife, Louisa, "little green blanket"; and John Stuart, guardian to Roderick Mackenzie's still-unmarried daughter, Nancy. When the meeting broke up, Angus and Louisa, Nancy Mackenzie, and John Stuart headed west and, for the first time, David Thompson and Charlotte pointed their canoe east and paddled through Lake Superior and on to Montreal. They would never see the West again.

♦♦♦

When the War of 1812 began between the British (the Canadians) and the Americans, the North West Company was smarting. They had wanted but missed out on Fort Astoria, owned now by the American Pacific Fur Company, as their base on the West Coast. But now, with the war keeping the American military busy in the East, the

George Simpson, governor of
the Hudson's Bay Company,
portrait by Stephen Pearce

Nor'Westers saw opportunity. They would, it was decided, "invade"
Astoria with a flotilla of trade canoes. The leaders of the "invasion
force" included Angus Bethune, John Stuart, and another North West
partner, John George McTavish.

Just as wives and children went with husbands on exploration
missions, so women went with the men to this "war," such as it was.
Nancy Mackenzie was in the canoe with her guardian John Stuart
as they paddled downriver. It was a remarkably friendly invasion.
Everyone, Americans and Canadians, knew each other; they had all
traded together, helped each other out of dire situations, and when
the "Canadians" discovered that Fort Astoria could be had by nego-
tiation, that there was no military victory to be had, they all shook
hands, had a fine feast, and worked out a business deal. The Pacific Fur
Company agreed to sell its assets to the North West Company. When
the Canadians went home in 1813, Fort Astoria had become Fort
George and Nancy Mackenzie left Astoria as Mrs. John McTavish.
John Stuart had engineered, at least on paper, a good marriage for his

ward, but where Charlotte Small's marriage to David Thompson is held up as a great Canadian romance and a fine example of cultural liaison, Nancy Mackenzie's marriage to John McTavish turned out to be anything but.

♦♦♦

The source of Nancy Mackenzie's unhappiness was HBC Governor George Simpson, brusque, intolerant, and judgmental. Simpson had several country wives himself. He referred to one as "his article…an unnecessary and expensive appendage," a bit of "circulating copper." For him, there were no "tender ties," and he discouraged any such affection in others. When one of the Selkirk Settlers, Colin Robertson, wanted to bring his country wife to Red River to visit her children at school, Simpson wrote,

> Robertson brought his bit of brown with him to the settlement in the hopes that she would pick up a few English manners before visiting the civilized world.... I told him distinctly that the thing was impossible which mortified him exceedingly.

Nancy Mackenzie's marriage began well enough. Her husband, John McTavish, was moving up in the company hierarchy and he became chief factor at York Factory. Nancy was the Lady of the fort. Everyone called her "Madam" and deferred to her; she was not only married to the man in charge, but she was also a Mackenzie from the aristocracy of the fur trade. She had servants and she and McTavish, over the course of their marriage, had seven daughters. But Nancy McTavish was sitting on the cusp of the growing racial divide. Beyond the Red River settlement in what became Manitoba, there had been relatively few white women in western Canada. Now white wives began to appear more frequently. (In eastern Canada, the number of European settlers went from sixty to four hundred thousand.) Métis wives had distinct skills; they could cook, make frontier clothing, and paddle a canoe: abilities that were valued in the west. The self-importance of the new white wives rested entirely on their husband's position in the company hierarchy. The measure of a woman's worth was changing.

John McTavish was George Simpson's closest friend. Nancy and John had been married for seventeen years when—at George Simpson's suggestion, it's said—the two men traveled back to Great Britain, McTavish to Scotland, Simpson to England, on what amounted to a wife-hunting trip. Simpson married his eighteen-year-old cousin Frances, and John McTavish married the daughter of a prominent Scottish lawyer. McTavish sent word from Montreal, and asked another trader to tell Nancy Mackenzie McTavish that she had been "discarded." She was devastated. One of the traders wrote, "The first blow was dreadful to witness but the poor girl is fast becoming resigned." What was even more serious to many was that McTavish had broken the ethical code and made no provision for her or their children. Nancy Mackenzie was well-connected. After all, her father, Roderick, was a retired chief trader and cousin of Alexander Mackenzie, her uncle, Donald, was the governor of the Red River Colony, other uncles were prominent in the fur trade—the "family" rallied around. Her old guardian, John Stuart, took her and her daughters in and her uncle Donald Mackenzie wrote to McTavish:

> What could be your aim in discarding her whom you clasped to your bosom in virgin purity and had for seventeen years with you? She was the wife of your choice and has borne you seven children, now stigmatized with ignominy. If with a view of domestic happiness you have thus acted, I fear the aim has been misused and that remorse will be your portion for life. I think it is well our correspondence may cease.

The two senior men pressured Simpson and McTavish into making a settlement—two hundred pounds, they wanted a thousand—and, using the money as a dowry but without consulting Nancy, they arranged a second marriage, this time to a carpenter named Pierre LeBlanc. As Mrs. LeBlanc, wife of a tradesman, she became a servant to the governor's new white wife, Frances Simpson, and cared for her after her first child was born. White women were expected to display a measure of politesse to Indigenous women—not Frances Simpson. She wrote that Nancy Mackenzie, now Nancy LeBlanc, was a "complete savage with a coarse sort of woolen gown without shape and a blanket fastened round her neck." Always the blanket.

Very few if any discarded wives had a family army like the Mackenzies behind them, but that was no longer enough. The arrival of white wives and, not incidentally, more clergy to solemnize marriages brought a new attitude. Until now, Charlotte Small, Louisa and Nancy Mackenzie, and the many women like them were part of the "mutually beneficial fusion," as it has been termed, between First Nations and white society. Now, as George Simpson wrote, "the greater distance at which they are kept the better."

✦✦✦

Angus Bethune, Nancy's brother-in-law and Louisa's husband, was part of the 1813 "invasion" of Astoria, and then stayed on the other side of the Rockies for the next five years. Louisa was put on hold in eastern Canada. Angus Bethune returned frequently enough to father six children, two of them born in Fort William. The company sent him, like so many before him, to Île-à-la-Crosse in Saskatchewan— then to Moose Factory in Northern Ontario, where their son Norman was born in 1822. As he grew up, Norman was sent to the most prestigious boys' school in Canada, Upper Canada College, then to Europe for medical training, becoming a doctor and a professor of surgery in Toronto. There's no record of Norman Bethune Sr. ever proclaiming his Métis heritage or praising his Métis mother.

Angus Bethune was not a well-liked man. George Simpson called Louisa's husband "a very poor creature, vain, self-sufficient and trifling." One of Angus Bethune's last postings was to Sault Ste. Marie, where their final child was born. He retired to Toronto in 1839, and family connections smoothed his reintegration into "society." Angus Bethune became a director of the Bank of Upper Canada and a municipal politician. It would have been a comfortable if unfamiliar life for "little green blanket," Louisa Bethune, but she never saw Toronto, never saw her sister again. By 1839, she had been in her grave for six years. She died at forty in Michipicoten—now Wawa, Ontario.

$$\blacklozenge\blacklozenge\blacklozenge$$

Charlotte and David Thompson arrived in Montreal in 1812.

The city must have been overwhelming. David and Charlotte saw streets with traffic for the first time and had to teach their children to watch for carriages and runaway horses. They had never seen brick houses. Charlotte stepped into shops that sold dresses and hats and jewelry. There were churches—Presbyterian, Catholic, even a synagogue. And there were people, thousands and thousands of people. Montreal had a population of twenty thousand. There was no solitude, no open prairies, no magnificent mountains.

Patrick Small, Charlotte's father, had gone back to England. Alexander Mackenzie had been knighted and retired to Scotland, and a few months before Charlotte and David arrived in Montreal, he had married his fourteen-year-old cousin, Geddes. But there was never any question—David Thompson would stay in Canada; for one thing, company policy meant that he couldn't take his wife and children back to Britain, and his family was everything to him. This country was Charlotte's birthright. And how could David Thompson leave? No one knew Canada, as it became, better. He had mapped it all, surveyed its borders, climbed its mountains, canoed its rivers, hunted and eaten its game.

Within a few weeks of their arrival in Montreal, Thompson had the children baptized at the St. Gabriel Street Presbyterian Church, the church founded twenty years earlier by Angus Bethune's father, and a month later, Charlotte and David Thompson got married in a Christian ceremony at their little brick house in the village of Terrebonne. Terrebonne, fifty kilometers north of Montreal, was the home of Roderick Mackenzie and his second wife, his white wife. His youngest Métis children from Fort Chip and his white children grew up together. Terrebonne was popular among retired Nor'westers who had, for the most part, done well for themselves.

This was David Thompson's social circle. He was a good story-teller and much in demand at dinner parties. John Bigsby, a medical

The Bethune-
Thompson house,
Williamstown,
Ontario

officer in the British army, sat at table with him one night and wrote
about the evening in his book, *The Shoe and Canoe*. It is one of very few
descriptions of David Thompson:

> ...a singular-looking person...plainly dressed, quiet, and
> observant. His figure was short and compact, and his black
> hair was worn long all round, and cut square, as if by one
> stroke of the shears, just above the eyebrows. His complex-
> ion was of the gardener's ruddy brown, while the expression
> of his deeply furrowed features was friendly and intelligent,
> but his cut-short nose gave him an odd look.

> Never mind his [John] Bunyan-like face and cropped hair....
> He can create a wilderness and people it with warring savag-
> es or climb the Rocky Mountains with you in a snowstorm,
> so clearly and palpably, that only shut your eyes and you
> hear the crack of the rifle or feel the snowflakes melt on your
> cheeks as he talks.

Was Charlotte sitting at that dinner table as well? Had she cut his hair
with "one stroke of the shears?" Was she wearing a silk empire-waist

gown and growing tired, as wives do, of these oft-told stories? It's unlikely. They had money enough in those early days for a silk dress for Charlotte, but she was ill at ease in this world. Thompson says in his diary that in Terrebonne they hired a housekeeper as "company" for his wife. Besides, there were the children. She had eight more children after they came east. Their first five, born in the wild, carried by canoe and in saddlebags for hundreds of kilometers, children who had lived through the coldest of winters, were thriving when they arrived in Montreal. Within two years, two of those children had died. Thompson wrote in his diary, "John Thompson, deceased, January 11th, 1814, at 7 A.M. in the Village of Terrebonne, buried in Montreal the 12th inst. Aged 5 years and near 5 months, a beautiful promising boy."

Five-year-old John died from roundworm, parasitic and contagious. By February, Emma was gravely ill with "a gentle rattling in the throat. Swallows nothing. Comatose as usual.... At 7.25 PM it pleased God to take her quietly from this world—poor innocent Child, now near 8 years old, that never in her life willingly gave one moment's uneasiness to her Parents, or anyone else."

They stayed three years in Montreal as David worked on his magnum opus, his huge map of Canada. In 1815, with the American-British war over, Thompson was hired to be the astronomical surveyor of what was to be the new US–Canada border. They moved to Williamstown, Ontario, and crossed paths again with the Bethunes. David Thompson bought the house that had belonged to Reverend John Bethune. It was a solid, well-built house with a river running in front and a hundred acres of land. There was a good, big kitchen with an open hearth and an underground oven, a "great" room where children could play, and Charlotte could do her mending by the window. One of the younger ones scratched the initial "T" in the glass—that T is still there two hundred years later. There was also a map room for David. He said that the years they spent in Williamstown were the happiest of his life.

Charlotte spent much of the time alone with the children but not entirely alone. Her sister Nancy and her North West company–partner husband had come east as well and lived what would be twenty minutes away by car today, closer to a day's travel then. Nancy Small's husband, John MacDonald of Garth, a good friend of David's, had built them a fine, big house. When he decided that he and Nancy had outlasted their relationship, she—another Métis wife—held her ground. She remained chatelaine of the big house and could look out the window and see the new, much smaller house where her husband and his new wife lived.

Charlotte had her sister close by, she had work to do on the land, and she watched her children grow up.

+++

Nancy Mackenzie's life had another chapter. In 1838, she and her carpenter husband Pierre had headed west, getting away from Fort Garry and all that had happened there, and were waiting at Fort Edmonton, about to climb aboard the Columbia Express, as it was known, bound for the Pacific coast. They would be traveling through territory mapped by David Thompson. There were more passengers than usual—twenty-six, including two missionary priests, two young English botanists, and the LeBlancs with their four children and thirteen-year-old Grace McTavish, Nancy's youngest from her first marriage. One of the young botanists, Robert Wallace, had fallen in love with Maria Simpson, Sir George's daughter, and against all advice they had married only days before.

It was a long, arduous, but well-established route—first six days on horseback, then by canoe up the Athabasca River to Jasper, then south overland, and finally the canoe trip down the Columbia to the coast. They were well on their way on the first leg when suddenly, the LeBlanc's eldest daughter, Henrietta, died. No warning, no explanation. When he heard the news, the factor in Edmonton wrote to a friend, "Poor m. Leblanc, when he left.… Did not think that 2 days after his fine young Daughter would be a corps, yes, my friend, 2 days after he had left that place she was no more. What a change in that poor woman [Nancy]."

Nancy was once again distraught. But there was nothing to be done. They buried Henrietta LeBlanc on the banks of the Athabasca and carried on. In Jasper, the missionaries christened babies—with Nancy often as witness. She was looking after her other children and carrying on. By mid-October, after six weeks of travel, they arrived at the final leg of the trip, the canoe voyage down the Columbia River. Because there were so many passengers, they split into two groups. The first group

Lady Amelia Douglas, Métis wife of BC Governor James Douglas, c. 1885

got through and the canoes came back for the second group, including the LeBlancs. A full-sized canoe could carry a great deal, but a complete complement of passengers and crew, luggage, and more than twenty pieces of cargo, was tempting fate. They were overloaded, and when they reached the aptly named Dalles des Morts, Rapids of the Dead, the boat took on water. The young English botanist, Robert Wallace, knowing nothing about canoes, took his new wife in his arms, stood up, calling, "Courage, my friends!" and jumped. The canoe overturned, throwing everyone into the river. The foolish young botanist and Maria Simpson both drowned, and so did Pierre LeBlanc and the other three LeBlanc children. Nancy stood on the riverbank battered, cold, dripping wet, and watching while the survivors searched for the bodies of her babies. Her husband and all her young children dead on one trip. Her fourteen-year-old daughter, Grace, all that was left of her family, was next to her.

Weeks later, they arrived in Fort Vancouver. What was going to happen to them? But grief-stricken Nancy was still a Mackenzie.

And on the strength of her name, she found a husband for Grace, her daughter. Grace McTavish married Charles Dodd, captain of the SS *Beaver*, the ship that sailed up and down the BC coast from post to post. The daughter looked after her mother, Charles Dodd did well enough, and the three of them moved to newly established Fort Victoria on Vancouver Island.

There they were again, two Métis women in corsets, hoop skirts, and hats—full Victorian costume. But as had happened back in Manitoba, Nancy and now her daughter found themselves increasingly squeezed out as more white women arrived. They were not alone in their discomfort. No one felt it more than Amelia Douglas, wife of James Douglas, the BC governor. Douglas was the son of a Creole woman from Guyana and a Scot. When he was knighted in 1864, Sir James Douglas and Lady Amelia, first leaders of the province of British Columbia, were a mixed-race couple. Amelia Douglas was relentlessly criticized by the white wives first for not entertaining enough, then for entertaining too much. Increasingly, she kept to herself.

Nancy Mackenzie MacTavish LeBlanc died in 1851. In the one very fuzzy photograph of her that has survived, she is sitting in her widow's weeds, thin, wiry, and smiling—a sixty-one-year-old Métis woman, a survivor.

✦✦✦

David Thompson's luck ran out in the 1840s. He could not find work, could not meet the mortgage payment, the family's lands were seized, and they were forced to move back to Montreal. All the while, Sir George Simpson continued to send Thompson's survey data to a mapmaker in London who used it without either paying or crediting Thompson. In 1842 he wrote in his diary, "We are without wood," and a few weeks later, in April, "I am the morrow 73 years old and so destitute that I have not wherewithal to buy a loaf of Bread." Their daughter, Eliza Landell, walked around Montreal looking for a room for her parents when they were evicted yet again. Eliza eventually took them in. Her husband had a job that came with a house.

As they aged, David and Charlotte went on long walks together at night and looked at the stars, the stars that had been so important to David when he had surveyed the country. Charlotte had her own Cree stories of the stars. But in the last years of his life, the stars faded; David Thompson was eighty-seven and nearly blind when he died. Charlotte, sixteen years younger, lived only three months more.

There was no money for a headstone and the plot where they were buried, so near the graves of Allie Vibert Douglas's family, belonged to the Landells, their son-in-law's family. And that is where Charlotte and David Thompson rested unnoticed for seventy years.

Charlotte Small gave David Thompson the family, the support, and all he needed to map this country. She traveled forty-two thousand kilometers by his side. Nancy Mackenzie McTavish LeBlanc began life as a fur-trade princess and ended knowing and feeling increasing and vicious racism. And her sister, Louisa Bethune? She left a genetic legacy. She became a many-times-removed cousin to a twenty-first-century mayor of Vancouver, Gregor Angus Bethune Robertson, and great-grandmother to Norman Bethune, doctor and revolutionary hero in Communist China.

Her husband, Angus Bethune, despite a checkered career in the fur trade, earned one mark of distinction. The North West Company chose him to develop the Company's new fur market in China. Louisa Bethune's husband landed in Canton (Guangzhou) in 1814, 124 years before his great-grandson.

# 6. ISABEL

*So much character....*

Isabel Crook had not expected to be watching history march by when she woke up that morning. It was the beginning of February 1949, she was six weeks past her thirty-third birthday, and the People's Liberation Army had liberated Beijing only days before. Isabel, tall and fresh-faced, was in Tiananmen Square, up on the wall with the military leaders. This was the victory parade. The proclamation of the People's Republic of China was only months away.

A military truck had brought her into the capital first thing that day. She had climbed out, stretched her legs, and been spotted by her old friend George Hatem. Hatem was the Lebanese American doctor who had been on the front lines with the Communist forces since the thirties. It was George Hatem who had brought Canadian doctor Norman Bethune to China eleven years earlier. He called out to Isabel, "I'm going up on top of the wall. Come with me!" and now there she was on the parapets with Lin Biao, Mao's second-in-command, and Nie Rongzhen, the military commander of Northern China—men who had been leading Mao Zedong's army for twenty years.

The troops, thousands of young men, exhilarated and exhausted from years of fighting, poured down Chang'an Avenue, showing off the

American guns and tanks they had captured from the Kuomintang National Army. Then came the Mongolian cavalry and hundreds of black-and-brown ponies, then a snake tail of students each holding on to the person in front and doing the Struggle Yangge dance, three steps forward and one back—how they rallied support in the villages. It was one big party.

"We stood there at the gate," Isabel said seventy years later, "and watched along the street at the masses of people. Students from everywhere welcoming the People's Liberation Army. Six hours it lasted." Then she chuckled. "And I was pregnant."

There was no one else up on the wall that day who could say that.

✦✦✦

Revolution, to quote Mao, is not a dinner party. It is chaotic, catch-as-catch-can, and full of pain and purpose. Isabel Brown had grown up in the early chaos of China, born in 1915, the daughter of Canadian Methodist (United Church after 1925) missionaries. As a young woman, she came to the conclusion that Christianity was not the solution to the misery she saw around her and cast her lot with the Chinese Communists.

She was not alone among Canadian missionaries in making that move. There is an oft-told story about another born-in-China missionary child—Norman Endicott, the son of James Gareth Endicott, missionary, socialist, and supporter of China's Communist Party. In the 1930s, when Norman was a child of six, he went with his parents when his father was invited to talk about Christian ethics to a group of jailed Communists. As they left the jail, little Norman looked up and asked his mother and father, "Do Communists try to help the poor people?"

"Yes, they do," said the senior Endicotts.

"Well, isn't that what Christians try to do?"

"Of course."

"Then why are the Communists in jail and you aren't?"

It was a story that resonated with Isabel Crook. She watched as the People's Liberation Army took over Beijing, and when most Westerners scuttled back home, she stayed. She lived in the poorest villages, produced pioneering anthropological work, taught diplomats to speak English, went through three years of house arrest during the Cultural Revolution—her husband was in prison for five—and, in her old age, had awards heaped upon her. Isabel Brown Crook turned 106 on December 15, 2021, and celebrated in the same third-story walk-up apartment in Beijing where she had lived for the past sixty-five years.

+++

*We are being initiated into the stirring side of China.*

—Lina Jolliffe

Christian missionaries started arriving in China in the early years of the nineteenth century—some even before Canadian fur trader Angus Bethune and his ship full of otter pelts docked in Canton. Inland from the coast of China, the interior of the country was a writhing mass of economic mayhem, corruption, and fiefdoms controlled by drug barons and warlords; it was territory virtually unknown to Westerners. In the mid-nineteenth century, the British and the French fought China in the Opium Wars. The treaties that followed opened up the vast interior of China to foreigners, and Christian missionaries from every country and denomination plunged in. By the turn of the twentieth century, a contingent of Canadian Methodists had settled in Szechuan in Western China and over the next sixty years, their numbers grew to more than five hundred. Half of those missionaries were single women. Missionary work had its attractions as both morally satisfying and promising adventure.

Isabel's mother, Muriel Hockey, arrived in Shanghai in 1913. She was an accomplished young woman, having won the "oration" prize in her first year at Victoria College at the University of Toronto and more prizes before she graduated. She met Homer Brown in China. He had arrived the year before, in 1912—only a year after the Qing dynasty, China's last imperial dynasty, was overthrown; the last emperor, a boy named Henry, was still living in the Imperial Palace in Beijing. The change in the country was cataclysmic: two thousand years of imperial rule and tradition was over; a very shaky Chinese Republic was struggling to stay on its feet.

Homer and Muriel married in 1915. Isabel was born later that year and her sister, Julia, two years after that. Homer Brown became dean of the Faculty of Education at the missionaries' West China Union University, and Muriel Brown set up the first Montessori kindergarten in Chengdu—the same kindergarten system that Mina Benson Hubbard's children were attending in England—and she worked with her husband to develop what was seen at the time as a progressive education system in Szechuan. They were busy and did it all in the name of the Gospel.

Chengdu, 1,900 kilometers west of Shanghai, where the Brown girls grew up, was a walled city of half a million people. They lived in the mission compound and went to the school for missionary children, a big brick building four stories high with traditional Chinese swooping eaves. It looked like a Chinese building, but the classes were all in English. Although she has lived in China for a lifetime, Isabel Brown Crook still speaks with an accent, and when she had children, she made a point of sending her boys to Chinese schools. They did not learn English until they were eight. Isabel and the missionary children watched their parents build a large Christian congregation throughout the 1920s. Homer Brown supervised the Chengdu city church where services attracted five hundred people, and they took the gospel beyond the cities. The West China Canadian missionaries proselytized over an area of more than 25,000 square kilometers. Homer and Muriel would climb on their horses and ride to the outstations around Chengdu. Isabel went west with her father into the mountains of Tibet—what is now the Tibetan prefecture of China. Then there was the mission hospital; in just six months in 1916, the hospital performed five hundred operations and logged ten thousand visits. The

Canadian West China missionaries were energetic, full of ardor and enthusiasm, and exulted in their success. Their mantra was, "The future of the West China mission is with those who pray."

To get to Szechuan from Shanghai meant a long and frightening journey up the Yangtze River. There were rapids so fierce that in places the boats had to be hauled through by two hundred men onshore pulling on massive steel cables. Life for anyone in China, including missionaries, was difficult and dangerous. Government was weak, much of the country was controlled by brigands, and foreigners were despised. The Reverend Richard Orlando Jolliffe and the woman he would marry, Celina Matilda Dunfield, had come up the Yangtze for the first time in 1904, almost ten years before the Browns. In 1916, Orlando Jolliffe reported, almost by way of warning, on the reception that missionaries could expect when they came to China:

> To be slapped or stoned in the streets, as well as reviled, to have their servants terrorised into leaving them so that supplies were cut off, to have to leave their homes with a few minutes notice to crowd on the gunboat to go down river, sleeping on decks, to their summer houses that had been looted [within] half an hour of their leaving is an ordeal to shake even the stoutest.

In 1911, when the revolution that overthrew imperial rule reached Chengdu, the missionaries, including the Jolliffes, by now married, were herded into the mission compound and held for three months. Anarchy prevailed in the city, all the mission property was destroyed, and the British eventually evacuated them to Shanghai. The Jolliffes took a furlough in Canada and returned to China in 1912. They had made that trip up the Yangtze before and thought they were prepared. Once again, they boarded the boat in Shanghai, this time with their two young children, John, six, and Grace, two. Halfway up the Yangtze, the boat was attacked by bandits. Guns blazed and everyone rushed below deck. Someone grabbed little Grace, but six-year-old John was shot and killed. Celina Jolliffe would write in her diary in the years to come: "October 14, 1915. John would have been nine"; "October 14,

1917. John would have been eleven"; and on it went. Yet, she never considered giving up on her mission. She had signed on for China, and this was what China was.

Celina Dunfield came to China as a qualified, certified Methodist missionary. She had been through two years of training. The Dunfields lived in Manitoba and, as a young woman, Celina Matilda visited prisons in Winnipeg and embraced all manner of other social causes. Missionary work had been her dream; then she met her Orlando on the boat going to China and she was faced with a difficult choice. If she married him, she would lose her position, her missionary status, all that she had worked for. Before she was allowed to marry, she had to resign from her job. She chose husband over career, and they were married by the British consul in Shanghai. As Mrs. Jolliffe, she was the wife of a missionary, never a missionary in her own right. Those were the rules. She stayed in China with her husband and her children for more than forty years and, for the first twenty, she kept a diary. Like Muriel Brown, she was an industrious woman with projects always on the go. She barely wrote about political events, concentrating instead on her immediate world—a world that permeated all her senses.

> When we entered the city gate after quite a long ride I thought we might strangle the odours were so terrific. You may have a vivid imagination but I think it will fail you in trying to give you an idea of Chinese odours and noises. Only those who have been there can know. Dogs and degraded piggies were to be seen all along the way—dogs too have lost any respectability they ever could have prided in and are mongrels of most defective kind. There is no privacy in Chinese life, they have their hair combed and faces washed in the street.

And she goes on:

> As we walked leisurely along we noticed coming behind us a group of about six men and one younger than the rest, with very little clothing...in the midst. He was cut across the lip and shoulder and quite bespattered with blood. My first

thought was that an accident had happened and all these men were friends or sympathizers but as they came nearer...we saw that the poor lad's hands and queue [his single plait] were tied together behind his back. But his face. My heart aches when I dare to let it come before me, poor, poor boy. I never saw, though I've seen many faces behind prison bars, one so utterly hopeless. It was blank despair.... Some of our party could understand Chinese so when in passing us the man said, "He stole clothes and is going to the *yamen*...." Some faces of China are so ugly it is distasteful to write them...if that poor laddie's head did not hang from the city gates that night as a warning for others—just because he stole clothes—I could hardly blame him—though the flowers are blooming and at times the sun is very hot yet my fur coat or golf cape are not a burden to me and he, poor boy had only a light cotton cloth about his loins—his back bore the welts of the lash. We went on our way but could not help but wonder how his home people felt when he did not return that night.

By evening, the "poor boy's" head did indeed "hang from the city gates." It was a regular occurrence. Celina Matilda's youngest daughter, Mary, when she was an irascible old woman in her eighties, remembered walking with her father alongside the nineteen kilometers of Chengdu's massive city walls, ten meters thick and twelve meters high. When they reached the gates of the city where everyone came and went, she saw severed heads on pointed sticks. Mary Jolliffe and Isabel Brown were schoolmates, and Isabel had similar childhood memories.

I remember going on a journey with my sister. We were facing each other, going out of the city gates. On the outside there was a straw mat and on it was a body and a head. "Don't say a word," I said to my sister. It was near the gate where the soldiers were guarding and they looked at us and laughed their heads off.

It was a visceral experience of the earliest days of Republican China that stayed with both women for a lifetime.

+++

Orlando and Celina Jolliffe and Mary Jolliffe with a group of Japanese soldiers, 1927

*The missionary compounds in China are lovely havens of rest, after trudging through filthy streets to come upon a high wall and passing through a gateway find within a lovely garden, with palms and ferns, flowers and birds, you rejoice that Christianity brings beauty and rest.*

—Lina Jolliffe

The missionaries, like many strangers in a foreign land, created their own enclaves. Orlando and Celina Jolliffe set up a missionary outpost in the city of Tzeliutsing—another walled city with, even in the 1920s, a population of more than a million. They built another four-story brick school, another huge church, and another missionary compound where they lived with their five children just as the Browns lived in Chengdu. The houses verged on the luxurious and Celina Jolliffe wrote in her diary that right from the start of her time in China, she regretted some aspects of missionary life. Even the boat that brought them up the Yangtze was uncomfortably opulent.

> …instead of being a hardship…it was like a palace car—the finest fitted up of any boat that had gone up. Of course this could only be said after the ladies had done their part in beautifying it with all the necessary knickknacks…. There are four good big living rooms in this one.

Inside the mission compound, their houses were big and well-staffed, although the missionary women did not hesitate to complain about the "help." One day, Celina Jolliffe summarily fired all her servants because they were stealing and then almost immediately rehired the cook. There were just too many big dinner parties coming up. For fun as a child, Isabel would play with her sister out on the sloping roof of their house and watch the world go by. It was a contradictory life. Inside the walls of the compound was luxury and comfort; outside, miserable poverty and violence. As Chinese social structures disintegrated with the end of Imperial rule, the lawlessness and violence between warlords and the government of the Republic increased. The missionaries filled the void, their compound became a sanctuary for the many refugees, and they became a source of not only spiritual but also civic guidance.

The West China Mission Canadian Methodists did not understand or have much faith in Chinese society. How could they? Celina Matilda was shocked and upset by the sight of a prisoner's head on a pole and convinced that the Chinese did not care about each other or value the sanctity of life. Christianity could change all that, she thought. She was equally convinced that China would never be able to drag itself out of its feudal past without the help of the West.

> No wonder Chinamen feel sensitive to the incoming foreigners. I feel very sorry for them. They realize at this late date that they are away behind every nation and that great haste must be made if they are to have any standing and yet cannot hasten—the new railroad to be put through to Szechuan will be a very difficult undertaking—no Chinaman or body of Chinamen can do it. They know they must call for help from foreigners and that almost entire control must be given them.

Her husband, Orlando, had no faith that the Chinese had the character to "lift themselves out of the morass of antiquity." He added, "In disposition they are pleasant, but still retaining some of those unpleasant sharper qualities, so common among primitive races."

This was the atmosphere in which both Mary Jolliffe, born in 1923, and Isabel Brown grew up: with a missionary community who saw it as their duty to persist in the face of danger with no comprehension of either the people to whom they were ministering or the concept of self-determination. Homer and Muriel Brown were more "with the people" than some of their missionary colleagues—Isabel's future husband, David Crook, called the Browns Christian socialists propelled by deep belief, commitment, and faith, qualities that were imbued in Isabel. But crucially, Isabel did not share her parents' Christian faith.

> My mother and father were very devoted people. They had a belief.... I was very happy living and working in China but I was uneasy because I didn't have a belief. I said to my

mother, please send me some religious things to inspire me so I can have some belief, so she sent me some tracts. But hard as I tried couldn't get inspired.

Isabel Brown was at one with the idea of Christian service, with the building of hospitals and schools to serve the individual, but as Michael Crook, her middle son, said, "Christian missionary work cannot change society." And for Isabel, that was the inspiration that was missing, something that would change society and lead her to a meaningful life. It was not Christianity.

Sitting up on the roof of their big family house in the Chengdu missionary compound in the mid-1930s, Isabel Brown must have looked down at the crowded streets, at the people who spent their lives as beasts of burden, at the refugees from what was fast becoming a civil war camped out in the compound, and she must have wondered what the nature of that meaningful life would be.

In the fall of 1934, eighteen-year-old Isabel Brown went back to Canada and registered, like her parents before her, at Victoria College at the University of Toronto (U of T). She lived in Annesley Hall, the

Isabel, Muriel, Homer, and Julia Brown, c. 1936

first women's residence in Canada, joined the music club, became part of the Athletic Society—she won the Victoria swimming cup—and discovered a new academic discipline, anthropology, offered for the first time at U of T. Margaret Mead, the young American anthropologist, had just published *Coming of Age in Samoa*, her study of youth and sexual life of teenagers, primarily adolescent girls, in the Samoan Islands. Margaret Mead published three more books while Isabel was at U of T. Her message was clear: culture shapes people; we can learn from other cultures. Mead was also studying the society of women and was one of the first women to do fieldwork. How could Isabel Brown *not* have been influenced?

By the time she got back on the boat for China, Isabel Brown was twenty-three. She had a new *academic* passion, but she was still looking for something to believe in, a key to change. It was 1938 and the China she was going back to had been invaded by the Japanese. War was never-ending in China; it was the enemy that kept changing.

+++

*I went to New York…to become a millionaire, to restore the bankrupt family fortunes and to donate money to Zionism. Fortunately, I chose the wrong time.*

David Crook was a middle-class Jewish kid from England. His family kept kosher; he went to synagogue every week, loved his mother, and respected his father. His Russian immigrant parents sent him to the very upscale Cheltenham College, from which he emerged with a good education and a cut-glass English accent. Then his father's business failed, there was no family money, and so at nineteen, David Crook went first to Paris then New York to see what he could make of himself. It was 1929. Wall Street crashed seven months after he arrived.

He found work in the fur trade—his father was a furrier—and

then in the early 1930s, David Crook enrolled at Columbia University in journalism. Within weeks of his arrival, he joined what was euphemistically called the Social Problems Club, led by two young communists. He went south with his newfound friends to "observe" the coal miners' strike in Kentucky and was deeply affected by their work conditions and the violence meted out to the strikers. The net result: after six years in the US, David Crook had become a leftist, a scrappy, noisy student radical. He left America with a journalism degree in his pocket and a much-heightened social conscience, arriving back in England in time to witness the Oswald Mosley–led anti-Semitic, fascist marches and pitched battles in the East End of London. He was twenty-five.

Where Isabel was an understated, clean-cut young woman still finding her way in Canada, David Crook was an opinionated, loud, and articulate young man who was ready to plunge into whatever came next. He joined the British Communist Party and within months volunteered for the International Brigade to fight Francisco Franco's fascists in the Spanish Civil War. David Crook, like Isabel Brown, was looking for a way to live a life that counted. As he wrote to a friend from the civil war in Spain, "I came here because life in England was too useless to be living at such a time like this. If I'm to be among those who don't get back, I'll have concentrated so much into the last short space that it will be as good as having lasted a normal span."

On January 2, 1937, along with 150 other young British men, David Crook arrived in Spain. By the beginning of February, barely knowing one end of a gun from the other, he was sent into battle in the Jarama valley, just east of Madrid. Two-thirds of the British Battalion were either killed or wounded in that battle, and David Crook became very aware that he might not make it out of Spain alive.

It was late afternoon. We fired now and then when we thought we saw something move.... Then I was hit twice in the thigh; another shot landed in the heel of my right boot and one went through my water bottle.... Lying on the ground behind the banked up olive tree I wished the bastards would leave us alone. All we could hope for now was that it would get dark before the enemy could reach us.... At last a wisp of a sickle moon rose. All through the past 50 years I've never seen such a moon without thinking of Jarama.

He was wounded on his first day in action and taken for medical treatment to Madrid. When he got out of hospital, he spent time convalescing, sitting around talking to people, and what people they were: he was in the midst of a galaxy of literary stars. Suddenly he was having long philosophical conversations deep into the night with Ernest Hemingway and his then-partner Martha Gellhorn. They talked of war. And Love. And Death. There was the British poet Stephen Spender—an Oxbridge man, withdrawn and a little standoffish. Herbert Kline, the American documentary maker whose first documentary on the Spanish Civil War had just been aired on CBC Radio, took him to an underground theater production. There was the Canadian filmmaker Ted Allan and Allan's friend, Dr. Norman Bethune, then developing the mobile blood transfusion technique that he took with him to China two years later. In his diary, Crook called Bethune "a colossal egoist."

David Crook was thoroughly seduced by the romance and fatalism of war. He, in turn, seduced and had an affair with Jean Watts, the Canadian Communist Party journalist and the only woman to join the Canadian Mackenzie-Papineau brigade, the Mac-Paps. Watts was staying at Bethune's headquarters, and putting his feelings about Bethune aside, Crook spent most of his time with Bethune's circle of friends. One night he was a vigorous participant in a living room debate on the relative merits of Soviet leader Joseph Stalin and the exiled Leon Trotsky, by the 1930s living in Mexico City. Crook came down solidly on the side of Stalin. Within days, having nailed his colors to the mast, he was recruited and became a Soviet Stalinist spy. One of the men who "ran" him and trained him introduced himself as Frank

Jacson, traveling in Spain on a Canadian passport.

He gave Crook a brief course in surveillance, and one of his first assignments was to find and ingratiate himself with Eric Blair, better known as George Orwell, who was in Spain with the British Independent Labour Party—a leftist but vehemently anti-Stalinist group. As he went in search of Orwell, Crook would almost inevitably have sniffed out William Krehm, a classical violinist from Toronto, one of Orwell's Barcelona café companions and a Trotskyist. Trotsky was a man with a price on his head, Stalin wanted him out of the way. Some years later, William Krehm, then living in Mexico City and working as a journalist, was screened by Trotsky's people, approved, and scheduled to interview Trotsky the following week. It was an appointment Trotsky never kept. A few days before Krehm's scheduled interview, another visitor, less well-screened, plunged an ice pick into Trotsky's skull. It was William Krehm who stood guard over Trotsky's body at his funeral.

One night, as the Spanish Civil War was ending and Franco's fascists were about to declare victory, Crook was hustled into a limousine by two of his handlers who asked, as they drove around in the dark, "Would you like to continue working for us, this time in Shanghai?" He did not refuse the offer.

In the late 1930s, Shanghai, a massive and strategic port city, was surrounded by Chinese revolutionaries and Japanese troops. At the height of its power, Japan controlled more than a third of China's population and occupied 25 per cent of China's territory. Shanghai had been designated an International Settlement. It was a refuge for Western nationals and a law unto itself. At night, Crook could smell the opium wafting through the air and watch the peasant girls making a living on the streets. Municipal trucks drove down the streets in the winter, picking up the frozen bodies of refugees and beggars. During the day, he played tennis with expat Brits. He took riding lessons from disaffected white Russians and dancing lessons from Chinese transgender dancers. He made his living teaching at the prestigious St. John's University and continued to spy for the Soviets. One evening, a year into his stay in Shanghai, he went to his regular Soviet rendezvous only to discover that there was nobody home. He had been dropped. David Crook was now an unemployed spy.

A little puzzled and uneasy, he decided it was time to move on. He found another teaching job, this time with Nanjing University, which, because of the war with Japan, had relocated to Chengdu in Szechuan. Midway through the very long bus ride from Shanghai to Chengdu, he got off the bus to get something to eat and he heard the news: on August 21, 1940, Leon Trotsky had been murdered in Mexico City. The man who had the ice pick concealed under his raincoat was Frank Jacson. Many things fell into place. "Frank Jacson" was indeed the man whom David Crook had met in Spain. He was not a Canadian, but a Spaniard named Ramón Mercader. As he got back on the bus, David Crook had a lot to contemplate during the rest of that bus trip—he thought about both where he had been and where to go. Chengdu? It was as good a place as any. He stayed on the bus.

"Chengdu, eh?" he remembered one of his friends saying. "You'll either end up marrying a Chinese girl or a missionary's daughter."

"A Chinese girl maybe," said Crook, "a missionary's daughter —never."

✦✦✦

*I'm sitting on the grass by the wayside right at the top of the pass and spread out before me are the most incredible snow mountains. They seem to pierce the sky. In the valley are dozens of fluffy white clouds. This is the life.*

Isabel Brown, the missionary's daughter, came back to Chengdu from Canada as the Japanese began bombing Szechuan. The mission school relocated from city to village to mountaintop, but Isabel was pointed in a new direction. Her degree was in this new discipline of anthropology, and that is what she wanted to do, to learn more about the mountain people.

I set out in March 1939, to travel through Yi territory with an American missionary Emma Broadbeck.... We walked across the mountain pass and...it was through Emma that I met clan leader Li and was invited to stay in his village.

The village was Zhaohoumiao, in one of the Tibetan mountain valleys, a week's walk from Chengdu. Her way had been paved by her father on his trips to the missionary outposts years before. She taught some English in the village and made an impression. More than seventy years after her time in Zhaohoumiao, a very elderly Yi woman—with the black, heavily embroidered rectangle of cloth that characterized Yi women perched on her head—talked about Isabel: "Her father told my father that he had a daughter who wanted to come. My father invited Isabel to stay. We had someone who would cook for her and we had a place for her to sleep." And then the elderly Yi village woman chuckled and picked up her Huawei tablet. She looked at the screen, clicked her Zoom link, and waved at Isabel in Beijing. Together they sang, "Row, Row, Row Your Boat."

The various shifts and changes at work in China were encapsulated in this small village. When Isabel arrived, the Chinese Civil War had been underway for more than a decade, and the Long March of the Red Army had come through these valleys five years earlier on retreat from the Kuomintang, the Nationalists. The slogans they had painted on the rocks were still visible. Rewi Alley from New Zealand, another friend, had set up one of his Chinese Industrial Co-ops intended to support the war effort against the Japanese. This one made spinning wheels and more than once Isabel, precariously balanced on a rope-and-pulley bridge with the river raging below, brought spinning wheels from one side of the valley to the other. Rewi Alley called his co-ops "gōnghé," meaning to work (enthusiastically) in harmony. The term "Gonghe" was appropriated by an American Marine Corps major, a friend of Alley's. He and his marines turned it into "Gung Ho." Isabel Brown stayed in this very traditional Yi village teaching English for eight months.

David Crook, meanwhile, had begun teaching at the university in Chengdu, his daily schedule punctuated by Japanese air raids. (Chengdu is 3,300 kilometers from Tokyo, but the Japanese were taking the war deeper into China.) Not long after he arrived in Chengdu,

Crook had been invited to a black-tie dinner in the mission compound. It was a mark of the times that Crook, a card-carrying Communist living in the middle of a war, had a tuxedo in his cupboard. One day after Isabel returned from Zhaohoumiao, David Crook was playing tennis when the Brown sisters walked by. "There's the new Englishman," said Julia, the younger sister. Isabel took a quick look over the hedge and replied, "Too short for me."

"Back then," her son Michael says, "Mother was political but not a communist. She was still mainly a pacifist." But she was thinking about things. Some of the missionaries were part of underground Communist study groups, and Isabel had become friendly with another teacher at the West China Union University, Ruth Weiss. Weiss was an Austrian Jew who had gravitated to Shanghai like so many Jewish refugees. She taught at the Shanghai Jewish school, worked as a journalist, and was briefly a secretary at the Canadian embassy. By 1939 Weiss, like David Crook, had decided that it was a good time to get out of Shanghai and she too wound up in Chengdu. On Sunday, May 7, 1939, Isabel's diary entry noted that she went to church in the morning, "then to Ruth Weiss to get some communist literature. I never took the time during my university course to learn how to be a communist if I wished. Now's the time to get my ideas sorted."

At the same time, she was getting to know David Crook. With the influence of Ruth Weiss and the stories of the Spanish Civil War that David Crook must have told her, Isabel Brown got her ideas sorted. "David had fought in Spain and was very political so I found it much easier to have a cause and have it to be communism." Now she had something new to believe in.

+++

*...we hired horses and with their Tibetan owners rode across the wild-flower-strewn grasslands and up the mountains to our objective...*
*to glimpse (not scale) Minya Gongka, a 25,000 foot peak topped by a*

*pyramid of ice…. Minya Gongka had been climbed by an American expedition eight years before…. The monks told them that at the top there was a crock of gold. After reaching the summit and returning to their base the monks asked if they had found the gold. "No," they replied, "there was no gold there." "Then," the monks answered, "you didn't get to the top."*

They traveled through the mountains for six weeks. Through Isabel, David Crook met the hill tribesmen and marveled at the fortitude of the Tibetans. She introduced him to the people and the country beyond the foreigners' compound in Chengdu. Six weeks together on horseback tests any friendship, but after those six weeks David Crook wanted to marry this woman. He proposed at the legendary Luding Bridge, a three-hundred-foot suspension bridge over the Dadu River. The story, more myth than fact, has it that a few heroic Red Army soldiers grabbed the suspension chains and went hand over hand across the river under machine-gun fire and defeated the enemy. But myths are captivating, and when David Crook, ever a romantic, proposed at the bridge, Isabel Brown accepted. Her Christian missionary parents gradually came to terms with a Communist, non-observant Jew for a son-in-law.

✦✦✦

*Oct 13 1940 It is market day today and so the rural members of the congregation park their products at the church while they attended the service. Two chickens that sat across the aisle from me had several disputes. But we just ignored them.*

In 1937, David Crook had gone to Spain to fight the fascists, and by the early 1940s, there were a lot more fascists to fight. He and Isabel agreed that the war came first, that they would go to England and enlist—he in the Royal Air Force and she in the Canadian Women's Army—then they would get married. Crook left China almost immediately. Isabel stayed in China and began work on the project that seventy-three years later would make her academic reputation in the West.

On the strength of her missionary background, her time in Zhaohoumiao, and her new academic expertise, Isabel was recruited by an American missionary group to work on a rural reconstruction project, another Yi village, Xinglongchang, "Prosperity's Market." It was halfway between Chengdu and Chungking (now Chongqing), the wartime capital of China's Kuomintang government. The project leaders wanted to know more about the people who lived in the area before launching their project—call it applied anthropology. Isabel was the only non-Chinese person on the project. She worked closely with a medical social worker named Yu Xiji, and together they surveyed nearly fifteen hundred households scattered over more than fifty square kilometers. It was a working friendship that lasted the rest of their lives.

The Japanese air raids by now had reached the countryside. They remained remarkably predictable, and Isabel and Yu could schedule their survey work around them. Some projects stop for a lunch break, they stopped for an air-raid break. The two women walked the territory armed with big sticks to ward off angry dogs and asked questions about every aspect of village life—marriages, arranged or voluntary, divorce, land ownership, and a secret robed brotherhood that proved to be the greatest obstacle to reform in the village. They also discovered that women had a much stronger economic role in village life than villagers would admit to. They surveyed by day and typed up their notes by kerosene lamp at night.

They were active observers doing more than asking questions. The project built a clinic, a village nursery, set up a salt cooperative (that ultimately failed), and conducted literacy classes. For the better part of the next two years, as World War II preoccupied the rest of the world, Isabel documented life in Xinglongchang. But the Japanese air raids were gaining strength, and in 1942, her parents, who were still living in Chengdu, decided it was time to go back to Canada. Xinglongchang was a finite project and that same summer, Isabel Brown packed up and headed to England to meet David. She took her field notes with her.

They got married in London, and Isabel Crook, as she now was, joined the British Communist Party. "During the war, in 1942," she said, "it was so easy for me immediately to want to be communist. I was longing for something." Everything was falling into place. David Crook immediately enlisted in the Royal Air Force, where with his knowledge of French, Spanish, and a little Chinese—despite his Communist Party membership—he was put in intelligence and spent, in his own words, a relatively comfortable war in the "Far East."

Isabel had something to do before she signed up. Not long after her arrival in England and armed with her field notes from Xinglongchang, she went to see Raymond Firth, then teaching anthropology at the London School of Economics (LSE). Firth, a colonial like Isabel, was from New Zealand. He too was a lapsed Methodist and something of a Marxist. He had wanted to do work in China, but his plans had been stymied by the war. Now here was this young Canadian woman with a bulging file of notes from China sitting in his office.

He admitted her to the LSE PhD program. In 1942, it was the right university for Isabel Crook. Unlike Oxford and Cambridge, the London School of Economics had awarded degrees to women from the day it opened in 1895—one of its founders was the Fabian feminist Beatrice Webb. Its mandate was to foster and legitimize the social sciences, working specifically on issues of poverty and inequality. Yes, this was the place for her. But she was not about to give up her war effort. Isabel Crook enlisted in the Canadian Women's Army, served in England, and when the war was over, went back to Canada to be demobilized. She was given a Canadian government study grant, and their thinking was that they would stay in London while Isabel worked on her PhD.

Before he was demobilized, David Crook discovered that because he had given China as his home address when he signed up, he and his wife were entitled to a free boat ride home. Isabel was eager to go, but David was not so certain—he saw himself as a man without a profession, something that haunted him all his life. He got himself press credentials with *The Times* and Reuters, called himself a journalist, and by the time a passage to China came up, they had a plan.

Isabel Crook, 1940s

They would go to China, stay for a year and a half, then come back to London for Isabel to finish her PhD.

They left England with a letter of introduction from the British Communist Party. World War II was over, Japan had surrendered, and China was in the final phase of the civil war. They were going back to work with their Chinese comrades.

◆◆◆

*They floated on a barge down China's Grand Canal through no-man's land between the territory held by the Kuomintang, the Nationalists, and the Communists. By November of 1947 they arrived in Ten Mile Inn.*

The Crooks talked their way past the Kuomintang customs agents and got themselves on the barge bound for the "liberated areas" controlled by the Communists. Their letter from the British Party would take them the rest of the way. The Kuomintang, led by Chiang Kai-shek and backed by the US, controlled the cities; Mao's Communists held the countryside.

The sign above the Ten Mile Inn city gate said, "Mao Zedong is the great star of salvation of the Chinese people." When they arrived in the city in the late fall, they settled in an empty room in a peasant house and submitted their plan—to study the process of land reform that the Communists were implementing in the villages—for approval by the party. Up until then, no one had been allowed in. As a party member, Isabel figured she had an inside track. They got the go-ahead.

A liberated area to David meant green fields, well-fed livestock, and happy peasants. Instead, he had to come to terms with abject rural poverty, hunger, and exhaustion. Isabel had seen it all before. They were also plunged into Chinese winter—as the missionaries had said decades earlier, "some foreigners wear more outer clothing in China than they found necessary in Saskatchewan." They had wool and leather to break the wind and the ubiquitous Chinese peasant jackets quilted and insulated with cotton. David Crook wore his like a badge of honor.

Isabel taught her husband the discipline of anthropology, how to conduct surveys, what questions to ask, and they spent eight months in Ten Mile Inn documenting land reform. The villagers, from the richest to the poorest peasants, met, measured land, and then divided

Isabel in 1949

it equitably. The Crooks watched it all, took volumes of field notes, and wrote three books on Chinese land reform over the next twenty years. When the American journalist Anna Louise Strong, another missionary daughter, asked Mao if he thought he would win the civil war, he answered, "Yes, because of land reform." Most historians agree.

They slept on primitive *kangs*—simple brick platforms that were part raised beds and part heated stoves; they ate peasant food—millet and sweet potatoes. They lived with people in the village, but much as they tried to fit in, they couldn't. They were different. For one thing they were not as strong as the villagers, and they could not keep up.

> I saw a boy of ten or twelve swinging along with two tins of water he had hauled up from the well. "Let me have a try," I said. I could hardly stand up under the weight of the load.

They were privileged foreigners, welcomed because they were needed. The party was desperate for foreign expertise, and the Crooks found themselves celebrated. When their work in Ten Mile Inn was done and they moved on by mule cart to the newly liberated city of Shijiazhuang, they were feted with a huge banquet. David and Isabel Crook intended to take their field notes, go back to England, and start writing the book on land reform. Then came the knock on the door. A ranking party official asked them, with great ceremony, to delay the book, stay in China, and become teachers at the Foreign Affairs

David and
Isabel, 1949

Training Class. Victory over the Kuomintang was around the corner, and the Communists had to create a country that could function internationally. The Crooks agreed.

In the beginning, the Foreign Affairs Training Class was nothing more than half a dozen teachers and students who studied, ate, and slept together in peasant houses. Today, it is a full-fledged university in Beijing that teaches 101 languages—and a lot more—to nearly nine thousand students. In 1948, the windows of the huts were papered over because of air raids, and curious children would wet their fingers to make the paper translucent and peer in. Isabel would make herself hoarse repeating English phrases over and over to every student; there were no tape recorders. When the crops were ready, teachers and students would harvest together, practicing conversational English as they went. The leaders stayed close to their followers; theory and labor were intertwined. This was "guerilla learning." David Crook reveled in it. Isabel had been teaching this way all her life.

When the air raids got too close, the school would relocate, students and teachers marching en masse at night and hiding in villages during the day. Late in 1948, when the liberation of Beijing was foreseeable, David set out with everyone else on the last three-hundred-kilometer march to the capital. Isabel stayed behind in the city of Shijiazhuang. She had had a miscarriage not long before and was pregnant again; this time, they were being careful and that is how at the beginning of 1949, Isabel came to hitch a ride in a truck into Beijing for the victory parade. When she found David the next day, they knew that everything was about to change.

Isabel's old schoolmate, Mary Jolliffe, had gone back to Canada in 1945, traveling with the legendary "Flying Tigers" over the Himalayas—no navigational aids, no weather charts, no pressurized planes—to get her degree at the University of Toronto. Her parents, Orlando and Celina Matilda, had also left China in 1945, never to return, and all her siblings were back in Canada. Most missionaries had seen the last of China, but Mary Jolliffe, like Isabel Crook a woman of conviction, had decided to go back by herself even as the civil war was still going on. In 1949, she was the twenty-seven-year-old matron of the missionary boarding school for girls in Chengdu. When Mao and the Chinese Communist Party took control of the country, she, like other foreigners, was given a choice: stay in China and become a citizen or return to Canada.

There was an attachment to China that held many Westerners —Mary Jolliffe almost as much as Isabel Crook. Almost. They were two sides of the same coin. They had both been born and brought up in China; they had both been inculcated with the same sense of integrity and service, the same Protestant work ethic—although Mary, who loved elegant and expensive clothes, was never frugal—and they were both determined to do something worthwhile with their lives. Isabel had become a Communist, and Mary, like so many of the Methodist missionaries, leaned left. Her cousin, another missionary

Mary Jolliffe, 2013

child, was Ted Jolliffe, a socialist and first leader of the Co-operative Commonwealth Federation party, the CCF, in Ontario. But Mary was not politically motivated. Isabel Crook stayed in China; Mary did not.

She came back to Canada, found her feet, and became the first to promote the new world of Canadian theater and dance, ultimately becoming a member of the Order of Canada. As Mary Jolliffe left China, undoubtedly with some regret, Isabel and David Crook, fueled by the idealistic zeal of newly won Communist victory, changed their plans and stayed.

Mao Zedong proclaimed the founding of the People's Republic of China on October 1, 1949. The new national anthem was played, and the new flag was raised in Tiananmen Square. This time, the Crooks both had seats in the official viewing stand. The baby Isabel was carrying on the day of the Victory Parade was now two months old and being looked after in a nursery on the other side of the very wide Chang'an Avenue. For hours, the parade of troops flowed like a river between mother and an increasingly hungry baby. Military parades are not designed with women and babies in mind. Isabel was becoming more than a little anxious and took matters into her own hands. She climbed down from the viewing stand, pushed her way through the crowd, and, with Chairman Mao looking on, the parade stopped for an instant as she ran across the avenue to feed her son.

+++

*Your Chinese students are wonderfully enthusiastic, just as ours were right after the revolution. It's the romantic phase. It'll wear off.*

—Vera from Leningrad

The school moved into Beijing and grew as the country began to define itself. There were more and more students but still no desks, no books, and they needed more teachers. Soviet teachers began to arrive. One, a woman named Vera from Leningrad, became close enough to the Crooks to speak frankly. But when Vera said that the post-revolutionary enthusiasm would be short-lived, they were dubious. She was right. The bloom wore off the rose quickly enough. David Crook was now deputy dean of the English department and rapidly found himself embroiled in the ideological debates that permeated every aspect of life. There was growing friction at the school. When a lecture or a speech was called for, Isabel would take a step back and keep her counsel. Not David. "I, setting lower standards," he wrote, "would take it on without much ado."

There were power struggles over pedagogical practice. The Crooks were native English speakers, something to be valued. But Isabel maintained, correctly, that it was less about native versus non-native than about power, ideology, and tradition. David Crook held on to his guerilla style of teaching—conversational, functional English learned by doing—practice not theory. But now he was doing battle with tradition. The Chinese advocated the "stuffed duck" approach to teaching—force information down the throats of students, much as the infamous Peking ducks were force-fed prior to slaughter. He was told, "Comrade Crook does not understand Chinese society."

"I comforted myself," he said later, "with the thought that my approach was more practical and productive than theirs.... I secretly saw myself as defender of a Communist approach to education against bourgeois academic snobbery and pedantry."

It was false comfort.

✦✦✦

*Lenience for those who confess, severity for those who resist.*

"They decided I was a spy," said Isabel in 2019. She was then 104 years old, a venerable elder, one of the very, very few who had witnessed the revolution still alive—with age came some license to speak. She laughed. "I was doing a lot of talking in the West about China and writing articles, so they had a lot of evidence that I was in touch, working with the West. So, it was easy to say I was a spy."

The Crooks were out of the country in the UK when the "Great Proletarian Cultural Revolution" began in 1966. They were eager to get back and to be part of this ideological reassessment. Isabel came first with their three sons, Paul, thirteen, Michael, fifteen, and Carl, seventeen. David followed. Deeply entrenched factions had developed: everyone took sides. At first, there were marches and slogans; then came the violence. When the Cultural Revolution ended seven years later, millions had been murdered, more dispossessed.

Students were regularly trucked off to work the farms, and within a year, Paul Crook, the youngest son, was sent to harvest pears and sweet potatoes. He was not away long and when he came back, his brothers said, "They've arrested a spy at the university. Can you guess who it is?" The spy was their father. His sons were incredulous and were convinced that David Crook's arrest was some kind of joke. "He believes in all this, supports the revolution," thought Paul at the time. "How could he be a spy?" And then their mother disappeared.

Isabel was detained by one faction but never actually arrested. The evidence against her was not strong enough—or perhaps her personal popularity protected her. The faction holding her were "...very embarrassed because if they let me go they would lose all credibility," she said, "so they didn't let me go.... They had to watch me, they had to make sure I didn't commit suicide so I had to have guards all the time.... I was not in danger of that. I never tried to jump out of the window." And she laughed. "It wasn't too bad."

Her biggest concern was her children. The two eldest, Carl and Michael, were more or less on their own. Carl was sent to work at a farm machinery factory. But Paul was still attending his Chinese school. She would see him ride by on his bicycle at 7:30 every morning.

> ...so I would stand at the window and watch. He happened to look at the window where I was. The girls [the guards] were in the room so I couldn't wave. I lifted my cup...so he saw that and...he rushed back and told Michael. Michael and a friend came over and knocked on the door. It happened

there was an important meeting and the guards had gone to the meeting. They [the boys] saw me and I thought they would get into trouble so I told them, "Go away" and closed the door.

Michael went away. "Oh, they think I'm being terrorized," thought Isabel. "I must ask to see them." It was arranged, and the boys said, "Oh, Mum. Of course you weren't terrorized. We knew."

Isabel was held under house arrest for three years. David had been arrested by state security and was held in different prisons for five years, much of that time in solitary confinement. He was interrogated repeatedly and only allowed outdoors to exercise once every two months. Remarkably, David Crook came out of jail with renewed determination to advance the revolution. He said that his fear was for his sons, then he added, "Isabel of course, could cope."

There was no need to worry about Isabel, he was saying. He was taking a lot for granted but indeed, Isabel had always coped. In the murderous days of the early republic when the mission kids would compete to see who could collect the most cartridge shells in the fields; as a young woman living for eight months in first one Tibetan village and then another, she coped with air raids every day. Then when she was pregnant, she harvested crops at Ten Mile Inn during the day and worked late at night on her surveys. And now she had coped through three years of house arrest. Isabel Brown Crook more than coped. David Crook maintained that it was the influence of her Christian upbringing. She had purpose, was seemingly unflappable, clearly had courage, and stuck to her principles. One early suitor said of Isabel Brown, "So much character scares the hell out of me."

David Crook was released in January 1973. As a condition of release, he was required to sign an admission of guilt, and he was prepared to sign. Isabel stopped him, stood on principle, and prevailed. The verdict in the case of David Crook was revised three times; the final version in 1982 stated that the charges were trumped up and that this latest verdict should be and was publicly acknowledged.

All three of their sons left China within months of their father's

David and Isabel,
1960s

release. David Crook had registered them at the British embassy when they were born, entitling them to British passports. They were young men who wanted to see the world, and they were angry and disgusted about all that had gone on during the Cultural Revolution and what followed under the Gang of Four. Carl, Michael, and Paul Crook left the country, yet Isabel and David Crook chose to stay. China was now their country, they said, and these events should be taken in historic perspective. It was an attitude that exasperated their children. Carl Crook, writing to his girlfriend at the time, said of his father, "He doesn't even know how to read between the lines (of the newspaper). Simply takes it at face value. It's pathetic."

♦♦♦

Was Isabel Crook ever critical of a Chinese regime? Judiciously so. The Crooks went back to Ten Mile Inn in the 1980s, and an old friend said, "Now I can tell you the truth about certain things which I wasn't free to tell you." David Crook seemed surprised. Isabel was more sanguine. When Head of State Zhou Enlai died in 1976, his burial was kept secret by the ruling Gang of Four for fear that thousands of mourners would appear in support of Zhou. Word leaked out that he was to be buried in the Cemetery of Martyrs to the Revolution. Isabel quietly got on her bicycle, rode out to the cemetery, and waited for the hearse. It never came, but she had made her position clear. By frequently boycotting China's pro forma International Women's Day celebrations, she also sent a message. The Chinese Communist government had not, despite the slogans, given women an equal place in government and society. Isabel Crook recognized the need for an independent women's movement and set up a Women's Studies program.

The Crooks both continued to teach at the Foreign Affairs Institute. Isabel trained the first group of English Chinese-language interpreters and today is credited with laying the groundwork for English-language education in China, developing a reputation as a fair but uncompromising teacher. She kept what amounted to diagnostic notes on every student, a recognition of individuality that her Chinese colleagues found difficult to understand at first. As China opened up, Isabel and David gained more status. In 1980, they were both appointed "Advisors to the Institute," a rank equivalent to university president. And in 1988, as retired, respected elders, they had a private meeting with Premier Zhao Ziyang and criticized the amount of money that China spent on education—2.43 per cent of GDP compared to an average of 4 to 5 per cent in other developing countries. They wrote letters to *Chinese Daily* on everything from the evils of car culture to the overgrazing of Mongolian cattle. Those letters were published; David Crook's letters on anti-Semitism and the arms trade were not. Following the government massacre of protesting students at Tiananmen Square in 1989, they protested in the Chinese language of food and banquets and declined several official invitations, maintaining that the time for feasting and celebration would come when "those responsible for the firing of the guns and the crushing by the tanks of students, workers, stall keepers and common folk condemn their own deeds.... When it is officially proclaimed that June 4 was a massacre."

+++

Isabel Crook was in her seventies when she pulled her carefully stored and never-forgotten field notes of her time in Xinglongchang out of the drawer. She got in touch with her old friend Yu Xiji, who had returned to medical social work, and they picked up where they had left off.

There were notes on foot binding. For thousands of years in many parts of China, a prized feature of a Chinese woman's beauty and status were her tiny and distorted feet. A young girl's toes were folded under the sole of her foot, pressed down until they broke, then the arch of her foot was broken, and the broken foot was wrapped tight for years. Women were literally hobbled. Foot binding had only begun to disappear when Isabel was a girl. There were notes on divorce: women could not divorce men, and they were married young. The village of Xinglongchang had a secret robed brotherhood with enough power to defeat reconstruction projects—these were all features of village life that she had surveyed in 1940. Surveyed but never published.

Yu Xiji and Isabel worked into the 1990s reviewing their field notes, and Yu added Chinese archival material that had become available. Remarkably, her original academic adviser, Raymond Firth, was still alive and pushed them to publish. Isabel was persuaded that to make the book work, it needed a historic perspective, and they recruited American historian Christina Gilmartin, who had worked in Beijing throughout the late 1970s and early 1980s. The three women worked together and made return visits to Prosperity's Market. Isabel was by now in her eighties. Yu Xiji was not a young woman, and she became ill and died in 2007. Five years later, Christina Gilmartin died of cancer.

But this was a project that would not be defeated. Two feminist China historians from the University of California in Santa Cruz, Gail Hershatter and Emily Honig, came on board, and in 2013, seventy-three years after Isabel Crook walked down the mountain pass into Xinglongchang, *Prosperity's Predicament* was published. Isabel Crook was ninety-eight. The book was the earliest anthropological study of a remote Chinese village. The story behind the book made the *Wall Street Journal* and various academic journals. At the official book launch, Isabel Crook "spoke gently and firmly" of the importance of China's rural people "in the new era of urbanization." *Prosperity's Predicament* also contradicted the Chinese position that reform only began after the 1949 revolution. Reforms to the marriage law, provisions expanding divorce, and prohibiting extravagant weddings had started under the old Kuomintang government in the 1920s.

As Isabel worked on the book, she and David turned their apartment on the campus of the Beijing Foreign Studies university into a space for Chinese students wanting to practice their English conversation, and, as early as 1973, when they were first allowed into China, Canadian students were often invited for dinner and conversation. One of those students, Margaret McIntosh, then a philosophy undergraduate from McGill University and now a family physician in Vancouver, recalled that Isabel Crook spoke about where socialism in China was working and where it was not working. McIntosh described Isabel Crook as a woman who had borne witness to the changes that made modern China.

As time went on, Isabel's home became a mecca for not only young Canadian students but also old friends—and their children and grandchildren—who had connections with those original missionary families. In 2011, more than twenty sat down with Isabel Crook at a long table covered with a huge white linen cloth. Then in her mid-nineties, she held court and talked about the long socialist experiment. "Ever since I came to China after I graduated from college, I have watched it," she said and talked about the speech that Mao had given at the liberation of Beijing in 1949, a speech that she and David were there to hear. This was just the first step, Mao had said. "Look at all the time that has gone by since then." Then Isabel smiled and added, "There are a lot of lessons to be learned...some good points and some problems. [This experiment] will take another sixty years at least"; forever the anthropologist and observer, she referred to the building of socialist China as a "great scientific task." One of the other women at the table in Beijing that day was Valerie Endicott, granddaughter of James Gareth Endicott, who had known Isabel Brown as a child; with her was her husband, Stephen Douglas, great-nephew of the astrophysicist Allie Vibert Douglas.

✦✦✦

*...so much of our life was spent on campus here [at Beijing Foreign Studies University]. Our closest friends, the people we cared about most, were right here in Beijing.*

There is a larger-than-life-size granite bust of David Crook on the campus of the Beijing Foreign Studies University. The inscription reads "1910–2000, David Crook, British, Jewish, Communist." Every so often, in the twenty years following her husband's death, Isabel would sit on a bench next to granite David, take out a big handkerchief, and polish his head, and then go home and climb the stairs to their third-floor apartment that they had shared for nearly half a century. The

Isabel, 95, at the dinner with old friends and grandsons and granddaughters of Canadian missionaries in Beijing, 2011

University of Toronto gave Isabel Crook an honorary degree in 2008. Ten years later, China named her "the most influential foreign expert"; the next year, she became an honorary citizen of Szechuan. That same year, she was by now 104, Michael Crook held his mother's arm, and they walked together out from the wings of a vast stage in Beijing. She was wearing a purple silk jacket and black trousers that day and she gently shook off her son's hand and made her own way to the center of the stage, where China's president, Xi Jinping, hung a very large gold medal, the Chinese Medal of Friendship and the highest honor that can be given a foreigner, around her neck. Isabel Crook knows China well enough to understand that any medal comes with political baggage, but Xi, whose face and manner betrays very little, was clearly a little in awe of this white-haired, sharp-eyed woman—one of the last eyewitnesses to the Chinese revolution.

# 7. PARASKEVA AND ALEXANDRA

*Art being so much greater than ourselves, it will not give up once it has taken hold.*

—Emily Carr

*I have too much respect for painting.... It has to have guts, some sort of guts, some sort of strength.*

—Paraskeva Clark

It was nearly dark, and the surface of the Neva River was glassy and smooth. There was no one kicking and splashing about. Everyone who had come down to swim that warm July day had gone home, back to Petrograd, as it then was. Paraskeva kept scanning the water as the sun went down. She had not gone with them to swim—she had never learned how and there was the baby, her little boy, to look after. Her sister-in-law, Olga Allegri, had come up from the river, toweling her hair, hours ago, but where was Oreste? She scanned the water again. Nothing. The darker it got, the more certain she was—he was not coming back; Oreste had drowned. It was 1923, she was twenty-five, and now she was a widow.

Two years later, a world away, it was another hot summer day.

Margaret Smith was four months married, pregnant, and she too was twenty-five. That day, she was tweaking her twin sister's wedding veil, making sure it hung well, when a voice called from the other room, "Marg, there's a telephone call for you." She turned, picked up the earpiece, and listened to a tinny voice, no one she knew, shouting down the line. "Mrs. Smith?" and she held the receiver away from her ear. "Mrs. Smith? I am so sorry to tell you, Mrs. Smith but Marcus has died." A heart attack. Her young husband had had a heart attack. He too was not coming home.

Two twenty-five-year-old widows, single mothers with little boys to raise, separated by seven thousand kilometers, a continent, an ocean, and a language. When they wept and buried their husbands in the 1920s, who could know that three decades later, they would talk about art with the same people, they would each lift a glass of wine from the same tray and cast a critical eye over the same exhibition, and that painting in Canada would owe so much to Margaret "Alexandra Luke" Smith McLaughlin and Paraskeva Clark? At twenty-five, Alexandra Luke had no intention of becoming an artist. Paraskeva did.

◆◆◆

"Why do you want to talk to me...? I'm an old lady," said Paraskeva to Gail Singer, but talk they did. In Singer's film, *Portrait of the Artist as an Old Lady*, Paraskeva is spontaneous yet calculated, passionate and thoughtful, both morose and joyful—the embodiment, as she would see it, of the deep, dark Russian soul. Her paintings draw you in. The self-portrait from 1933—her in a black hat tipped a little rakishly over her left eye, a woman with a pale face, a pale neck, wearing a black dress, and standing with her big paddle hands crossed over her belly. She pulls you in and she stays with you.

Alexandra Luke did not, for the most part, paint people; she was an abstract artist. Where Paraskeva was passionate, Alexandra was cool and intellectual; where Paraskeva wore slinky satin dresses, Alexandra arrived at an opening in her mink over a tweed suit and pearls. Where Paraskeva laughed from her belly with her mouth wide open, Alexandra didn't; where Paraskeva was born poor and a self-declared socialist, Alexandra was wealthy and part of one of Canada's most successful business families. They were never friends, they seldom met, yet they were in some ineffable way connected.

♦♦♦

The Russian revolution launched Paraskeva. The Bolsheviks gave her a chance, and she ran with it. When she was born in 1898 czarist Russia, her father, Avdey Plistik, was a peasant in a worker's cap who had come in from the country to work in a St. Petersburg shoe factory; her mother made wonderful, intricate artificial flowers and brought in at least as much as her husband; and they all lived in workers' housing. There were three children, and it was a hand-to-mouth existence, yet her parents had done what parents do and somehow found the money for Paraskeva, their eldest and brightest, to go to secondary school. But she had stars in her eyes and wanted to go to theater school, to be a performer. She was a performer all her life but never, it turned out, on the stage. When she was a little girl, she saw the czar, the grand duchesses in their furs and jewelry, drive by in their carriages on their way to the opera and the theater, while she lived in a world of open sewers and families living ten to a room. This was a time of workers' strikes and peasant marches when soldiers shot two hundred people and left them bleeding in the snow. World War I broke out, prices went up, food shortages got worse, and Paraskeva's mother got pneumonia and died. Paraskeva was seventeen. As the war went on, Paraskeva got an office job at the shoe factory and started taking art classes at night school. Theater school was too expensive, out of the question, but she could draw and night school at the Imperial Academy of Art was manageable.

When Gregor Katznelson, father of cellist Zara Nelsova, went to the music conservatory in St. Petersburg, across the river from the art school, he was hard-schooled in classical flute technique—the scales, the études—and was rapped across the knuckles if he strayed. The Russian approach to art instruction was no different—start with the fundamentals. Paraskeva was schooled in form, in perspective, in color. There were weeks of drawing in charcoal from a plaster head before she was allowed to paint or work with a live model. She drew cones and cylinders, the constituent elements of figures, and by the time she was in her early twenties, she had a solid technical foundation. Yet there was revolutionary fervor in the air, the Bolsheviks were getting stronger, and discussion all around her was all about Cézanne, Picasso, everything modern that was going on in Europe, in Paris.

As a student, she had to learn to draw figures, to understand the human form, how muscles and bones worked, to explore the shadows and the tensions in a human body, where her teachers told her that character is rooted. To draw and paint the human body well meant live models and nude models, a problem for young women students. In England, major art schools admitted women as early as 1855, but in life drawing classes, only the men worked from live models. In the life class at the Royal Academy in London in the early part of the nineteenth century, the model for the women was a man in a full suit of armor. At one art school in Pennsylvania, it was a cow. In Russia, it was different. Paraskeva learned life drawing alongside the men, and together they drew from nude (female) models.

By the end of 1917, the Bolsheviks had triumphed and were in control of government. Over the next year, under the direction of an artist-run commission, the Petrograd Academy of Art was reformed. Private art studios were closed, and the Academy reopened in October 1918 as "Svomas," the Petrograd Free Studios. Not only was tuition abolished but students were given a stipend. Paraskeva quit her day job and became a full-time student. Her course was set, and she was jubilant. Among young painters, revolution in Russia brought with it a philosophy that scarcity—of food, of heat—could be transcended by artistic vision. The avant-garde thrived.

Not only did the art schools change; so did the theater. Many of the old set designers and painters left, and students, including

Paraskeva holding
a Picasso catalog in
front of her portrait of
Philip, c. 1939

Paraskeva, moved in, and that is how she met the Allegris, a legendary Paris-based family of set designers. She married the eldest son, Oreste, in 1922. Their son Benedict was born, and the senior Allegris left Petrograd to go back to Paris the next spring, months before Oreste drowned. Paraskeva was on her own, living with a baby in a room in the theater. Not only was she distraught, but she knew how difficult life would be for a single woman with a small child in Petrograd, a city still rife with food shortages and post-revolutionary chaos. She made up her mind, and she and her son got on a train and made their way to Paris to her in-laws. She left Russia but never did she say that she had "escaped" Russia.

To the world, Paris was the most exciting city on earth; for Paraskeva, it was security.

*Prisoner of an ordinary life.*

—Joan Murray

The consensus was that Oshawa, Ontario, was enterprising but never exciting. Margaret Alexandra Luke Smith would not have disagreed. In the fall of 1925, the *Oshawa Daily Reformer* ran columns on the latest recipients of the Victoria Cross and the visit of the Queen's Own Rifles. There were speculative articles over the forthcoming federal election—Oshawa had gone Conservative since 1878—and the front page included a story about a $2,000 civil judgment against the Oshawa chapter of the Ku Klux Klan.

The same edition of the paper advertised "Saturday Specials" at Luke Brothers's Furniture Store—hardwood chairs for ninety-five

Paraskeva Allegri and
Ben, Chatou, France

cents—and reported that Sam McLaughlin and his brother George had each donated $5,000 (the equivalent of $80,000 in 2020) to the brand-new Banting Research Foundation.

These were her people. Margaret's family, the Lukes, were merchant pillars of Oshawa society. She grew up a few doors down from the McLaughlins, the most powerful—and philanthropic—family in Oshawa. The nineteenth-century McLaughlin Carriage Company, the largest in the British Empire, had become General Motors Canada. Colonel Sam McLaughlin was president of the company, and George was vice president. The Lukes and the McLaughlins swam in the same social pool, so it was not surprising when the George McLaughlins steered their eldest son, Ewart, still unmarried at thirty-two, in the direction of the newly widowed Margaret. The McLaughlins needed a wife for Ewart, and neither the Lukes, the Smiths—her deceased husband's family—nor the McLaughlins wanted Margaret to remain a single mother. It was a tidy, but in the long run not a particularly happy, solution. Ewart was looking for a conventional wife, a woman who would can peaches, as his mother had done, and attend to his needs. Margaret, in all likelihood, did not know what she wanted but was there a choice? She had trained but never worked as a nurse. Her daughter said that she regarded scrubbing floors and changing bedpans as demeaning. She had a son, she needed a husband, so in 1928 she married him. They did not see life the same way; as one friend said, "He took margarine, she took butter, and they did not compromise." Ewart McLaughlin was notoriously frugal—it's said that he gave his wife an allowance equivalent to the amount he was allowed as a spousal exemption on his income tax.

Margaret's sister-in-law Dorothy, Ewart's younger sister, was interested in art, and not long after Margaret Smith became Margaret McLaughlin, Dorothy brought a Dutch landscape artist to Oshawa. Margaret took lessons, she dabbled, and became a Sunday painter. She had done what was expected of her and found a new father for her son. Now she had to behave like a well-bred wife. She was expected to be subservient and to show herself incapable of deciding much more than the dinner menu. She was allowed "hobbies." Queen Victoria had been dead for a quarter of a century, but for a young woman, a young wife, hobbies meant playing an instrument—preferably the piano—and painting or drawing, but not too well. One late-nineteenth-century private art instructor in France wrote a letter to the mother of two of his better pupils, warning her: "Considering the characters of your daughters, my teaching will not endow them with minor drawing room accomplishment, they will become painters. Do you realize what this means? In the upper-class milieu to which you belong this will be revolutionary, I might say almost catastrophic."

Catastrophic when contemplating marriage. Many, if not most, of the women who became serious artists were unmarried. Dabbling was the expectation, a little something to augment the serious business of husband and family. The young Russian painter Marie Bashkirtseff, studying in Paris in the 1880s, wrote in her diary, "What I long for is the freedom of going about alone, of coming and going, of sitting in the seats of Tuileries…of walking about the old streets at night; that's what I long for and that's the freedom without which one cannot become a real artist."

As Paraskeva Clark put it, "An artist has to be able to lock the door and throw away the key." It took a long time, almost twenty years, before Margaret Alexandra Luke McLaughlin threw away the key.

✦✦✦

By 1929, Paraskeva Clark had a job as a shopgirl at René Joubert and Philippe Petit's very upscale, very Art Deco Décoration Intérieure Moderne showroom in Paris. She was lifting herself up out of the web of grief and confusion that, for almost five years, had kept her in the suburbs living with and keeping house for her in-laws and looking after Ben. She did some painting, not a lot, but this was when she first painted an image she came back to repeatedly: a dejected woman seated in an almost empty apartment with her baby in her arms, a large window looking onto a dark city sky behind her. *Memories of Leningrad*, she called it.

In Paris, she taught herself French and slowly began to think about her future. That's when she decided that it would be a good idea to follow up one new language, French, with another and learn English. There were, according to one estimate, forty thousand Americans in Paris in the twenties. These were *les Années folles*—the crazy years. Paris was retaking the aesthetic leadership of the western world. In 1925, fifteen thousand exhibitors of the *style moderne* were in Paris for the International Exhibition of Modern Decorative Arts. (Herbert Hoover, then–American secretary of commerce, declined America's invitation, saying, reportedly, that there was no modern art in the US.)

Fitzgerald, Orwell, and Hemingway were in Paris; Picasso was in Paris; the surrealists Man Ray and René Magritte were in Paris. Russian expats painted in garrets, going as hungry as they would have at home. And there were hundreds of art students. Isabel McLaughlin, third of Sam McLaughlin's five daughters and now Margaret's cousin-in-law, had arrived and she and Prudence Heward were taking classes together. The Group of Seven's A.Y. Jackson would call Heward one of the best painters in Montreal. Ten years earlier, Emily Carr studied at the Académie Colarossi, one of the schools that allowed women to draw nude models. The Toronto sculptor Frances Loring followed her two years later. Yvonne McKague Housser, one of the first female instructors at the Ontario College of Art, was in Paris; so were Emily Coonan and Lilias Torrance Newton from Montreal. Canadian women painters were thick on the ground between the two wars. But what did Paraskeva know of Canada in 1929?

Every morning, she got on the train in the suburb of Chatou, traveled to the center of Paris, and walked to the elegant Art Deco design shop. Her clientele included designers, artists, and those American tourists. One day, two Canadian men strolled through the Place de la Madeleine and saw a small sculpture in the Décoration Intérieure Moderne shop window. They went in and a small, wiry young woman, striking in her shopgirl's black dress, looked up as the little doorbell jingled. "*Bonjour, messieurs. Je vous en prie?*" she said. That was about as far as they got. Murray Adaskin, the shorter of the two men, spoke a little French, but his taller, leaner friend, Philip Clark, barely knew a word. Paraskeva's English lessons had only just begun, nonetheless, the shopgirl smiled, used what words she had, and sold them the sculpture. Adaskin, the child of Latvian immigrants, heard the Russian accent behind her French and was curious; Clark was smitten.

Philip Clark was a Toronto accountant, a jacket-and-tie man, restrained to the point of repressed. He came from a strict Presbyterian household where women were expected to dress modestly and wear no makeup. Paraskeva looked fabulous with her scarlet lipstick. He found his own family dull; most of the women he knew were pale, bloodless, and didn't say much; he was tantalized by the exotic. All his life he would be drawn to artists, writers, and musicians. His friend Murray Adaskin was a violinist, and Philip played the piano but, he was told, not well enough to make a career. The arts were, for him, the path not taken.

Paraskeva may well have had a secret smile on her face when she took the train home that night. There was something about Philip Clark that she found attractive, but she declined his invitation to dinner. That pleased him; he would have considered her too "easy" had she accepted. "Wholesome" he called her when he wrote to his father. Paraskeva was called many things throughout her life, but seldom if ever wholesome. She had, when she met Philip, overcome her grief and started an affair with Paul Allegri, her dead husband's younger brother, who would soon ask her to marry him. Philip Clark knew none of this.

When he went back to Toronto at the end of that summer, he realized he didn't know much about her at all. He knew that she was a widow with a small child—Ben was seven—but he had no idea that she was an artist until one day she sent him a self-portrait. He could see immediately that she was no student. They wrote to each other, he in French and she in English, correcting each other's mistakes. Love letters? When they were both much, much older, she told him that he didn't know how to write love letters. "He's chartered accountant." (Her Russian English never made room for "a" and "the.") Somehow, through his fractured French and her beginner's English, they connected. Gradually, he began to think of her as a possible wife, although like Ewart McLaughlin, for him a wife was a helpmate, a woman who supported her husband. Painting, he thought, for Paraskeva was a hobby. Unlike McLaughlin, however, Philip Clark had more elasticity in his soul.

Paraskeva, far more than Margaret McLaughlin, needed security; she had no family, nothing to fall back on. Marriage to Paul Allegri, when he offered, was a viable option, but when Philip came back to Paris in the summer of 1931 and proposed, that was a better option. This was a man who had liquidated all his investments *before* the 1929 stock market crash, who had a job that lasted through the Depression, and who would take her to a new country and a new world. He was, certainly in his old age and must always have been, a courtly gentleman, and a kind man, prepared to accept her son, and that was important. It wasn't a difficult decision; she once again packed her things, gathered up Ben, and was gone from the Allegri house before the mystified Paul Allegri got home. They eloped to England, where it was easier to get a marriage license, and by June of 1931, she was Paraskeva Clark and on the boat to Canada.

+++

*There was a period when there was great anxiety in Canada. There was no reflection, there was nothing but Group of Seven, landscape, landscape, landscape! Nothing but the bloody Group of Seven, bah! They don't consider social content but I was interested in somehow participating in that expression.*

—Paraskeva Clark

The title was daunting: *An Exhibition of Seascapes and Water-Fronts by Contemporary Artists and an Exhibition by the Group of Seven.* Paraskeva had only been in the country for six months when Philip took her to see this show at what was then the Art Gallery of Toronto. It was the Group of Seven's last show as a group, and it was their paintings that dominated. Paraskeva was not impressed. She didn't know the history of the Group of Seven—what they were trying to do, why they painted "landscape, landscape, landscape!"

They had banded together in 1920; seven men, nearly all in their

The Group of Seven (and their friend Barker Fairley) lunching at the Arts and Letters Club

thirties, nearly all working for the same commercial art firm. Every one of them wanted to see painting that reflected the Canadian identity, at least the English Canadian identity. They were pushing back against what was then calling itself Canadian art, paintings that were essentially European, certainly in style and often in subject matter. Their work—strong, bold Northern Ontario landscapes—was about Canada. This was, in the 1920s and '30s, radical new painting. It wasn't her only objection, but Paraskeva thought it was also very male.

A.Y. Jackson, Lawren Harris, Arthur Lismer, and the rest lunched regularly at the Arts and Letters Club in Toronto, where they talked about nationalism and Canadian identity. Her husband was a member and Paraskeva would have liked to join Philip for lunch and to have told them what she thought. *Landscape wasn't enough to define Canadian painting*, she would have said and added that they didn't understand in the least what it was like to be a woman artist. "She was very controversial," said her daughter-in-law, Mary. "She went on about the Group of Seven and how they didn't understand menstruation, and how hard it was for a woman like her."

Yes, she would have liked to have lunched at the Arts and Letters Club, but she could not get past the front door. The Arts and Letters Club was a men's club. It did not admit women for another mind-numbing fifty-four years. Even then, it took a ten-year battle, kicked off in February of 1975 when sculptor Anne Lazar Mirvish and a couple of her friends picketed the club. It had refused to let her in to hear her husband, Ed Mirvish, by then a Toronto theater impresario, speak.

The men of the Group of Seven, particularly Lawren Harris, were supportive of several women painters, most notably Emily Carr, but when one of the seven left the group, and then another, they never invited a woman to join.

There were many strong women painters in Canada—remarkably, fourteen of the thirty-two artists in that big 1931 Art Gallery of Toronto show were women. Prudence Heward's painting *Girl Under a Tree*, a striking, dramatic, and controversial nude, was included in that exhibition. Arthur Lismer called it "the best nude ever painted in

*Myself*,
Paraskeva Clark,
1933

Canada." Nude paintings were difficult. Two years later, Lilias Torrance Newton's *Nude in the Studio* was excluded from another exhibition because it was a painting not of a nymph or a goddess but a "real" naked woman. Heward painted strong, independent women who made their own way in the world, who voted and smoked and went out in public unescorted. The Canadian artists studying in Paris were just the tip of the iceberg. There were Heward and the Beaver Hall Group in Montreal, nearly half of whom were women—and all but one of them unmarried. In Toronto, Paraskeva Clark got to know Yvonne McKague Housser; "the girls," sculptors Florence Wyle and Frances Loring; Mary Wrinch Reid, the first Canadian woman to make a living from her art; Marion Long; and, floating among them all, Isabel McLaughlin, another of Margaret McLaughlin's new sisters-in-law.

Paraskeva was painting vociferously in her new country. In 1933, she did a portrait of Philip and that big, bold, black self-portrait, *Myself*. Invitations to show her work began to come in, and in 1934, she and another young woman, Pegi Nicol, were hired to work on the new Eaton's College Street Art Deco hall. When she went to openings, she appeared in dresses that were elegant and a little shocking—low-cut front and back—and she made the social pages. Paraskeva Clark became a presence in Toronto, a strong, opinionated presence. A.Y. Jackson was reportedly afraid of her. No question, she and her painting had landed. When she was invited to show a 1931 self-portrait at the Art Gallery of Toronto, she wrote on the back, "foot in the door into the Temple of Canadian Art."

◆◆◆

Margaret McLaughlin would have seen Paraskeva's self-portrait at the Art Gallery of Toronto, and she would have gone to that final 1931 show of the Group of Seven, the show that rankled Paraskeva. At that point in her life, McLaughlin might have been only a "Sunday painter," but she kept up with what was going on in the art world. She went to shows in Ottawa and in Montreal, she probably saw the Beaver Hall

Paraskeva reclining

Group exhibitions, and she went to New York. The Brooklyn Museum brought in an exhibition called Paintings by Modern French and American Artists; Georgia O'Keeffe was on display at her then-husband Alfred Stieglitz's Intimate Gallery; there were the paintings by Edward Hopper and a great deal more. New York had seen the avant-garde, Fauvism, and Cubism as early as 1913. Margaret took it all in.

At home in Oshawa, she kept painting, dabbling in landscapes, and did what wealthy women were supposed to do: organized events for the betterment of her town. There was the Oshawa Skating Club, art classes for children, and art exhibitions at the Young Women's Christian Association. The Oshawa YW must have been one of the few—if not the only—chapters in the country that made art a priority. Adelaide House, home of the YW in Oshawa, had its own gallery. In the late 1940s, Margaret and Dorothy Van Luven presented sixty-nine exhibitions over five years at Adelaide House.

Ben, Paraskeva, and Philip Clark, 1931

In 1933, as Paraskeva was painting her *Portrait of Philip* and *Myself* in Toronto, the Oshawa Lyceum Club—a women's club—was hanging its annual exhibition. Sir Edmund Wyly Grier, esteemed portrait painter, president of the Royal Canadian Academy of the Arts, and one of the founders of the Arts and Letters Club, was invited to open the show. Sir Edmund was a fossil with no time for modern art. Standing up in front of the Oshawa ladies in their fine hats and their gloves, he said, "It [modern art] was founded on a passion for the limelight…written up like advertising for poor breakfast food…and would not stand the test of time."

Many applauded. Margaret McLaughlin was incensed and, at the risk of betraying her social position, wrote to the *Oshawa Daily Times*:

> As an exponent of modern art I would like to refute the stand taken by Sir Wyly Grier. Sir Wyly belongs to that group of traditionalists who can see no good in new or different methods of approach or technique in art and who cannot

tolerate the change from old to new, from static to dynamic. His unjust criticism of Modern Art provoked many of his audience who studied the modern school. I sincerely hope that those who heard Sir Wyly Grier will not be prejudiced by his condemnation.

To underline her point, Margaret McLaughlin and her friend Dorothy Van Luven incorporated increasingly more "modern" art in the exhibitions they mounted at the YW in Oshawa.

Not only did she travel to New York and other eastern Canadian cities, but she went further afield, taking her son with her for the benefit of his allergies and sinus trouble. They went to Bermuda, where the McLaughlins had a family house, and to Arizona; then, in 1938, she took both children—she'd had a daughter with Ewart McLaughlin in 1930—to Santa Fe, New Mexico. The children were looked after by a nanny in Santa Fe while Margaret traveled to Taos, which was increasingly becoming a mecca for modern artists of all sorts. There was painter Georgia O'Keeffe and photographer Ansel Adams. British novelist D.H. Lawrence "discovered" New Mexico in the 1920s. Margaret signed up for lessons with a Hungarian American modernist Emil Bisttram, a member of the new Transcendental Painters Group—nine painters who aimed to "create painting[s] that finds its source in the creative imagination" rather than in landscapes or people and aimed to "carry painting beyond the appearance of the physical world to imaginative realms that are idealistic and spiritual." It was in Taos that Margaret McLaughlin began her search for a spiritual identity that could be articulated in her painting. She was becoming more confident in her own vision.

*It is a long and complicated process for any young painter to find his own personal voice and keep it intact and natural. It is a painful triumph over the self and when it is carried out sincerely and profoundly, in depth, it is bound to be a heroic undertaking.*

—Margaret Alexandra Luke McLaughlin

*Those who give their lives, their knowledge and their time to social struggle have the right to expect great help from the artist. And I cannot imagine a more inspiring role than that which the artist is asked to play for the defence and advancement of civilization.*

—Paraskeva Clark

"We went to Paraskeva's and wrecked a very pretty party," wrote Pegi Nicol to her lifelong friend, Montreal artist Marian Dale Scott. Nicol, Scott, and her husband, poet F.R. Scott, were part of the self-described "pinko" artistic set in Montreal. It was 1936; Paraskeva and Philip were mid–dinner party when Pegi Nicol showed up. Murray Adaskin, his wife, Frances, artist Bertram Brooker, and J. Campbell McInnes, a singer and a robust drinker—although Paraskeva could match him shot for shot—were between courses. Nicol walked in, bringing with her another Montreal artist, Fritz Brandtner, and their friend "Beth"— Norman Bethune.

"Anybody got any beer?" said Bethune and threw himself into a chair. "Philip, get me some beer."

They were off and running. That year, 1936, was the lead up to the Spanish Civil War—communists versus fascists—and feelings were running high. On another evening, an argument between Bethune, who had just returned from the Soviet Union and joined the Communist Party, and the articulate Brooker came close to fisticuffs. Paraskeva was in her element; well-mannered Toronto was being shaken up. The arguments always came down to the role of the artist. In Montreal, Bethune was known as both a doctor and an artist. With Brandtner and Marian Scott, he had set up the Children's Art Centre in his apartment, giving workshops and classes to poor children. "The function of the artist is to disturb," maintained Bethune. "He [the artist] is an agitator, a disturber of the peace." Paraskeva was with Bethune all the way; this was what she believed in. It was more than shared belief—Bethune was alive, an unrestrained man who lusted after life every bit as much, if not more, than Paraskeva. It didn't take long—Bethune did not have long—before she was sharing his bed. They went to New York City together, fundraising for the International Brigade and the Spanish Civil War. When they came back, Bethune, who was staying with the Clarks, asked Philip—in a perversely well-mannered gesture, as though he was asking to borrow his umbrella—for his permission to sleep with his wife. Not that Paraskeva needed or wanted his permission. Philip told Paraskeva that he would not stand in her way, writing later to a friend that he regarded sex as "a minor aspect of human life." Perhaps that was part of the problem.

It was a grand passion. Long after Bethune died in China treating soldiers in Mao's army in 1939, his memory stayed with her. When she spoke about Bethune as an old woman, she would tremble. She said that she understood the sacrifices that Philip had made to have a life with her. Philip, in turn, said of his wife, "I consider her to be a remarkable and beautiful woman." Paraskeva Clark's biographer Jane Lind writes that when years later Bethune came to be regarded in Canada as a hero, relative strangers would ask her, "Did you *know* Bethune?" With Philip standing at her shoulder, she would stare them down and say, "I *fucked* Bethune." At this point, Philip would say, "Paraskeva, it's time to go home."

Bethune spoke of Paraskeva as "a great artist and a great human being." He reinforced her thinking, her view that art could be both a vehicle of expression and a tool of change, and he influenced her painting. He wrote to her from Spain and sent mementos—a pamphlet, a cap of the International Brigade. The gifts became a political still life, *Presents from Madrid*, that she painted in 1937. Much as she believed in Bethune, she did not put up with his artistic liberties. One day when he was in her studio, her painting *Petroushka* was on her easel. He casually reached over and painted a brown building blue. Really? She repainted it.

Bethune had joined the Communist Party of Canada, but Paraskeva never did. It would have made life difficult for Philip, and during the Cold War of the 1950s, she was glad she had not signed up. She was, however, deeply and loudly involved in the related debate over the role of the artist and the function of art. It had started, in large part, with the Group of Seven's push to create a Canadian identity and to foster nationalism through their landscape painting. By the late thirties, the debate centered on the political and social issues playing out in Europe. Those whose thinking sprang from the goals of the Group of Seven maintained that art and the artist should embrace the purity of nature and rise above the misery of everyday life; Paraskeva and those who agreed with her, saw art as a means to remedy that misery—or at least put it squarely in the public view.

Elizabeth Wyn Wood was a Toronto sculptor who, like the Group of Seven, was inspired by the Northern Ontario landscape, the Precambrian Shield. In 1936, in an article for *Canadian Forum* magazine, she argued that while European artists might be caught up in the social and political upheaval that surrounded them, Canadian artists did not need to be. Wyn Wood asked somewhat contemptuously, "What should we Canadian artists do—paint castles in Spain? Crumbling. Paint the Russian proletariat standing on the fallen

The photograph that
Norman Bethune sent
Paraskeva from Spain

Cossack? Such things are not authentic stimuli to the Canadian artist." To Elizabeth Wyn Wood, authentic stimuli to the Canadian artist were the woods and the lakes and the trees; she added that Canadian artists "have always had some doubts about civilization."

Paraskeva would have none of it. Writing publicly in English for the first time in an article called "Come Out from behind the Pre-Cambrian Shield," published in the journal *New Frontier*, she wrote, "Is [the artist] not a human being like ourselves, with added bits of finer understanding and perception of the realities of life, and the ability to arouse emotions through the creation of forms and images? Surely. And this being so, those who give their lives, their knowledge and their time to social struggle have the right to expect great help from the artists." The impact of her views was ironically heightened, coming as they did from the well-dressed wife of a successful accountant who by then was living in Rosedale, Toronto's "best" neighborhood.

Paraskeva continued to decry the lack of social engagement in art, as her reputation grew. In 1937, she mounted her first solo show; one of her paintings was included in a show of British Empire artists in London, and in the same year she painted *Petroushka*. Paraskeva Clark painted a capitalist puppeteer waving his bags of money and cheering on a policeman as he beats a man senseless while the people shout back. Far more than cartoonish propaganda, she considered it her best painting. It has been exhibited widely and is now owned by the National Gallery of Canada. Not only were her paintings widely shown, they were also selling. Paraskeva Clark now considered herself well installed in the "temple of Canadian art."

Not only did she have a seat in the temple, but she was also becoming part of the club. Visual artists in Canada have been organizing themselves since the 1920s; in contrast, Canadian composers did not get themselves organized until 1951. A decade later in 1961, they were still only forty strong and included only four women. The Group of Seven disbanded in 1931, and two years later the Canadian Group of Painters, a group with no specific artistic mandate, was born. By 1935, it had admitted forty-six artists, including Paraskeva and thirteen other women.

Paraskeva was an immigrant, by now she had a place in the temple of Canadian art, yet she never stopped feeling Russian, not only in the food she cooked and the music she loved; she was Russian—almost Soviet—in her beliefs. "I hate capitalism," she would say. When the Soviets were allies in World War II, that was tolerable. She raised money for civilians in Russia and donated the proceeds from the sale of twenty-seven of her paintings. It was not only a point of principle: it was personal. Many of her family—her brother, her sister, and some cousins—were in Leningrad (Petrograd had been renamed five days after Lenin died in 1924), throughout the sixteen-month-long German siege. Her brother died during the siege, and by the end of the war, her sister was dead as well. Cousins, men and women in the countryside, were shot. Paraskeva had no Russian family, no connections left.

Things got worse. In 1943, her twenty-year-old son, Ben, had

New Year's Eve party, late 1930s. Front Row: Elizabeth Wyn Wood, Paraskeva, Will Ogilvie. Second Row: Doris Davies, Charles Comfort. Back Row: Unidentified, Emanuel Hahn.

what was then called a nervous collapse; he was hearing voices, hallucinating. Paraskeva and Philip didn't know what to do. Eventually, they found a psychiatrist who diagnosed Ben with schizophrenia. Her lovely boy, whom she had cared for by herself in Russia and protected as he grew up in France and then Canada, her lovely boy had gone. Treatment—electroshock and insulin therapy—was primitive and ineffectual, and mental illness was seen as a mark of moral weakness. Blame for schizophrenia was often laid squarely at the mother's feet, and if others did not blame her, she blamed herself. Ben was in a psychiatric hospital for the better part of a year the first time, and every time she thought he might be getting better, there was a recurrence. For the rest of her life, she looked after him, lived with him. She was his mother. What could she do?

♦♦♦

*Painting is not a women's profession. It needs a strong fellow to do it....*
*But sometimes a woman is strong too.*

—Hans Hoffmann

In 1944, when Paraskeva was trying to understand what was happening to her son, Margaret McLaughlin met a Winnipeg landscape artist named Caven Atkins, not particularly well-known but respected. That summer, he had been teaching at Queen's University. Knowing that Margaret painted at least a little, Atkins asked her, "Would you like me to look at your paintings and tell you what I think?" Never afraid of criticism, she said yes, and Atkins came to Oshawa to see her work. He did not pull his punches and told her that her landscapes were not particularly interesting or original; she was painting pieces that were in the style of, almost duplicates of, Group of Seven paintings, and in Atkins's view there was no point in going over old ground. Atkins had spent time in Montreal in the thirties and met Norman Bethune and Paraskeva's Montreal friend Fritz Brandtner, who had introduced him to abstract expressionism. If Margaret McLaughlin wanted to continue to "dabble," he told her, the landscapes were fine, but if she wanted to be a serious painter—she needed to dig deeper. Years later, whenever those early landscapes surfaced, she would shake her head and burn them.

It is impossible to know if there was any one thing that pushed her, but during those war years, there was a great deal that was new and different going on around her. Oshawa, at its heart a manufacturing town, was key to the Canadian war effort. Its factories had been churning out field guns and anti-aircraft cartridges; GM Canada had moved from making cars to building troop carriers, wireless trucks, ambulances, and armored cars. In 1941, the Duke of Kent, brother of the king, came to Oshawa to watch the five hundred thousandth

Margaret
Alexandra Luke
McLaughlin

military vehicle come off the line. Sam McLaughlin rode with the duke in the official car, and it was Colonel Sam who tightened the final bolts for the newspaper photograph. Margaret, because she was a McLaughlin, had to be, and she wanted to be, involved in the war effort. Given her nursing training, she worked with the Red Cross on blood drives. Every time she put on her uniform and went to work, she would have seen hundreds of women in their uniforms—coveralls and kerchiefs—clocking in to work on the GM line. Women were going out to work as they never had before, doing things they never had before. Why not her?

On May 7, 1945, she cheered and waved her Union Jack at Oshawa's Victory in Europe parade. A few weeks later, she left Oshawa like a shot and headed for the summer session at the Banff School of Fine Arts in Alberta. She was going to get serious about painting.

At forty-four, Margaret McLaughlin was a middle-aged woman, but she was a young artist. That summer in Banff, she was every bit as disciplined and committed as Paraskeva Clark had been twenty years earlier in Russia. And just as Paraskeva had relished and talked about what was new and important in her long talks with other students and teachers, so did Margaret that summer in Banff. Since her letter to the *Oshawa Daily Times* in the early thirties, it was clear that Margaret McLaughlin was interested in where painting was going, not where it had been. She had now discovered the color and energy of abstract expressionism, the concept of painting emotions and ideas, not things.

Her teachers were the much-respected A.Y. Jackson, a leader among Canadian artists long after his Group of Seven days, and Vancouver-based Jock Macdonald, an immigrant from Scotland who became one of the most influential people in Margaret McLaughlin's life. Macdonald, captivated by the force and grandeur of the BC landscape, had already begun to experiment with a painting style that could capture the spiritual aspect of nature, and he found it in abstract expressionism. He was painting and showing semi-abstract paintings in Vancouver as early as the 1930s, well before the wave hit Toronto.

While she was at Banff, Margaret drew, painted, and read everything that Macdonald gave her about spiritualism and painting. Half the class thought it was nonsense, and the other half embraced it. "He makes one see deeply," she said, "what a very deep and searching problem it is." Her work became stronger throughout the summer, and Banff included one of her pieces in a traveling show of student work; sixty-five were chosen from fifteen hundred submitted, and another piece was selected for Banff's permanent collection.

When she came back to Oshawa, Margaret McLaughlin and her sister-in-law Isabel McLaughlin, by now a well-established painter, were offered a two-woman show. It was her first opportunity to show her new work in the East. But two women named McLaughlin in the same show? Confusing, she thought. And ostensibly to avoid confusion, she created a new identity. She became Alexandra Luke (her middle name and her birth name). From then on, it would be Margaret McLaughlin, "Marg," at home and as the wife of Ewart McLaughlin, Alexandra Luke in the art world. The new name did more than avoid confusion: it provided a cover—as all pseudonyms do—if she fell on her face. It would be Alexandra Luke who had failed, not Margaret McLaughlin.

✦✦✦

*I feel ready to start anything. I phoned A.Y. for advice. He told me to go for a week to country and thus get some fresh material…for s.s. [silk screen]. Well—here I am—on a farm.*

—Paraskeva Clark

The war effort took many forms. Paraskeva was commissioned to contribute to the Silk Screen Project, a federal government project to boost troop morale. How encouraged the men would feel if they had an image of Canada hanging on the barrack walls, a landscape! A.Y. Jackson and the National Gallery's H.O. McCurry were in charge. McCurry wanted Paraskeva, despite her earlier public disavowal of Canadian landscape. He knew how to get her onside—he told Paraskeva that several sets of the prints would be going to Russia. She made her peace with Canadian landscape.

Another letter came from McCurry telling her that the National Gallery was going to purchase another of her self-portraits. Then McCurry told her that he had recommended her to the Royal Canadian Air Force (RCAF) as a war artist, adding, "but do not know if the minister will agree to appoint a woman artist."

He was right; the minister was reluctant. Two women had applied to be official war artists in World War I, Mary Riter Hamilton and E. Dorothy McAvity. They were both rejected. Riter Hamilton later made her own way to the battlefields of Belgium and France and came back with three hundred paintings—an unexpurgated and unequalled view of the residue of war. In World War II, one woman, Molly Lamb Bobak from BC, was named an official war artist. Paraskeva wrote back to McCurry, "The adventure would be great and would've done a lot of good to my painting, but, on the other hand, I was worried about my family…and please believe me that I feel a great honour Canada gave to a Russian that came here 13 years ago—so utterly unsuspecting it might be waiting for her."

She was genuinely flattered, and she wanted to be part of it all, but she could not leave Ben. It did not end there. McCurry engineered a National Gallery commission for Paraskeva to paint the Women's Division of the RCAF in training. She would not have to travel far from Toronto or leave Ben for any length of time. Her friend Pegi Nicol MacLeod, the woman who had crashed the Clarks's dinner party with Bethune, had been thinking about the Canadian war artists program and had written to a friend, "It is unfair enough to leave out the mothers of soldiers, the nurses, the factory girls. What an obvious flaw to neglect also the women in the armed forces." Pegi MacLeod was also commissioned.

One of the major criticisms was that military service would destroy a woman's femininity. Nicol's first piece was called *CWAC Beauty Parlor*, a painting of an army corps woman sitting under a hair dryer reading a magazine.

Paraskeva went to Galt, Ontario, and HMCS Conestoga, the site where less than a year before, "Trixie" Worsley had done her basic training. She was looking for drama, for tension, but most women in the Women's Division of the RCAF were telephone operators and filing clerks, jobs without much drama. Two paintings came from that visit: one of women packing parachutes and the other of three women working—repairing—an airplane in a hangar; the message was clear, here were women working to protect the lives of men on the front lines; but more importantly, she came away thinking about hidden drama and different priorities. Paraskeva wrote,

> You see I feel that dramatic subject in Canadian Women's life is not among CWAC [Canadian Women's Army Corps] but among millions [of] women who stayed in their homes carrying on some jobs, some responsibilities plus their normal home duties—with their hearts full of constant pain and longing and sorrow for their men going fighting. Being CWAC was the easiest thing to do, the most pleasant. Throwing off the eternal chores and drudgery for women's life—women entered a regulated orderly life with one duty set upon each, for so many hours each day, with the glory and glamor of uniform to top it!

> If I see a dramatic subject here in Toronto, it is like this group of 3 or 4 legless young soldiers laughing and joking, pushing along in their wheel chairs with few others hopping beside on crutches. A promenade—a narrow crooked window in the second storey of a slum house, elaborately decorated with flags and inscription "Welcome Home son"...such a home...! But National Gallery wouldn't want such war records and I am not sure that I would be able to put on canvas the drama and pathos of such subjects.

✦✦✦

*I put my work up first as the others all seemed bashful about it and also I knew if I didn't I wouldn't have the courage later.*

—Alexandra Luke

The year 1947 was a big one for Alexandra Luke. This was the year that she signed up for Hans Hofmann's summer school in Provincetown, Massachusetts. Hofmann was a German American painter and one of the most influential teachers of the twentieth century. Nearly every prominent American abstract expressionist had worked with him. Luke went to Hofmann every summer, bar one, for the next five years and she flourished. Early on, the student at the easel next to her leaned over and whispered that he had never seen anyone "get it" as quickly as she did. She brought other Canadian painters with her—Isabel McLaughlin, Yvonne McKague Housser, and William Ronald, one of the Toronto young Turks, the next generation.

In 1948, she was given a solo show at Trinity College at the University of Toronto; in 1950, she had a work accepted at the annual spring exhibition at the Montreal Museum of Fine Arts; and she was one of the few abstract expressionist painters included in a Canadian Group of Painters show, certainly one of even fewer abstract expressionist women. Alexandra Luke was developing a reputation and as an abstract expressionist painter, she was venturing into a very male world.

The American abstract expressionists were the cowboys of painting, and the Canadians "The Wild Ones" of Canadian art. Their work was "astonishingly assertive" and "emphatically large." Large was a challenge in and of itself. Alexandra Luke's grandchildren peered into her studio at the family farm and seeing a canvas eight feet by nine, wondered how their grandmother managed. "And she didn't paint on the floor," said her grandson. She was climbing ladders and reaching up, her brush slathered with paint. She did not hesitate or hold back.

All the time she was painting landscapes and exhibiting quietly, her hobby was accepted at home. But this new work, this big painting with its loud colors, was beyond Ewart McLaughlin's ken. He didn't

Alexandra Luke in her studio at Greenbriar, 1950

understand her new paintings. He didn't like her new friends. When Jock Macdonald moved east to Toronto, he and his wife came to dinner. They talked about painting and spiritualism and they smoked. Ewart McLaughlin, true to his conservative Protestant roots, did not approve of smoking or drinking and called the Macdonalds "the puff-puffs." He did not know what to make of them. When Alexandra Luke went off in the summers to study with Hofmann, Margaret McLaughlin's husband would take her paintings off the walls and put up what made sense to him: his traditional Victorian paintings. He liked cars and racing boats, not modern paintings. No one can remember Ewart going to any of her openings. She had a studio on the third floor of the big family house in Oshawa, and he never appeared up there. Having been married to her husband for more than twenty years, she must not have expected anything more; she just got on with things.

Support came from her friends, like New York gallery owner Martha Jackson, whom she met in the early fifties. Jackson invited her to New York and, when Alexandra Luke hesitated, said, "What's the good of being married to this rich man who pays you so little attention unless you can spend some of his money and come to New York."

One way or another, she knew where she wanted to go, what she wanted to do. As one family member said, "She had such a hard time to get anybody interested and to help her. She had to do it always herself."

✦✦✦

*I grew so scared of critics and of my own feeling about my painting, which I feel is so void of excitement, originality, adventure—in comparison to what is going on. I am always scared to face my works.*

—Paraskeva Clark

As Alexandra Luke was pushing forward, breaking new ground, Paraskeva was pulling back. In the years after the war, the trajectory of their respective careers crossed. Paraskeva was pulling back in part because of Ben. She loved her son and, most of the time, liked cooking and looking after her house, only going to her studio to paint after she had done the housework. But equally important and unsettling, she was not comfortable with her painting. She felt out of step and frustrated with her work. Which is not to say that she was out of the public eye. There was an article about her and Clive, her and Philip's son, in *Saturday Night* magazine, and there were more shows—the benefit of a recognition coming as it often does a decade after the work that earned it. One of those exhibitions was with the Canadian Society of Watercolour Artists, of which she was president. A critic called her work "sensitive and powerful." She showed twenty-six of her paintings at Victoria College at the University of Toronto and had a two-person show at the Art Gallery of Toronto in 1954. Nonetheless, her anxiety and insecurity about her work did not go away.

In 1956, Paraskeva was invited to be the out-of-town juror for

Paraskeva in her studio, c. 1949

the Montreal Museum of Fine Arts' annual spring show, and Lilias Torrance Newton, the much-respected Montreal portrait painter, held a party for her, a great and very personal compliment. She had another one-woman show at the University of Toronto, this time at Hart House—still a male bastion; university women were only allowed in the gallery for two hours on a Wednesday. The Ontario premier sent her a congratulatory note after that show. Paraskeva Clark was becoming an establishment figure, a grand old lady of Canadian visual art. Not a role she had ever imagined. She pushed herself for the Hart House show, tried to "modernize" her style. "I am so happy and so scared," she said, "but it is not in my character to refuse meeting the challenge—and I'll try to work as hard as possible for an old girl."

The old girl met the challenge of the new by painting an abstract, a form she never really took to, that she called *Kitchen Cupboard Aspect*. When the show opened, she wrote, "I am bragging about the fact that 4 members of the Painters Eleven honoured me by visiting me that evening—I think there is no greater satisfaction than to get a word of recognition from young avant-garde. One feels then not quite useless."

Painters Eleven were eleven of the biggest, boldest new Canadian abstract expressionists. She didn't name which four came to her show. Harold Town, then barely thirty, was almost certainly one. A few years before she died, they met at his house, and she saw one of her paintings hanging on his wall. He smiled and spoke to her with great affection. "I remember you being grumpy," Town said, "marvellously grumpy. You had a kind of universality." Then he said, "Every time we'd try to give you a hug, you'd say 'all you men ever think about is sex.'" She laughed but didn't give an inch, "You weren't going to accept the role of women," she said.

Another one of the four members of the Painters Eleven, those "bad boys" of Canadian art who came to her show, might well have been Alexandra Luke—Painters Eleven would not have existed but for Alexandra Luke. Both women were in their fifties; Paraskeva was audacious while Alexandra was the epitome of decorum. Yet Alexandra Luke was now the young revolutionary.

+ + +

*I became an abstract painter because every damn tree in the country had been painted.*

—Graham Coughtry

Alexandra Luke was, in the words of respected art historian and curator Joan Murray, "the best organized, most energetic, most practical woman who ever wore shoes." She organized everything from the Oshawa Skating Club to pageants with her grandchildren to the Painters Eleven.

The American abstract expressionists, Jackson Pollock, Willem de Kooning, Mark Rothko, and the rest, had been recognized and regaled since the early 1940s. Commercial galleries in New York were selling their work. In Montreal, avant-garde Quebec artists published a manifesto, a declaration of artistic freedom that is credited with giving impetus to Quebec's Quiet Revolution. The American and the

Quebec modernists were noticed. The work of Toronto abstract expressionists—Alexandra Luke, Harold Town, William Ronald, Jock Macdonald—was included in group shows, but as Macdonald said, they were tired of seeing their paintings hung in dark corners. When Alexandra had a solo show of her big, bold canvases in 1952, no one noticed, no one reviewed it. No galleries, no one in Toronto were paying attention to abstract expressionism. They needed a coming-out party.

Alexandra Luke's experience as a committee woman gave her the skill to do what no one else in that crowd could. She brought together the work of twenty-six abstract artists and organized a traveling show, the Canadian Abstract Exhibition it was called, that started in Oshawa and went on to seven more galleries in Ontario, Quebec, and New Brunswick. Jock Macdonald wrote in the catalog about new concepts of nature, time, and space that the abstract artists tried to pull together. Luke wrote, "Painting should not stop with the already discovered beauty but should continue searching." People began to notice, and these "new" painters began to know each other better and find pleasure in each other's company.

In 1953, William Ronald, still in his twenties, was working at Simpson's department store when the head of interior design asked him for paintings to complement window displays of modern furniture. He called his friends, including Alexandra Luke who he knew through the classes with Hans Hofmann, and seven Canadian abstract expressionist painters found their paintings on display in Simpson's shop windows. Shoppers stopped and stared; never had as many people looked at their paintings. When the photographer was taking the publicity shots, he said, "You should show more of your work together." That's all it took. Alexandra invited the six other painters in the Simpson's display along with four more, including another woman, Hortense Gordon, to her cottage in Whitby, and in October 1953, Painters Eleven was born. It was never going to be an easygoing group.

Jack Bush, who had the biggest career with major international exposure, said, "We're making history." Harold Town answered, "No, we're not," but he brought along a tape recorder and taped the meeting

Painters Eleven L–R: Tom Hodgson, Alexandra Luke, Harold Town, Kazuo Nakamura, Jock Macdonald, Walter Yarwood, Hortense Gordon, Jack Bush, Ray Mead. The canvases facing forward represent the late Oscar Caen and those facing the wall represent William Ronald, who had left the group in 1957.

just in case Bush was right. He was. There was strength in numbers. Their aim was to make a noise, to get noticed, and Alexandra was with them all the way.

They drank—a lot—they swore inventively, Ronald was full of himself, Town brawled. Alexandra ignored all that and drew energy and inspiration from all of them. The first Painters Eleven show was at the Roberts Gallery, the gallery that represented Jack Bush, and they were nervous. As Ronald put it, "A painter is like a flasher, an exhibitionist. You literally expose your soul each time you have an exhibition." At first, no one showed up. Harold Town went out in the street and yelled, "Free drinks!" When all was said and done, more people had come to the Painters Eleven show than any other show in the Roberts Gallery's hundred-and-ten-year history. The *Toronto Star* said, "It gives conservatism a polite but firm kick in the pants and blazes independent trails." Alexandra Luke had dragged Canadian art kicking and screaming into a new era.

The Painters Eleven showed in 1956 in New York, where the Canadian consulate backed them, and the McLaughlin name might well have helped make that happen; they showed in Montreal in 1958. Alexandra and Hortense Gordon, Alexandra called her "Hortie," rode on the train together and became friends. Back in Toronto, she organized one more show, and she wrote in her diary, "Great praise from Jack Bush. Great praise from Yarwood, Bush, Town.... I was completely bushed...10:30 pm checked out of the Park Plaza and drove home. At last it has come and gone. May 5 1958."

Her peers respected her and her work, and she got good reviews when the Eleven exhibited in New York, but in Canada her work was either ignored or trivialized. Jack Bush said, "We wept blood over the way the Canadian art establishment treated Alexandra." Bush, Town, Ronald, Nakamura became names that art lovers recognized. No one knew Alexandra Luke. She never attributed her lack of recognition to being a woman; it was not in her nature.

✦✦✦

*Painting is not a woman's job. If I were a man I could be hard-hearted,*
*selfish, and paint modern art. But I'm not and I can't.*

Paraskeva Clark could not find room in her life to be the painter she wanted to be. She ranted, "For women it's no good. They are not good painters. The lord made them to be mothers and that's all...their hearts always taken by anxiety or something while in painting you have to close the key on the door from everything." She was angry. Paraskeva Clark was often angry. Alexandra Luke had a cooler disposition. She split her life. Whether that was any more satisfying is a moot point.

Paraskeva had more success in her lifetime than Alexandra Luke, she naturally drew attention to herself, but none of those women painters—Paraskeva Clark, Alexandra Luke, Yvonne McKague Housser, Isabel McLaughlin, Pegi Nicol MacLeod, Prudence Heward—are much remembered. Were they any good? The argument usually goes something like this: If women had artistic genius, then their work would crowd the great galleries. But their work does not crowd the great galleries, therefore they must not have artistic genius. What

Paraskeva Clark, the "angry old lady" and her painting *Philip Clark, Esq*, completed in 1933

about the frame of reference, the perception of genius? Does genius only flow through the paintbrushes of white men? Or does it have something to do with the galleries? Institutional support has been hard to come by. Alan Jarvis, director of the National Gallery in the 1950s, let it be known that he had no time for "liberated housewives who aspired to paint." According to Jarvis, they should "relax and play bridge." Alexandra Luke began as a "liberated housewife." In the UK, the National Gallery holds more than two thousand pieces of art; only twenty are by women. In the US, the feminist artists Guerrilla Girls asked, "Do women have to be naked to get into the Met Museum? Less than 5% of the artists in the Modern Art section are women, but 85% of the nudes are female."

In the 1940s, Prudence Heward painted unsmiling, unpretty women, bulky, strong women who stared out from the canvas. When she died in 1945, her fellow painter Edwin Holgate wrote an obituary that praised her work, then he added, "her works had no political implications of any kind."

Both Alexandra Luke and Paraskeva Clark are long dead. Alexandra Luke was only sixty-six and just coming into her own when she died in 1967. Her husband, Ewart McLaughlin, died a year later. Before they died, they funded the new Robert McLaughlin gallery in Oshawa. It houses Alexandra Luke's personal collection of work by Painters Eleven—the paintings that Ewart McLaughlin could never understand. Many Alexandra Luke paintings are on display at the McLaughlin Gallery but as is often the case with women painters, many more have stayed with her family. At one of her last openings, when she was in her eighties, Paraskeva Clark wore a bright red dress and was as defiant and outspoken as ever. She died when she was eighty-seven. Her paintings hang in major public galleries, and they have been reproduced on posters and book covers. That's the thing about artists—their paintings last. A hundred years later and you can still see what these women were thinking.

*I have too much respect for painting. It is a serious business. It is not repeating...like technical exercises. It has to have guts, some sort of guts, some sort of strength.*

—Paraskeva Clark

# 8. MINNIE AND THE GRENFELL MAT-MAKERS

*It's just them old mats. Who would be interested?*

"Can you tell me the name of the woman who made this mat?" asks the woman in the third row.

"Well, no. I'm sorry. I wish I could but they were never signed—no one kept a record."

This was Paula Laverty, the expert on Grenfell mats. When there's an "expert," it's a sign that there is value, sometimes undiscovered value, in whatever they are expert about.

Value and a story.

It was a Sunday afternoon in Cobourg, a town on Lake Ontario an hour east of Toronto. There were three or four Grenfell mats on the tables at the back of the room. Paula picked one up—it was not big, sixty-six by a hundred centimeters. On the face of the mat three Canada geese flew across a mottled purple evening sky, the shading as subtle as a painting. The mat felt silky smooth; it was silk. The crowd in the room pressed in as Laverty turned it over, folded the corner back—gently. "Look at the stitches—so tight and so straight—made in the nineteen thirties perhaps."

There were thousands of Grenfell mats made by women up and down the Labrador and Newfoundland coast and made well. All but one or two are unsigned—at least in the early days those mat-maker women did not know how to sign their name. The raw materials cost next to nothing, and the makers were paid in used clothing. It's the old story, today they are collectibles and some sell for thousands of dollars. The settlements, the outports, where the fishermen and their families lived, were so small, so remote, so unknown that the people who lived there seemed not to exist. But the women who lived there had worked those mats, and in the years when the fishery failed, when there were no cod in the traps and the herring didn't come, and when there was no game in the winter—then it was those mats and those women who stood between their families and starvation. A hook, a piece of burlap—brin—and a pile of old silk stockings, that's what kept them alive.

+++

For some reason the codfish along the coast have also become more liable to fail of late years, to such an extent that most of the northern stations have been entirely abandoned. The herring too...this fishery also has been practically abandoned.

At Black Tickle the situation was pathetic. The families were sorely in need of clothing and mothers begged for work....

At Boulter Rock I stayed with a dear old lady...her heavy stiff shoes hurt her feet.... She literally danced with joy when, in payment for her hospitality, I gave her a pair of white tennis shoes.

At Capstan Island a mother of eight apologized for her appearance...she told me she did not know what to give her children to eat. We paid them in brown flour. It would not last long. I have since heard that they caught no fish. How will they exist under such circumstances I do not know.

Silk stocking mats,
*Flying Geese* and *Dog
Sleigh Team*, 1930s

At Poverty Cove, one woman, the mother of six children, stood with tears in her eyes, repeating over and over as she patted the baby clothes, "The little lamb, the little lamb." I doubt that she had ever seen so many garments. We unravelled our own scarves in order to have some wool to give out as work. The people have a quiet modesty and deference which is the most real sort of courtesy.

These are notes a Grenfell worker made after she was rowed ashore over and over again from the boat to the shore, from the shore to the boat, on her tour of Newfoundland outports in 1922. She was a young American volunteer enticed by the lure of the North and she wrote fulsomely. The Grenfell nurses had done the circuit before her. Their notes were more succinct yet equally telling.

31 villages visited; 11 glasses fitted (children were amazed that now they had glasses letters stood still on the page) dysentery and pneumonia; 181 cases of malnutrition.

1922 was sixteen years into the Grenfell Association mat-making project. Thousands of mats had been hooked, the women "paid" with bundles of used clothes. 1922 was a good year.

+++

*Dr. Grenfell's position on the coast is one of great authority. The prestige and honors which have come to him…are simply a recognition of the work which he has calmly done. His plans have been gigantic.*

—Cuthbert Lee

*At the beginning I was criticized for giving everything for nothing, now I am criticized for giving nothing for nothing.*

—Wilfred Grenfell, 1907

In 1895, the boat, a thirty-five-foot launch carrying the doctor, sounded its horn as it came into the bay partway up the Labrador coast. The men and woman onboard looked toward shore and caught sight of a young man as he came out of one of the huts, waved, and started rowing out to ferry the doctor to shore. There were three or four huts huddled together onshore, each one of them covered in peat—twenty or so people inside. The fishermen in their knee-high boots, coveralls, and jerseys pushed forward, their wives and daughters staying in the shadows. Inside the hut, the doctor bent over a man with a deep gash on his arm; he had been slicing blubber from a whale in the dark when the knife slipped. Another man asked the doctor, begged him, for a pair of glasses. "I'se can't shoot without, can't hunt," he says. Winter, when there is *only* hunting and trapping foxes, was a month away.

It's a fool who underestimates Labrador, as Leonidas Hubbard found out in 1903. There was no game that year, and Hubbard starved and died. Come February, those fishermen, their wives, and their ragged children would be living on hard tack—flour and water dried out hard and fried up—and tea sweetened with molasses. Living on it until the flour ran out—then they would starve.

Wind and cold and emptiness. It was godforsaken territory; its worth lay in the fishery. Every summer, the fishing boats came in from St. John's. When they were full to the gunnels and riding low in the water under the weight of the catch, they sailed back. The people who stayed were the "Labrador Liveyers"—people who "live here." To the merchants in St. John's, the fish were money, the people an inconvenience.

The doctor was Wilfred Grenfell. He arrived in Labrador in 1892, a young English medical missionary, only twenty-seven years old and full of Christian purpose. Newfoundland and what was simply called the Labrador coast was British territory. There were no schools, no hospitals, no nothing; just five thousand people in a quarter of a million square kilometers of land. To Grenfell, it was an unplowed field, an acreage of Christian opportunity.

Grenfell was a charismatic man, an inventive doctor, a first-class negotiator, and a brilliant fundraiser. He knew everyone who counted in London and New York. Grenfell and Mina Benson Hubbard wrote to each other about Labrador. In the 1930s, David Crook, then a young man finding his way in New York City, shook the hand of Wilfred Grenfell when he was on one of his fundraising swings through the eastern seaboard. Not only did Grenfell raise money for the hospitals he built, but he also pulled in young, well-educated volunteers. A season on the Labrador coast was an early twentieth century gap year, an international summer of service for the likes of Henry Cabot Lodge, Cyrus Vance, and Nelson Rockefeller and his brother Laurance, privileged youngsters who would grow up and become powerful men.

Grenfell recognized early on that it was not enough to build hospitals and nursing stations; the Liveyers needed to be pulled out from under the thumb of the merchant-traders who ran the barter system up and down the coast. Barter is all they knew. Most fishermen had never seen money, did not know what it looked like. The traders would sail in and say to the men, "You give me your fish and I'll give you a pair of boots, or flour, or tea, and if you haven't caught enough fish to cover the bill this year, I'll do you a favor and we'll hold the debt over till next year." A quintal of dried salted cod (fifty kilograms) was offered up for whatever the traders would give them. Atlantic salmon might be fetching three cents a pound; the trader would be charging $6 for a pair of boots—a fisherman had to pull a hundred kilograms of fish out of the sea to come home with a pair of boots. It was indentured labor. Trader debts lasted from one generation to the next.

"If you hand out charity—they will hate you," Grenfell maintained. Instead, he set up what became known as "the Industrials"—cottage industries for woodworking, stone polishing, and, for the women, making the mats. It meant someone else to trade with, another way to keep body and soul together.

✦✦✦

*I'se always been hookin' ever since I'd be big enough to hold a hook and sit on a stool. There's nothing in this world I likes better than hookin' a mat.*

In the 1500s, the waters of Red Bay—on the Labrador side of the Strait of Belle Isle—were thick with bowhead whales and Basque fishermen harpooning the animals from open boats. Red Bay was the largest oil-rendering plant in the world, and the whale oil was taken back to fuel the lamps of Europe.

But by 1893, when Grenfell arrived, the market for whale oil was in sharp decline and Red Bay was just another fishing harbor of no more than eight or ten houses. On that first trip up and down the Labrador coast, Grenfell saw more than nine hundred patients, every little settlement a mirror image of Red Bay. His medical ship was captained by a Red Bay man, Levi Pike, who brought with him his twenty-year-old daughter, Minnie. She was no fool, keen, but regrettably more than a little nearsighted. Minnie Pike must have impressed Wilfred Grenfell. One way or the other, she worked for the Grenfells for the next fifty years. She was guide, philosopher, and friend to the whole district around Red Bay.

It was a two-hour trip from Labrador across the Strait of Belle

Isle to the Northern Peninsula of Newfoundland, the long finger of land on the west coast of the island that points up into the Atlantic. Grenfell built his first hospital in Battle Harbour in the early 1890s, Mina Benson Hubbard waved good-bye to her husband from the little hill in Battle Harbour in 1903 and probably stayed at the hospital. By the end of the decade, Grenfell had moved on from Battle Harbour and set up what became his headquarters in St. Anthony at the tip of the Northern Peninsula—a thirty-bed hospital, an orphanage, and Grenfell House, where he and his wife, Anne, stayed when they were in Newfoundland. In 1910, prim little Minnie Pike came to live at Grenfell House and became "nurse"—nanny—to the Grenfell's three children, even going with them to England one winter. It was in St. Anthony that Minnie Pike met and began to work with Jessie Luther, an occupational therapist from Rhode Island whom Grenfell had brought over in 1906 to run the Industrial. It was Luther who decided that weaving, not mat-making, would be the industry for the women in the outports and figuring that Minnie Pike could do more than be nanny to three children, Jessie Luther began to teach her how to weave and how to spin.

Over the years, Minnie lugged spinning wheels on and off boats in Red Bay then in all the other little harbors on the Labrador coast. By now, Grenfell had corrected her nearsightedness and outfitted Minnie Pike with what became her trademark owl glasses—circular and dark-framed—that made her look even more prim and proper. She may have been the only woman on the Labrador coast with glasses. But glasses did not solve the fundamental problem of trying to set up spinning and weaving as a cottage industry. First, there weren't that many sheep. Sheep don't do well on a barren shore, and it was fine for Jessie Luther to get caught up in the craftiness of looms and spinning wheels, but this kind of equipment takes up space, and space was at a premium in fishermen's houses that might have six or eight children running around. It didn't make sense. Then a light went on and Jessie Luther saw what had been in front of her all along. The women in the outports—many of them descendants of rural English and Scottish settlers—had been brought up hooking mats, and in Newfoundland

and Labrador, they were never "rugs" always "mats." Mats were familiar; they were functional. Everyone had mats in their houses. Come the winter, those houses were cold. There was a woodstove downstairs—the wood was always green and coated with an inch of solid ice—and the rest of the house was heated by whatever warmth leaked from the pipe as it wound its way upstairs to the chimney. The floors were raw wood, splintery; linoleum was a luxury. Mats made those raw wood floors warm while the snow blew and drifted outside, and it did drift. Grenfell slept with the window open in St. Anthony and one morning he was found fast asleep under a foot of snow. Labrador Liveyers had more sense.

+++

*...all that can [be] heard is the howling wind. On the bench that runs three sides of the room sit a dozen men, they don't read, they don't know how and there is nothing to read anyway, they don't talk.... What is there to say...? And the girls? There is nothing to occupy their time, their desire, no means which they can contribute to the family income....*

There was nothing the women wanted more than to contribute to the family income. In the summers, women "made the fish"—dried them out on the flakes, the outdoor drying racks, cut and salted the catch. In winter, the women had time to make mats. February and March were matting season. The equipment cost nothing—a nail in a piece of wood with the head hammered out and the wood handle smoothed, that was the hook, and a piece of brin, burlap, was the backing. The burlap came from the big bags that held rice or grain or potatoes; the size of the bags became the size of the mats. It was simple. The frame—four pieces of wood lashed together—could be stashed against the wall. It came out after dinner. Minnie Pike and the then sixty or so other women up and down the Labrador coast hooked by kerosene lamp into the night—sometimes all night.

They had always made "scrap" mats, from bits and pieces of left-over material, the sleeve of a blouse that still had some life in it, the tail of a shirt, some part of an old pair of pants—waste not want not.

Wilfred Grenfell and Minnie Pike, 1932

Every mat-maker drew her own patterns, usually not more than lines and circles, on the brin with the end of a burnt stick. That's the way it had always been. There were no pictures, no books to inspire different designs. The traders, seeing an opportunity, began selling cheap and cheerful mat patterns. Grenfell became enthusiastic about the mats. He saw them as not only a new cottage industry but also an aid to public health—they became spittoons. There were mats with "spit here" hooked into them. Given the rate of tuberculosis, it was better to spit on a mat than on the floor.

Jessie Luther was looking for mats that could bring in money for the mission, sold for ready cash. The old scrap mats, she said, were not good enough.

> As a rule they are very ugly though often beautifully made. In many cases the material is what remains of a family garment, in many others scraps of color are used and the designs which are stamped on the burlap and sold by the trader are meaningless and/or ugly and not worth the fine work so often put into them…none of them are really saleable excepting as example of local unguided work.

She really did not like the colors. As she said in a letter to Grenfell, rolling her eyes as she wrote, "the colors in the mats designed by the women themselves we might almost ascribe to the futurist school"— garish, she thought. Something would have to be done about that. Jessie Luther was not interested in "authenticity" and was quite prepared to change things up. Fortunately, these women were not divas. They did not balk at the paternalistic tone. They wanted the work.

Luther set about guiding the mat-making, and Grenfell, who had a finger in every pie, drew new designs himself that would be stamped on the brin. The first mats were hooked from clean, new pieces of cotton and flannel, all donated. Workers in St. Anthony would sort and cut the material into quarter-inch strips that were then packaged up and delivered to the outports. Grenfell headquarters would include a small picture of what the finished product should look like in the package, what color goes where, how big the polar bear should be.

There was no room for creative license.

The new designs were full of polar bears, spouting whales, and sled dogs—popular images of the North. But the advertising emphasized the usefulness of the mats. "They are designed as furnishings to live with, not curios. We aim to have the colours fast and durable to last years."

Luther and the Grenfell workers cracked a whip hand. If a mat was flawed, then it had to be unhooked and done again, and it was much more difficult to unhook than to hook a mat. And each mat fetched its own price for the maker; better hooking meant better money. Jessie Luther wanted nothing but the best and, if she had her way, would only have given mat packages to the best "hookers." Anne Grenfell, Wilfred's wife, who was by now handling much of the administration, disagreed. Nineteen-sixteen had been a terrible year in the fishery, and a great many women *needed* work to clothe their families. Anne Grenfell was the boss' wife, and every woman who wanted mat packages got them. By 1917, there was a workforce of sixty women scattered among settlements on the Northern Peninsula and up the Labrador coast. Minnie Pike and the women in Red Bay, in Indian Harbour, and in Northwest River as far north as Nain were producing mats, not all of them perfect but saleable. Their payment came in the form of bundles of used clothes.

*The mat industry is a bonanza to our consciences and a solution to a difficult problem of putting clothing and a little ready cash within reach of many needy women and children.*

—Wilfred Grenfell

✦✦✦

In Red Bay, Minnie Pike lived in a big white building with a windowed porch that was perched on the low, smooth rocks. The house was a Grenfell center, part first-aid post, part community center, and

Minnie was the den mother. From the north-facing windows of her big hospital house, she could see half a dozen fishermen's houses and the well-worn footpaths that connected one to the other. There was always a group of girls living with her whom she trained. Everyone on the coast knew Minnie Pike and stopped by—she was an unselfish, friendly woman, but like Allie Douglas there was never a smile on her face in the photographs.

In the summer of 1920, Minnie, wearing her best clothes and carrying her leather suitcase, left her house and walked down the path to the wharf where she was ferried out to the steamer heading for Newfoundland. She always went out to the mail steamer when it anchored in the harbor and brought the mail back, but this time she was staying aboard. Minnie Pike was going to America. After what must have been days of travel, she arrived in Berea, Kentucky. The International Grenfell Association (IGA) was sending her to Berea College—the first coeducational, non-racially segregated Christian college in the American South. The IGA sent more than a hundred men and women to Berea over the years. Grenfell called it "a wonderful uplifting machine" and, at $150 a term for room and board, it was cheaper than anything St. John's could offer.

Minnie Pike stayed at Berea for a year and three other Red Bay women followed her. They were there to learn more about weaving and spinning. Jessie Luther and her successors never totally gave up on weaving. Berea appealed in more ways than one. It was a good price, and the thinking was that the women from Labrador had a kinship with Appalachian women from Kentucky—"sister spinners" they were called. One of the Labrador Industrial workers wrote that they had common qualities—"their handicap in book learning, their absolutely selfless devotion and sacrifice for their large families and," the Grenfell worker added, "their easygoing way of granting supremacy for the man of the house." Minnie Pike never married.

Back in Labrador, in Red Bay, she supervised the weaving and the growing number of mat-makers. Six years later, it was slim, little Minnie Pike in her neat gray dress and her dark stockings who was sent to the Third Annual Craftsman Show in Boston to demonstrate

Minnie Pike and two of her trainees, the blind twins, Clara and Mary Ellen Morris, 1920

mat-making and show the mats. Minnie Pike traveled well. She was sent back twice to Berea for more training, but she always returned to Red Bay. By 1929, Red Bay was shipping out $670 worth of weavings and rugs to headquarters in St. Anthony, and the IGA was sending back bundles of used clothes, payment, to the women of Red Bay. Julie Yetman was one of those Red Bay hookers whom the Grenfell mat expert Paula Laverty found when she went to the outports decades later. "Every Spring they'd send out their mats and then in the Fall they used to have clothing come in barrels. And each one, each parcel your name was on, whatever parcel was yours, your name was on it, hey. Whatever was in that parcel…that's what you earned."

There was no picking and choosing. You got whatever the IGA worker in St. Anthony put in your parcel. No one complained; anything could be remade—a coat too small became a pair of trousers, a sweater could be unraveled and knit up again. And if a mat-maker was looking for something in particular, she could always ask. "Just write a letter and tell 'em what you wanted," said Julie Yetman. "If you want nightdresses, or underwear, or pants or—you know—coats or whatever you wanted. And they would pick from what your letter said and send what they had to send you." The system worked for her; Julie Yetman hooked Grenfell mats for twenty-five years. "I often, like, thinks to myself, if I could only mat like that now, like I could then, I'd still have one in frame."

Minnie Pike would get on the boat and make the circuit and work her way down the coast. She would train the women in Forteau Bay down near what became the Quebec border; get back on the boat and head for George's Cove, Boulter's Rock, Seal Island, Spotted Island, and on it went. Between 1912 and 1921, the number of mats from up and down the coast rose to thirteen hundred. Minnie Pike kept a lot of payment flowing into households.

The designs changed but they were always about life in the North—the komatiks, Inuit sleds; seals; fish—always fish. Jessie Luther left as Industrial Supervisor and along came Rhoda Dawson, an artist in her own right from Britain. Her designs were good. Some of them veered toward the abstract—one in brown and beige of fish drying on the flake seemed a little odd, a little off to the women hooking the pattern. "I never see'd a fish look like that," puzzled one mat-maker. "They's supposed to be all white in the inside. Them's wrong side out and whoever's spread 'em only had a little bit of fish that day. They should be right up together." Puzzled or not, she hooked the wrong-side-out fish. Women hooked what they were given. This was a job of work.

Then there was Dora Mesher, a Labrador woman working for Mae Pressley-Smith, the next head of the Industrial. Rhoda Dawson wrote about Dora in a letter to a friend: "She was gentle, loving, kind but efficient and she did without a murmur the back work we all had to do, drawing out the mat, putting in the rag…weighing, writing the instructions. She also did the dyeing, quite a professional job. But more than that, Dora was a true artist. She has been sent to…an art school in the States and her taste was impeccable—far too good for the tourist trade on which the Mission depends."

Dora Mesher, like Minnie, had been sent to both Berea and

Philadelphia for training. Rhoda Dawson spoke more about her in a Christmas card to her father. "There is a woman who works with us of Indian descent…she designs the most beautiful rugs. Pressley is so naughty and makes me do fearful commonplace mats for stock and these magnificent things of Dora's roll in and I writhe." The artistic career of Dora Mesher, who was more likely Inuk than "of Indian descent," sadly did not go beyond the few Grenfell mats she designed.

The mats were shipped and sold in Montreal and Toronto, in the resorts of New England, and in swank stores in New York and Chicago. Saks Fifth Avenue ordered batches of two hundred. Grenfell Handicrafts had a booth at the British Empire Exhibition in 1924. One newspaper reported "many people…insist that the hooked mats are woven. They have never seen such fine hooking…." The Grenfell mats were recognized internationally. Outport women were providing for their families and at the same time developing a reputation for their artistry and bringing in money for the Grenfell mission.

◆◆◆

*"Simon Peter, show the lady the very last thing we got with the mat money." Simon Peter, aged four but great with importance, led me around the corner of his grandmother's low frame house to a pen in which dozed two small white pigs.*

*"If I'd had mats these last twenty years, instead of eight. I'd have had me a real house built by this time. And here's shoes and coats for the girls, and a little bit of a suit for Simon Peter come on the last Prospero [the Grenfell ship]. The girls and me, God willin' can hook fifteen for ye the winter."*

—Edith Tallant, 1929

Edith Tallant was a Vassar girl, Vassar being one of the elite American women's colleges. She had ambitions as a writer and by the 1940s had published three books of juvenile fiction. But in 1929 she was an Industrial worker in Labrador and writing about outport women, including Simon Peter's grandmother. "Her hard horny hands were rough from the sea, from cleaning fish, splitting wood, spading potatoes but possess a skill inherited from her great-grandmother in the old country and patience to hook through every hole in the fine brin to put, as she once counted, a hundred hours into a mat a[s] fine as tapestry."

The work done in this Labrador outport by those horny hands was as fine as anything in a European drawing room. A hundred hours and as many as two hundred stitches per square inch of brin, the density equal to that of a good Persian rug. In the mid-1920s, the quality and finesse of these mats went up another notch. Mae Pressley-Smith, the little Scottish woman now running the Industrial, had a revelation: silk stockings.

As hemlines went up in the 1920s, silk stockings had come into their own. Every woman in the cities wore them and every woman had to deal with "ladders," runs in their stockings. Snag your stockings, get a run, and it's done for, into the garbage. But, thought Mae Pressley-Smith, unwearable stockings could be used for mat-making. Rather than mats made from flannel and cotton, mats from silk stocking would be finer, smoother, and fetch a better price. Her imagination took hold—why not silk underwear as well—"step-ins," the new, shorter, wide-legged bloomers, panties, chemises. It could all be used.

Never one to miss an opportunity, Grenfell jumped on the silk-stocking bandwagon. At every fundraising drive, in every issue of the Grenfell newsletter, he put the word out to Sunday schools, church congregations, women's groups. "Save your old Silk Stockings, let them run to Labrador. We need silk stockings and underwear in Unlimited Quantities! Please send your silk stockings and underwear no matter how old or worn." And there were addenda: "Please cut the tops and the feet off your stockings to save mailing costs and don't send them in the winter. The huskies cannot pull a sled that is too heavily laden."

Freshly dyed silk stockings drying on the fence in St. Anthony's

There were "crotch parties" where girls armed with a pair of nail scissors carefully cut the cotton crotch gusset out of every pair of donated silk knickers. Wilfred Grenfell made a special and very successful appeal to the dancers at the Folies Bergère in Paris.

The stockings came in, nine tons of them one year. They piled up in the corner of the storeroom in St. Anthony, then they were sorted and dyed—blues, greens, turquoise, reds, and every shade in between—silk took the dye like nothing else. The newly dyed stockings drying and blowing in the wind on the fences in St. Anthony looked like a rainbow. Packages of silk stockings went out to women in the outports with new instructions. First, cut them on the bias in quarter-inch strips round and round each leg, then pull the edges tight. Every strip would furl up perfectly. A standard-sized picture mat—one hundred centimeters by sixty—took between fifty and sixty pairs of stockings.

Fifty or sixty pairs of stockings spilling from the mat bundle on an outport kitchen table—it was a wonder. Those Labrador outport women in their bulky skirts and wool socks had never felt silk before. Silk stockings were sensual, enticing. When a woman in the city pointed her toes, slipped a stocking over her foot, and then slowly unrolled it up her leg, she felt elegant, attractive—sexy. Stella Fowler from Capstan Island felt the lightness of the silk on her hand, felt it brushing against the inside of her wrist. She bent over and slipped the stocking over her foot, what a feeling, then she pulled it past her calf, over her knee, and up under her skirt. She looked down at her legs and smiled. These women wanted to feel something other than the splinters from fire logs or the slippery cold of fish. The feet of the stockings had been cut off, but it did not matter: "People would just pull the legs up over they own legs and they'd wore those 'jazz' stockings we calls them, with the pattern tops turned down." Stella Fowler almost blushed when she spoke. "Beautiful." Then she caught herself and laughed a little. "Some people never had enough to finish their mat coz they weared them." A little bit of heaven. But the Industrial workers in St. Anthony caught on quickly and in the name of efficiency stamped out the pleasure. "The feet was cut off at the Industrial. Then they started cutting through the stockings so's you couldn't wear them."

Mat-making and silk stockings created shared and sometimes secret pleasures. As Mae Pressley-Smith noted in her rather formal way, she knew this was the stuff that community is made of.

> An effort to produce something of creative worth cannot fail to react on the character of those who create and will assist in giving them balance, self-reliance and a certain dignity and purpose and surely for such a result almost any amount of effort and experiment is worthwhile.

In the 1970s, long after mat-making had ended, Stella Fowler became a leader in the Women's Institute, the first women's organization on the Labrador Straits; its seeds were in the mat-making.

♦♦♦

*More tables now show vegetables, butter and milk than ten years ago, the babies are fatter than those of ten years ago. The three thousand mats to be hooked this winter along the coast of Labrador and Newfoundland mean more money for nurses' fees, better food and warmer clothing for hundreds of families.*

—Edith Tallant

Three thousand mats—remarkable. Mats were bringing in enough to keep a woman's family clothed and fed, plus a little bit more. Now there were vouchers that could be exchanged for paint, wallpaper, even seeds. Gardens were women's work. They were sad little efforts; in Newfoundland and Labrador, topsoil is scattered on the rock like shaved chocolate on a frothy drink, no more than a little treat, and the growing season is short, but by now, mothers knew that gardens were worth the effort. Scurvy and rickets were rampant; there were cases of beriberi, and vegetables helped ward off disease. The food order that was given to the traders was always the same: white flour, molasses, lard. "It's Skipper orders food," they would say. They had no voice in what went on the table—except for what they grew in the garden. By the 1920s, the abject hopelessness the women had felt thirty years earlier had faded at least a little; they had now not only butter and milk and the occasional vegetable on the table but a growing feeling of self-worth and the smallest amount of power.

There were mats coming from as far north as Nain and south and west beyond the Quebec border into what was called the "Canadian Labrador." Mat revenues coming into the IGA went from $27,000 in 1926 to more than $63,000 in 1929, and payments to the mat-maker ran at about $3 per mat. Mat-makers were if not riding high, then

Mae Pressley-Smith assessing and buying mats, 1930s

breathing a little more easy.

Edith Tallant had written enthusiastically about the wonders that the IGA had wrought in the outports in the early fall of 1929. Three weeks after her article appeared in the IGA magazine, the stock market crashed, and the Depression began. The price of fish, never good or constant, plummeted. In 1907, Newfoundland had become a Dominion, an independent country with its own postage stamps, its own government, and its own economy. When the Depression hit, that economy went to rack and ruin. By 1932, corruption ran rampant; there were riots in St. John's. The Dominion of Newfoundland was deep in debt and in 1934, voluntarily gave up self-government and was once again under British control. It was less-than-lean times all round. In 1937, there were two thousand mat-makers on the books; eight years earlier, mat-makers were getting three or even four dollars a mat, and now they were taking home two or three dollars a year.

> Mrs. D. was the mother of many children. An industri-
> al worker asked her: "What would you do if there was no
> work—it's been 2 weeks now?" "Well I don't know what I'd
> do. I biys many a good thing with the money...lots of things

for all hands at home. My, my, miss, if there wasn't no work I don't know how we'd do at all." March and April are going to be terrible on the coast.

✦✦✦

*Yes, my dear, it was a laugh. Sit down for two weeks and hook a mat and gets paid $3.50…we gave up hookin' 'cause t'was too hard and too much work, for nothin'. But I hooked lots, my love. All different ones. Do 'em as fast as you can hook 'em we did. We had to. The place was different. You had youngsters and you had to work for 'em.*

The overgrown grass almost hides the headstones in the very small Anglican cemetery in Red Bay. It has been abandoned and many of the stones are broken, but push the grass aside and the names and the dates can still be read. There are a good many Yetmans and Moores and Pikes, thirteen of the thirty-one people buried in that graveyard never saw adulthood; only two lived past sixty. Minnie Pike is there. She was seventy when she died in 1943 in the middle of World War II.

It was "the war," not the Depression, that finished things off for mat-making. During the Depression, international sales dried up, but tourist boats went up and down the coast and kept business going. With the start of World War II, those boats were requisitioned, and the final nail in the coffin, the chemical company DuPont invented nylon; then came nylon stockings, and nothing was the same after that. Nylon didn't stretch and bend like silk, nor did it take dye in the same way.

Sales decreased; overhead increased, and the mat-makers were not making enough money to keep going. Aunt Esther Cox from Harrington Harbour on the Quebec side of Labrador looked after dyeing the stockings. Her daughter remembers bringing in buckets of snow in the winter to add to the dye pot on the woodstove and watching her mother throw in salt and vinegar to make the dye fast. In a month in the 1950s, Aunt Esther dyed 180 pounds of stockings and underwear. She was paid $53. Not enough.

The mat-makers had kept the wolf from their own doors and brought in revenue for the Grenfell Association. Were Esther Cox and Stella Fowler and Minnie Pike and the rest exploited? Taken in the context of the times—no; a bundle of used clothes for a hundred hours of hooking saved lives. Most importantly, when any of the thousands of women who hooked mats on the Labrador coast and the Northern Peninsula put a mat in the frame and hooked through the night, what they made was theirs and theirs alone. That was worth everything.

Come the 1950s and '60s, roads went in along the coast, communities were connected, women driving together to some meeting in the next little town got stuck in the snow, laughed, and dug themselves out. Strength in numbers, and now there were numbers. Mat-making has become a demonstration sport, a curiosity. The old mats are hard to find. Lives are hooked into every stitch.

# 9. MARGARET

*She was not a person who liked to be told what to do—ever.*

—Peter Herrndorf

*Nov. 7, 1990*
*Dear Sirs/Mmes,*
*Douglas Fisher in his Monday column...wonders wheth-*
*er I needed to claim the $21,000 redress offered to Japanese*
*Canadians, who in his eyes were scarcely "wronged...."*

Margaret Lyons had worked up a full head of steam that November Wednesday. Douglas Fisher, for the past sixteen years a columnist for the tabloid *Toronto Sun*, had gone too far this time. Fisher was irascible, outspoken, a former Member of Parliament and a World War II veteran. Margaret Lyons had spent her war interned as an "enemy alien" along with twenty-two thousand other Japanese Canadians. She had become, it was widely agreed, one of the most powerful women in North American broadcasting, and she was every bit as irascible as Fisher. He was known as the "dragon-slayer"; she was called the "Dragon Lady." It was an even fight.

Margaret's letter continued:

> *What, in Mr. Fisher's view, is a wrong?*
>
> *We were all compelled to be refugees in our own country. Like the international dispossessed, we lost our childhood collections, and some, childhood itself.*
>
> *We were rejected by our country, we had to survive split families, transportation, internment, dispersal and forced labour.*

This was Canada, not Stalinist Russia.

In his column, Douglas Fisher made it clear that in his estimation, the money the federal government had handed out in reparations—he called it "ethnic pandering"—would be better spent on Canadian veterans of Japanese action in Hong Kong. He had taken aim at three successful Japanese Canadians—Thomas Shoyama, the highly respected civil servant who had been integral to establishing Medicare in Canada; environmentalist David Suzuki, and Margaret Lyons. They, said Fisher, did not need the $21,000 in reparation money. That was not the point, wrote Margaret Lyons.

> *Yes, I have claimed it…part of it was given away in my father's name and the rest to educational institutions which opened their doors to Japanese Canadians at a difficult time. Theirs was a generosity which I can never repay…we might ask whether Mr. Fisher, a very successful journalist among other things, really needed to accept his MP's pension since 1965.*

She had pounded out the letter on her manual typewriter. Then she read it over—there is only one edit in the yellowed carbon copy in her files, and mailed it. In the morning, she took another look and reluctantly decided that line about Fisher's MP pension was below the belt. When Margaret Lyons set out to decimate a foe, she looked him in the eye. She thought for a minute, picked up her pen, and across the bottom of the letter wrote, "phoned to cancel."

When Douglas Fisher wrote a second column attacking the Japanese Canadians for accepting the reparations they had been offered, this time she did not hesitate.

*You can write what you like about the performance of my public duties but whether I claimed redress money or not is none of your business…. What do you really know about what happened to us?*

*Most of us were so traumatized that we did not want to talk about it for years…. Some Japanese Canadians survived by being inconspicuous and they did not want to call attention to themselves…. We left our farm, our home with everything in it and our dog. We never saw any of it again…. Do you think we should have been starved, tortured and gassed as well?*

*And please don't lay the guilt of the Japanese occupation army on me. I am a Canadian and the Japanese have less respect for me as an overseas Japanese female than they would have for you.*

*…I read your Wednesday column; the logic in it was even more incomprehensible than the Monday article…. I asked Mr. Downing [editor of the Sun] not to print the letter because you must be seriously unwell to be so uncharitable and so confused….*

*I hope you are feeling better.*

Parry, thrust, riposte. This was the woman who saved and revolutionized public radio in Canada, who took on all comers. Nobody trifled with Margaret Lyons.

✦✦✦

*Thanks to my father's attitude, I never noticed gender discrimination.*

Smoke poured out of the chimneys of the little houses in the Fraser Valley, split-rail fences separated one farm from the next. Yoshinobu Inouye was a first-generation Japanese immigrant, an *issei*. He and his father had cut down the trees, cleared out the scrub, followed the horse and plow as it furrowed the eight hectares of land that became their strawberry farm. By the time Keiko Margaret was born in 1923, there were more than twenty thousand Japanese immigrants in British Columbia—fishermen on the Fraser delta, an urban Vancouver community, and the berry farmers like her father up the valley. The Inouyes and their six children lived three kilometers outside the little town of Mission.

There had been racism brewing in Vancouver from the arrival of the first Japanese immigrants in 1870. It came to a head in anti-Asian riots in 1907 that were directed equally against the Chinese and the Japanese—"yellow" immigrants who the rabble shouted were taking their jobs. Japanese and Chinese people were systematically excluded from law, from medicine, from teaching, from the civil service; and when they could get work, they were paid less. They were also disenfranchised. The best place for Japanese Canadians to be was up the

Keiko Inouye, c. 1930

valley among the strawberries. The Japanese berry growers put their heads down, labored, and ran their farms so well that by 1941, they harvested 191 trainloads of berries. The following year, when the Japanese were interned and white farmers took over their farms, it was only thirty. The strawberry rows on the Inouye farm stretched across the flat of the valley and up the hill. Come harvest time, women, children, everyone knelt and squatted for hours on end between the rows, filling baskets.

When Yoshinobu Inouye's firstborn entered the world, he must have wanted a son to carry on both the name and farm as tradition demanded. Yet somehow, he did not seem to mind or notice that this baby was a girl. "I was quite a decent substitute for the first son he really wanted," she said. There were sons later, but in the meantime, he took Keiko Margaret with him everywhere and did all the things with her that he would have done with his boy. "I tried hard but never enjoyed hunting and fishing and looking for *matsutake* [mushrooms] in the cold, dank woods. I made up for it by being pretty good with the cross-cut saw and keeping the woodpile stocked for the kitchen stove." It was her job too to clean out the chicken coop, something she hated, but you got on with it. "When it's time to pick strawberries, you pick the damn strawberries; when it's time to clean the chicken coop, you clean the chicken coop."

Baby Keiko Margaret on her father's lap, her mother back left

There was no running water, no electricity. Everyone worked, hard, and while being a girl did not seem to make a difference to her father, being the firstborn made every difference. The firstborn was the leader and set the example for the younger children. Keiko Margaret carried more water, sawed more wood, and bore more responsibility.

Her mother, a forceful woman, saw things differently. To her, Keiko Margaret was a girl, and she would behave like a girl come hell or high water. There were qualities that were valued in a young *Nisei* woman, modesty, for one, which in her community meant silence, deference, and proficiency, but as with young white women of the era, never excellence.

"She was trying to fulfill her mission in life, which was to bring up modest daughters, educated, but not too much." Margaret understood her mother. "She did not want me or my sisters to succeed too well. Her girls would know how to sew and cook and how to manage a household, so they would be good fodder for the marriage market." Mother and daughter saw Keiko Margaret's future very differently. "My mother thought I was already overeducated in the wrong things and undereducated in feminine skills like sewing and flower arranging. She was planning to send me to Japan to a finishing school." Ironically, Margaret Keiko inherited from her mother the single-mindedness and determination that served her well in her career, but at home, the two women had diametrically opposed views of a woman's role. With the advantage of age, she could afford to be magnanimous, but Margaret Lyons is not entirely convincing when she says, "Looking back, I feel sorry for my mother.... My good fortune was in having a father who encouraged me. But I was a great disappointment to my mother."

Her mother's understanding of tradition and its value came from her father, who lived his life as though he had never left Japan. He built himself a Buddhist shrine in the woods, mastered perfect calligraphy, and while he conceded that his grandchildren had to speak English at school, at home they were only allowed to speak Japanese. English was a second language for Keiko Margaret Inouye, the little girl who grew up to run Canada's English-language radio service. Grandfather Tsuji also loved kabuki theater, and there were annual community

The Inouye family, 1920s

productions. "My grandmother made me a new kimono every year for the silent parts and the *odori* [dance] bits." She learned how to wear a kimono, how to fold the sash, how to make Japanese food, and called it being brought up "pure Japanese." Out there in the valley, a hundred kilometers from Vancouver, it was a very Japanese life until it all fell apart. Grandfather Tsuji did not survive the internment. He died puzzled and uncomprehending in one of the internment camp barracks hundreds of kilometers from his home, of spiritual as much as physical want. Every pattern in his life had been shredded.

The kindergarten where Keiko Margaret began to learn English was organized by the Nokai, the farmers' cooperative. Having decided that their Japanese-speaking children should not start their English education at a disadvantage, the Nokai hired a kindergarten teacher to teach them their new language and their numbers. Mrs. Barnet, whom everyone came to love, was a retired Baptist missionary; she taught them well, but those Japanese elders must have been a bit startled when they arrived at the little wooden schoolhouse and heard a classroom of young Buddhists singing "Jesus Loves Me."

They went from their own kindergarten into the regular school system, white and Japanese children together. Keiko Margaret was the smallest in the class. She was *always* the smallest; she was never more than 142 centimeters tall, less than five feet, and she railed against a lifetime of looking up at men—("up at" seldom "up to"). There is a photograph of her at a reception, chin in the air, talking to Robert Bourassa, then-premier of Quebec, and federal Cabinet Minister Donald Macdonald. She is less than shoulder height to Macdonald. "Why am I always surrounded by tall men!" she would say in exasperation. But she wielded other weapons in life's battles. Her best friend in school was a white girl who appointed herself Keiko Margaret's protector—"Not that I needed protecting," she said. "I could slaughter anyone verbally."

The Nokai and the collective responsibility of community was integral to her Japanese upbringing. It was imbued in her. Her daughter, Ruth, said, "In the Japanese culture you are not the center of the universe. It's about community." And that, Margaret Lyons maintained, was what made the Canadian Broadcasting Corporation (CBC), the public broadcaster with its legislated mandate of service, a perfect fit for her. Ruth Lyons saw the connection. "The [Japanese] idea that we are all responsible to the community and the idea of the CBC she thought of in exactly the same way. It [the CBC] is an amazing resource that we all had access to and we all owned a piece of, and that had a responsibility to all Canadians. That was very much driven from the culture that she came from." That sense of serving a higher purpose is scoffed at by many. But for Margaret Lyons, never ever a sanctimonious person, it was very real.

+++

Quebec Premier Robert Bourassa, Margaret Lyons, Liberal Cabinet Minister Donald Macdonald.

More tall men. Margaret Lyons with Ontario Premier David Peterson, left.

*I don't know where I picked up the idea but I always wanted
to be a journalist.*

Where did she get the idea—how could she ever get the idea—that she, a young Japanese girl, could ever be a journalist? It's easy enough to conjure up an image of Yoshinobu Inouye sitting in his chair after dinner reading the Vancouver Japanese newspaper, *Tairiku Nippo*, and, across the room, Keiko Margaret with her copy of *The Province*, the newspaper that her father bought for her. She wanted to understand how the world worked and in a great leap of imagination, she wanted to write about it herself.

In the first thirty years of Vancouver's history, there had been seven daily newspapers, and women were writing for nearly all of them, some even running them. The Canadian Women's Press Club, with sixteen founding members, although none west of Winnipeg, had been formed in 1904. Writing was something that women were "allowed" to do, and by 1920, there were 250 women writing for Canadian papers—most of them writing for the women's and society pages; those pages sold newspapers. But teenage Keiko Margaret would skip over the women's pages and stop to read the society pages only out of curiosity. Social gossip, church teas, and recipes were not what she was after.

There were women on the more consequential beats. E. Cora Hind had been agricultural editor at the *Manitoba Free Press* since 1901 and was an internationally recognized oracle in forecasting grain yields; Myrtle Patterson, on the police beat for the *Vancouver Sun*, was the highest-paid woman journalist in the country at $50 a week in the 1920s. (Women journalists working for regional papers in BC thirty years later were typically making no more than $30 a week.) Ella Johnson was marine and financial editor of the *Vancouver Sun* and wandered the waterfront with her revolver stuck in her waistband. In 1923, the *Vancouver Sun* hired Genevieve Lipsett Skinner, a woman with twenty years of reporting experience and a law degree, as its Ottawa correspondent, making her the first woman in the

Parliamentary Press Gallery. These were successful women journalists. The Canadian Women's Press Club, which, by the 1930s—when Keiko Margaret was thinking about journalism—had chapters across the country and had been an adjunct to the suffragist movement. Suffrage champion Nellie McClung was a member of the Canadian Women's Press Club and in 1936 was appointed to the first board of governors of the CBC.

Long before Keiko Margaret was born, women—most women—had the vote federally and in every province except Quebec, and Nellie McClung was shouting from the rooftops, "Women are at last admitted to every department of labor. Women have gone into factories, offices, munition plants, everywhere that there is work to be done and even the bitterest critic has had to admit that they have made good." McClung had been an advocate for the Japanese, but Keiko Margaret, the women who would become head of a national journalistic organization, would have stood toe to toe with Nellie McClung, glared straight at her, and said, "No, Nellie McClung. You should know better. No, I have not been admitted to every department of labor. I am not enfranchised. I and my brothers and sisters are not allowed to be lawyers or teachers or doctors. No, I am Japanese. Think about it, Nellie McClung."

At eighteen, she graduated from the high school in Mission alongside white teenagers and wondered what was next for her. She knew the meaning of hard work; she was intelligent and as well-read as she could be. Her father encouraged her, but she was a prisoner of both the racial restrictions that kept her out of most professions and her mother's ambitions that would have her spending her days arranging flowers. Speaking her mind only made things worse. "My mother would say I was too opinionated for a well-bred Japanese woman, and that was my problem. I was too lippy."

*In prewar British Columbia I did not like being Japanese. Being Japanese*
*then meant that you lived in an emotional ghetto where your white*
*friends never quite accepted you and your parents would not let you join*

*them. And you knew that when you grew up you could have a university degree but you could not vote. Because of this discrimination, I felt ashamed of my Japanese parentage.*

—Keiko Inouye, *New Statesman*, 1957

✦✦✦

*We looked out of the back of the truck which had come to collect us.... It was a mild spring day with a thin drizzle washing the new maples' leaves on the hill behind our house, the house which we were leaving complete with furniture and all our belongings which could not be packed into 150 lb lots per adult, which was all that we were allowed to take.*

—Margaret Lyons, unpublished

It was nine years later, and Keiko Margaret was living in another country before she could write about that day in 1942 when they were taken away.

> The door was to be left unlocked so that the custodian could come to take possession. Annie, my pet spaniel, looked at us and whined. She whined because we were not allowed to take our pets. I found out later that they shot her. I looked back and with Annie at the door, the house looked as if we were leaving it only for a short visit, but I have never returned and I could not return now because they tore it down.

Keiko Inouye turned eighteen two weeks before the Japanese bombed Pearl Harbor. By the middle of January 1942, all Japanese Canadian men between eighteen and forty-five were removed from protected areas—anywhere that was less than 100 miles, 160 kilometers, from the Pacific Coast. Her father was working as a cook in a sawmill in the interior of BC, well outside the exclusion zone, and that's where he stayed, earning some money for the family. On February 24, the Canadian government issued the order that all "persons of Japanese origin" would have their property confiscated and men, women, and children, would all be removed from the protected area, that hundred-mile corridor. Japanese fishermen lost their boats, Vancouver storekeepers their shops, and the famous Japanese baseball team, the Asahi, was no more; in the valley, the berry farmers looked at their fields and knew there was no point planting that year. Twenty-two thousand Japanese Canadians were herded onto trains and moved east.

Carrying magazines and whatever else she could find for her friends, Keiko Margaret would go down to the Mission train station to say good-bye to those who were first to go. Her friends went, then her grandparents, her cousins, the uncles and aunts. Keiko, her two younger sisters, three little brothers, and their mother would be next. There were choices—they could either be involuntarily removed and sent to internment camps in the interior of BC—the New Denver camp in the Slocan Valley housed ten thousand Japanese Canadians before the war was over—or go east "voluntarily." Usually that meant to work on sugar beet farms in Alberta or in the Prairies. At least that way the family could stay together. Father was gone, and her mother, strong woman that she was, had never learned to speak English nor were her traditional Japanese feminine skills that she so valued any help. Keiko Margaret, criticized by her mother for her "lippiness," took charge. It was her decision that rather than be involuntarily removed to the internment camps in the Slocan Valley, the family would go "voluntarily" and go as far east as they could. They would join four thousand other Japanese Canadians working on the sugar beet farms in the Prairies.

With that last image of their house, the sound of Annie whining in their ears, and their packed lunches in their hands, they got on the train in Mission. Disheveled and very uncertain, they got off in Winnipeg. They were herded into the old Immigration Hall.

...the plumbing was rusty and did not always work. It was like an army barracks, no rooms or partitions, steel two-tier cots, women and children on one floor and men and boys on another. The plan was to move us to our final destination, sugar beet farms, as quickly as possible so home comforts were not necessary.

The building served as what Margaret described as the "slave market." Farmers came in, inspected the arrivals, and picked the labor they needed to bring in the crop. But the Inouyes—a middle-aged, Japanese-speaking woman, three teenage girls, and three little boys— were a problem family. None of them was strong enough for farm labor. No one knew what to do with them. Two months later, they were still living at the Immigration Hall. Eventually, friends of the chairman of the Security Commission proposed a solution. They would take Keiko Margaret and her sixteen-year-old sister, Yoshiko, as domestic servants, and their mother and the younger children would live out the war in a sod hut in the Prairies. They were not allowed to stay in Winnipeg. The city, like many others, had by-laws prohibiting enemy aliens, and that's what they were, from living within city limits. It was not only the cities; the municipal council of the high-end suburban community where Keiko and her sister were headed had to convene a special meeting and solemnly debate whether these two teenage girls would be permitted to live in their midst. "It made me extremely an- gry. In later years, it would have turned me into a political activist but people didn't take to the streets then. And you must remember the traditional Japanese respect for authority figures."

She and Yoshi became live-in help to this well-placed suburban family. Yoshi looked after the children; Keiko Margaret became the cook. She made the most of the hand she had been dealt. Yes, she would say, she was victimized, they were all victimized, but what were they going to do? Sit around and weep? You get on with life. She cleaned the bathrooms, washed the dishes, learned to cook "Canadian" with the help of the Mennonite cleaning lady, and thought ahead. A lifetime ago back in BC she wanted to go to university, and her mother had been an almost insurmountable obstacle. Now, her mother was out on the Prairie trying to keep warm in the winter and looking after the youngest children. "My mother could no longer prevent me being overeducated."

The internment became an opportunity.

Forty-five years later, when she was running CBC Radio, Margaret Lyons was at a conference at a country hotel with her department heads. On the second morning of the conference, CBC Radio's head of music, Harold Redekopp, turned on the radio in the morning in his room and heard that Prime Minister Brian Mulroney was going to apologize to Japanese Canadians later that day. "You must feel great!" he said when he ran into Margaret in the hall. "Well, yes," she replied. "Yes, it's...," and she paused. "Commendable." She wouldn't go overboard. "But I want to tell you that it suited my purposes.... I think the expectations were that I would become a dutiful Japanese wife and there was no way that was going to happen so the whole internment... it gave me a chance to break out." Redekopp never forgot what she said next: "And it helped me remake myself."

"Margaret never ever forgot who she was, where she came from, how tough it had been to get where she was." Redekopp, who was a Prairie Mennonite and an outsider himself, understood. "Every step she took was tough.... She was a born fighter. I don't think it ever left her."

Keiko Inouye saved every penny she earned in Manitoba. Two years after she arrived in Winnipeg, she had enough money for a train ticket to Ontario and in 1944, she walked away from her Japanese life.

*She was such a survivor, always looking forward. I don't think she believed in looking back. You can't do anything about what has happened so why look back.*

—Ruth Lyons

✦✦✦

Margaret, the coed at McMaster University, 1947

*...most of us were driven by the need to be at least the equal of other Canadians. To be equal you had to be educated, and to be educated, I had to go away.*

There are photographs of Margaret sitting on the steps of the big McMaster University brick building in saddle shoes and bobby socks; Margaret smiling and hanging out with other girls; and Margaret—by now "Keiko" had disappeared, she was just Margaret, sometimes even "Peg"—wearing a 1940s two-piece bathing suit, leaning back seductively at the beach. She was twenty-one and she was beginning to have fun.

She had left Winnipeg and come to Hamilton, Ontario, and McMaster University. Beginning as a Baptist university, McMaster billed itself as "a Christian school of learning," and it practiced what it preached and accepted Japanese students, still seen as enemy aliens, where other schools did not. In the mid-1940s, it was a small university, no more than a hundred students. When she arrived, the school gave Margaret a job as a chambermaid while she made up her admission requirements at night school. Once she started first year, she was off and running—joining every club in sight, and when she joined, she

Keiko Inouye, editor of the McMaster student newspaper, *The Silhouette*

often ended up running the club. She was editor of *The Silhouette*, the student newspaper, and president of the women's economics club. In 1948, she and a dozen or so other students got on a ship and went to postwar Europe. They climbed over the rubble of bombed-out Germany, went to Versailles, and then went on to the first international student conference in France. More photographs—Margaret lounging in sunglasses and shorts on the deck of the boat coming back, Margaret playing cards, and Margaret and Ed. Ed Lyons, in his cable-knit pullover and pleated pants, was her first and only boyfriend. As he told his children years later, he saw this tiny Asian woman sitting by herself on a bench and was immediately drawn to her. He put it down to both of them being outsiders—he was the son of a Jewish father and a Scottish Presbyterian mother and identified with the Jewish side of his family. They were also classmates in economics—a subject Margaret chose deliberately to separate her from the crowd. There wouldn't be many young women trying to make their way in journalism with a degree in economics, she thought. She was right.

In May 1949, Margaret slipped her arms into her academic robes and holding her mortarboard on her head with one hand and a bouquet of roses in the other, joined the parade of graduates. She and Ed received their honors economics degrees in the morning, stopped for lunch, and got married in the afternoon. Ed's mother was there, and Margaret's sister—no one else from her family. Fifty years later, less than 3 per cent of marriages in Canada were "mixed." Ed's family coped well enough, but it was one more division between Margaret and her mother.

They graduated, they got married, and that evening they put their bags in the car and left Hamilton. They were off to see the world. They never got beyond England, which suited them fine.

Margaret en route to
Europe, 1948

In the morning, Ed Lyons and Margaret Inouye graduated from McMaster University...

...and in the afternoon, they got married.

+++

*8 October 1951*

*Dear Mrs. Streatfield,*
*I have received word that there is an opening for typists*
*at the BBC for their twelve-hour shift....*

The only journalism that Margaret Lyons knew when she arrived in London was print journalism—newspapers, magazines. CBC Radio news was only a year old, barely tottering, and when she left, BC Radio in Canada was music and soap operas. In London, she discovered the BBC, radio that was all things to all people. Its news and current affairs coverage was rigorous and respected; its comedy and satire biting and wicked, and, if you wanted, there were serials and children's programs. The more she listened, the more she liked the BBC. Surely anyone with a good education could work in radio, she thought. She knocked on the front door of the BBC. "Come back when you know something about radio," she was told. Then she tried the back door. BBC journalists—all men in the 1950s—did not type, they dictated. Margaret Lyons could type. She typed her way into the BBC and worked her way up. Seize the stereotype.

Her daughter, Ruth, was born in 1952. (When her second child, Erskine, was born in 1958, the BBC—ahead of its time—gave her paid maternity leave.) She wrote letters home about her jolly, fat baby, about the Coronation in 1953, and the Lyons settled into a typically English life, with holidays on the Isle of Wight, Margaret making sandcastles with Ruth, with cheap theater tickets and, when they could manage, opera tickets. When she went to work, she left Ruth in the care of Aunt Silva, a Jewish Polish refugee—"a Communist!" Margaret said dismissively.

The BBC needed a clerk in its French service, and someone came to Margaret, saying, "You're a Canadian, you speak French?" She lied through her teeth and got the job. Then she faked her way into the Japanese section of the BBC World Service. "I did not mention that I never got beyond second-year afterschool Japanese in Mission." The World Service treated her like a pet. They borrowed a kimono from the Japanese embassy, dressed her up, and took her photograph interviewing a British Labour leader. Seize the stereotype one more time.

"I behaved with Canadian cheekiness rather than Japanese modesty."

She was clever, she learned quickly, and she was audacious. The BBC saw that she was worth training, and sent her to "producer school." Then she had to fight for a coveted job in production and went head-to-head with young Oxbridge graduates—callow young men, she called them. She bested them, and the BBC hired the little Japanese Canadian. The BBC taught her to double-check her sources, to be honest in her reporting, to probe and question, and to value a journalistic organization whose first obligation was to its public.

It was a heady time. She inherited the desk of Eric Blair—George Orwell—who had worked for the BBC's Eastern Service in the early 1940s, and she worked with and became friends with writer V.S. Naipaul. Fifty years later, Naipaul won the Nobel Prize for Literature. Back then, she and "Vidi" chopped up Shakespeare into fifteen-minute segments, and he knocked out scripts in Caribbean patois. It was fun.

She also worked in the field carrying what passed for a "portable" tape recorder in the mid-fifties, the cumbersome, 10 kilogram, Swiss-made NAGRA machine. Margaret Lyons was one of a handful of journalists, the only woman, invited to hopscotch their way across Asia as the British Overseas Air Corporation (BOAC) showed off its new routes. She hoisted that NAGRA over her shoulder and, working alone, gathered tape wherever they stopped. "Oh, I remember how heavy those NAGRAs were," she said to one very surprised young CBC producer who had no idea that Margaret Lyons, by then vice president of CBC Radio, had ever done "real" work. Standing there in her high heels and looking very corporate, she went on—"I used to have to lug one around Baghdad in the fifties." The young producer gulped.

She was one of the first BBC women to gather tape in the field, one of the first to produce interviews with major political figures, but later on, in her time at CBC, she did not trumpet her work at the BBC. She wasn't particularly self-effacing, rather, she separated different phases of her career and never looked back.

The decade spent in England also gave Margaret Lyons the time and distance she needed to think about herself both as a Canadian and a Japanese woman. Was she really "Canadian?" During the internment, Canada did not think she was. She looked Japanese, but was she? From Baghdad, the BOAC flight went on to Tokyo, and in July 1957, the *New Statesman* published the article she wrote about that visit.

> ...for some years I had wanted to visit Japan but now when I was expected to be Japanese I was afraid.... Do I look like those people? But I am a foreigner. Surely the cut of my clothes should show that I am from London. My face must wear an English-speaking expression.... I discovered how

Margaret at the BBC in a borrowed kimono

Japanese I seemed when the BOAC coach stopped in front of the Imperial Hotel and 3 pages rushed out to meet us with umbrellas to protect us from the typhoon rain. I was handed down by one of my fellow passengers, an Englishman, but when I stood on Japanese soil under the first umbrella it was quickly jerked away and offered to the Englishman behind me.

She, a Japanese woman, was not comfortable in Japan.

I stood in the drenching rain surrounded by men of both races and automatically, I picked up my own bags.... Once inside [the hotel] I suddenly came to my senses. It was important to me to establish my foreignness and to cling to it or I should be drowned in the habit of accepting the inferior status of woman which I was taught so long ago.

In Canada, she was a lesser being because she was Japanese, and now, among "her people," she was a lesser being because she was a woman. Today, they call it intersectionality, for Margaret Lyons in the 1950's, it was an awakening. "In school," she said, "I could see that boys and girls were educated equally. I thought they must therefore be equal at home and at work.... In those days, I was very green. The only discrimination I feared in the big world was against yellows, not against women."

Margaret Lyons donned what she called her *Nisei* armor—discipline, education, fearlessness—and marched forward ignoring this other discrimination. It was an attitude that made her unsympathetic to young women who later worked for her and wanted time off to look after their children or, as she saw it, played the "woman card." Margaret Lyons expected everyone to fight back.

In 1957, future Canadian prime minister, Lester Pearson, won the Nobel Peace Prize. On his way back to Canada after receiving the award in Stockholm, he too came into the BBC to be interviewed. Pearson was curious about this tiny Japanese woman who told him that she was Canadian. "He told me, as a Canadian, I ought to be at home doing public broadcasting.... He almost implied that it was rather a colonial thing for a Canadian to be working in London." What he said hit home.

Three years later, Ed carried eighteen-month-old Erskine and Margaret held Ruth's hand as they boarded the ship back to Canada.

+++

The stories about Margaret Lyons are legion. There was the time she was under a deadline and trying record a script in the old, falling-apart radio building in Toronto. She was all set to go when the sound of a

Margaret Lyons, the only woman embarking on BOAC's new Asia flights, 1950s

piano came through the wall. She waited a few minutes, but the piano kept going. Now she could hear humming and muttering between the notes. She pounded on the wall; the piano kept going, and so did the pounding. Margaret Lyons was teaching Glenn Gould, Canada's God of the piano, some radio manners. "Well, he was playing too loud," she said uncowed. "I couldn't get any work done."

When the family arrived back in Canada, she did not want to go back into radio. Her first choice was print but there was nothing for her in any of the Toronto newspapers. Television looked interesting, but when she went to talk to the TV people, they made clear she would have to be available twenty-four-seven—not possible for a woman with small children. Was it a manufactured excuse to keep a woman out?

Radio snapped her up—a BBC-trained radio producer, even a woman, was an asset. Radio was moribund. It had become wrapped up in itself, and no one was listening. The Toronto Radio building was more interesting than its programs. An old girls' school, it was a honeycomb of odd-shaped offices, furnished with whatever anyone could find, and mice fell from the ceiling onto producers' desks. Margaret came in every day, nodded, said hello, produced interviews, including one with American labor leader Jimmy Hoffa, made what she called her "long-winded" documentaries, and watched what was going on around her.

By the end of the decade, Canada and the rest of the world was infatuated with television. CBC Radio was in such dire condition that the CBC board of directors issued an ultimatum: revitalize radio or we will cancel the service. There was wide consultation, and a report was issued that did, on paper, revitalize radio. A report is one thing, making change is another. Doing things differently meant scrapping sacred programs, sacred at least to the relatively few who listened, demoting and firing producers and hosts with long careers, and taking big chances with new programs. It also meant difficult negotiations with broadcast unions, placating outraged listeners, facing colleagues in the hall knowing that you were going to fire them the next day, and constantly being second-guessed. Not everyone has the stomach for the job. One senior manager said as much. "I'm not prepared to make those choices," he said and stepped back.

But somebody had to. "There just aren't enough people around who are good at being bastards," said one producer, quoted anonymously in *Maclean's* magazine. "There are a whole mess of nice guys with good intentions but what this corporation needs is a director without a heart who will purge all the decrepit personalities, all the creeping vines who have become part of the masonry."

Margaret Lyons was prepared to purge. She wanted more edge, livelier radio, and better journalism, and she relished the battle. "She made no secret that she thought the place was full of shoddy, stalwart bores." Mark Starowicz, who became CBC's best-known and most-respected radio and television producers, started under Margaret Lyons. "She wanted to shake the place up—the most frequent word I heard from her was boring, boring, boring." This was the Radio Revolution. Margaret Lyons had the guts to sweep the decks clean and the imagination to see something new.

◆◆◆

In the early 1970s, Michael McEwen was a young man about to lose his job. He was an enthusiastic, if naive, radio producer from Calgary who had gone too far with a program. "I flew to Toronto in my cowboy boots and my jeans and I got down to the old radio building on Jarvis street and into Margaret's office. And there she was sitting in her chair, her feet not touching the floor, and she said, 'I hear they're letting you go in Calgary. Would you like to come and work here?'"

Margaret Lyons was recruiting, looking for new and different people. She wanted brash, she wanted smart, she wanted young, and she wanted good journalism. Mark Starowicz was still in his twenties and had just been fired by the *Toronto Star*. "I think she had a Rolodex of troublemakers who worked in newspapers; the common denominator was that they had all been fired and stirred up trouble." It was a risky strategy that took the confidence that she could manage these troublemakers. Peter Herrndorf, then–vice president of both English-language radio and television, had nothing but admiration for what she pulled off. "She hired some of the most brilliant and difficult people in broadcasting"—talent so good that Herrndorf poached many of them for television.

By the time Margaret was done, the radio building was full of new names—Gzowski, Starowicz, Fecan, Znaimer, Suzuki. There were newspaper people who knew journalism and, alongside them, neophytes. There were young women bored with their degrees in English literature; one with a doctorate in medieval studies; another who quietly admitted—but only among friends—that her degree was in home economics. There was a good sprinkling of disillusioned lawyers; a former secretary or two; a crop of "out"—or nearly out—gay men (male homosexuality was only decriminalized in Canada in 1969); a Saskatchewan social worker; and a few political science–types full of their own overstated opinions. Gone were the days when a radio announcer boasted of his "good pipes," his mellifluous voice: now what counted was attitude, a sharp wit, and a good brain.

Wilfred List, Margaret Lyons, and James Hoffa, seated, Washington DC, 1960s

People who previously would never have gotten an interview at the CBC were hired. "I've always looked for people who would take whatever they were doing one step beyond," Margaret Lyons said before she retired. "We were continually debating what we could do to make ourselves a more significant force in the country."

"The people she hired were scrappers, intelligent scrappers, mind you, but scrappers," said Harold Redekopp.

"She resented people who had the easy way up—usually they were men, usually they wore blazers and were graduates of Trinity College." Redekopp laughs. "She wouldn't limit herself to Trinity, but she wasn't sympathetic to the WASP 'establishment.'" The scrappers and the outliers were the people she understood and respected, people like her. "I felt I had to hire tough, aggressive people and then get them, persuade them, to agree with my objectives."

Redekopp heard it from her again and again: presentation—you can be as clever and well-informed as anything, just don't be boring on the radio. Format, writing, and much more—was as important to her as content. "We deliberately went out of our way to carry out radical ideas of presentation," she would say as she reminded stick-in-the-mud managers that the CBC mandate, what was set out in the act of parliament that defined the CBC, was not only that it must "inform and enlighten" but it must "entertain"—an equally important part of the mandate. Be cheeky, irreverent, and above all, no pomposity. Self-important academics, anyone who took themselves too seriously, were the kiss of death with Margaret Lyons. That emphasis on presentation eventually got her labeled a populist by her detractors.

"A lot of people resented what Margaret Lyons did to CBC Radio because she took it in a populist direction." Beth Haddon worked on the program *Sunday Morning*. "There was a constant battle between elitism and populism; standards and quality versus ratings and what we believed at *Sunday Morning*, and it must have come from the top, was that it's not one or the other. Our job is to put forward quality, intelligent programming that significant numbers of people would listen to or watch or care about. That's how you built your base, served your citizens. That was and remains the answer. That kind of programming was her vision."

+++

*I was nervous to meet her. She didn't have a cuddly demeanor. You didn't go, "Hey, hey, Mrs. Lyons, I love your work." The Radio Warrior—if I wrote a song about her I would call it "The Radio Warrior."*

—Satirist Nancy White

Margaret Lyons scared people. She was the Dragon Lady. Mark Starowicz, on the other hand, saw her more as a "den mother." There were weekends when she would appear in the CBC Radio building with a basket of apples or cookies she had made for the producers who she knew would be working all night to get the next day's program on the air. And when she became vice president of radio and someone won an award or put in a particularly hard year, they might be invited over for dinner, a reception, or a swim in the backyard pool; she would never claim expenses. If she knew that a colleague was having a hard time with a teenage daughter, a sympathetic note would appear. More than one CBC spouse said, "Is this the same woman?"

Because there was the other side: the Margaret Lyons who, if a producer was not up to scratch, ordered them gone, the Margaret Lyons who slipped into a studio unannounced while a program was on-air, intimidating everyone in the room. And in the evenings, in the early mornings, she listened—and fired off memos when she thought things weren't right. Margaret Lyons ran a tight ship. "She didn't raise her voice, didn't come on strong." She might not be pleased, but there were no surprises. Diana Filer originated the science program *Quirks and Quarks*. "She was very definite and that helped her. You knew what she was thinking." And when she agreed with her producer, she was equally low-key. "She just said okay. Do it."

◆◆◆

*Sitting in her office—her glasses would slip a bit, then she began to pronounce—as if she had an essay in the back of her mind. She always spoke in paragraphs, it was very impressive. She was very polite and very firm. I think people were almost aghast that she was so strong, so well-read, so thoughtful. So observant—and sometimes cutting.*

—Harold Redekopp

There came a time when the CBC committed to building a new broadcasting center in Toronto. It would have everything—the most state-of-the-art TV studios with room for audiences, purpose-built drama studios, executive offices near the people who made the programs. The list went on. What radio wanted in particular was an acoustically perfect theater for concerts and recordings. Inevitably, things did not go as planned, and there was talk of trade-offs. Equally inevitably, radio, the scrappy, older but by now very successful service, versus TV, bigger, more glamorous, and much more expensive. Margaret Lyons, who had risen to become vice president of radio, was determined not to lose that concert theater. One day, she fumed through yet another very long meeting and suddenly had an idea. She stormed back to her office on Bay Street. "Get me Harold," she said to her secretary as she was taking off her coat. Harold Redekopp ran the music department. "Harold," she said, "this is what you have to do…." There were no pleasantries. "Go and see the Glenn Gould people and tell them that we want to name the theater in the new Broadcasting Center after Gould and let them know that they are free to let it be known." Gould, now dead, had a foundation boosting his cultural legacy. With the Gould name and the Gould organization behind her, Margaret staked her claim. It would be great embarrassment if the theater was cut from the Broadcasting Centre plans. Who knows if what became the Glenn Gould Studio was ever at risk? Had she run the idea up the corporate flagpole—not a chance. Better to ask for forgiveness than permission.

This was Margaret the tactician, the street fighter. Long-term corporate strategy, she said herself, did not come naturally. "You have to drag out from yourself those qualities that you didn't know were in you, a sort of quiet calculation of various options. You cannot afford to be intuitive and spontaneous, you have to calculate the consequences of everything you say and do, which I found difficult in the beginning. Eventually you learn how to do it."

At the same time, she lost none of her take-no-prisoners attitude. The corporate Margaret Lyons has been compared to a Venus fly-trap—seduce and charm, then snap the trap. Redekopp said too, "She could be cruel—that was part of her." Displeased with a lieutenant on one occasion, she berated him so loudly that what she was saying could be heard at the end of the hall. When it was suggested that she could have gone a little easier on the man, she harrumphed and said he had no gumption, no self-respect. "He did not stand up for himself." It was behavior that made complete sense to her daughter Ruth. "She didn't cut herself any slack so she wasn't going to cut anyone else any slack. I think she was really tough on the people who worked for her too. Off with their heads, kind of thing. Either you rose to the occasion—my mother often said, get on with it and stop whinging—or you were out the door. That's what a lot of people experienced working for her."

Nor was she easy at home. Her hours at the office were predict-able—in every day on the bus and the subway before 9:00 a.m. and home by 6:00 p.m. And every night she took home a full briefcase that she dug into after dinner. There were no idle moments. She cooked and she sewed. There were the parties for colleagues and friends that she catered herself. And clothes that she made herself. She could never find clothes in the store that were both small enough and corporate enough. Her husband, Ed, she always pointed out, took a big part in bringing up the children and if either Ruth or her little brother Erskine felt shortchanged and said so, it was "stop whinging." Ruth rebelled and became the "daughter from hell"—her description—and then in the mid-eighties, when he was in his twenties, Erskine Lyons committed suicide.

The day her son died, a work day, she was called out of a meet-ing and given the news. She paused, thanked the messenger, and went back into the meeting. No one could quite believe it. "Heartless," people whispered. No. She had dealt with what was a massive emo-tional blow and drawn on her own cultural resources. It was not in her

Japanese upbringing to express emotion publicly. A few days later, she summoned two women, both of whom had children and worked with her closely into her office, sat them down across the desk, and closed the door. She talked about her son, about the difficulties he had had, about his dyslexia. She did not invite questions, there were no tears— Ruth Lyons said she only ever saw her mother cry tears of rage. After fifteen minutes, she stopped and said to the two women, "Thank you for letting me talk that through," and the day went on.

✦✦✦

*Mrs. T[hatcher] on election night was formidable. While all around her wilted she glowed. She became more animated as the returns improved. She went through 3 changes of outfits, mostly expensive Chanel-type suits, and had a fresher, blonder rinse on her hair. She was last seen on TV by me around 3:30 a.m., bandbox fresh telling everyone to "Get to Work!"*

Margaret Lyons's final CBC job took her back to London—full circle—where she became director of European operations. It was seen as a perk—a reward for years of service—a take-it-easy job. That was not her way. The executive assistant to the new vice president would come into her office at 8:30 every morning to the sound of the phone ringing. It was Margaret from London, asking questions, wanting answers.

She sent a report back to managers in Canada every week. Those reports were some of the best writing to ever come out of an interoffice envelope.

On the appointment of a Lord to the regulatory commission on obscenity: "His lordship was asked to be precise about his view on the depiction of sex. Singing Detective was fine because it was art. Allo Allo was also harmless because he enjoys it. It was all that unnecessary suggestive groping that he found offensive."

On the suicide of a high-ranking Church of England clergyman desperately afraid that his criticism of the Archbishop of Canterbury would be revealed: "With his suicide discreet tastefulness has descended on most journalists. Only a female religious writer spoke the truth and called him a moral coward for not standing by his own principles."

On myths circulating in London about the CBC: "…Had a fight over coffee with an otherwise sensible political scientist who believed them. Have offered to send him blow-by-blow refutation."

On TV viewing in the UK: "The masses are watching comedy shows (10 million each) which are usually subversive. The real political and social commentary is on these shows."

On the appointment of a new controller [head] of BBC 1: "He takes advantage of his cherubic appearance to needle his rivals outrageously. He can contradict himself without losing face. He is respected and loved by his staff. All this, and a sure instinct for picking winners—a true phenomenon. No doubt underneath he is ruthless and manipulative."

And on Britain's prime minister, Margaret Thatcher: "The PM herself sounds almost wet these days…. Last month, she was on TV talking about her clothes. Denis [her husband] likes frills and bright colours, and she affirmed that she bought her underwear at Marks and Spencer. This week she was on a kids show judging rock videos."

+++

Margaret Lyons retired from the Canadian Broadcasting Corporation in the late '80s and stepped well back. She lunched two or three times a year with her old friend Mark Starowicz. "Elfin," he called her. "She would march straight up to you 'Well,' she would say, 'Well, what's new?'—always fishing for gossip." She served on the senate of McMaster University, and she and Ed donated $100,000 for a new media lab, saying that what McMaster gave her could never be repaid. In 2010, Margaret Lyons became a member of the Order of Canada. When she wrote to her friend Rosemary Bates, she wrote about the event and the other recipients: the way distinguished academics, men of business, and politicians gathered like so many little boys around

Margaret Lyons, Director of European Operations conference delegate, in Tunisia

Margaret Lyons, vice president of CBC Radio

the hockey players; about the "ethnicity" of both Métis actress Tantoo Cardinal's dress and her red, almost Japanese jacket. Always the outsider looking in, she was being a journalist and reporting on the event.

She remained close to her siblings, who had all led modest lives, and came to terms with her Japanese heritage and accepted what internment had done to her. "Many of *us*," she had said in that letter to Douglas Fisher and the *Toronto Sun*, "were so traumatized by what happened to us that we did not talk about it for years." She did not talk about it and always fought for her Canadian identity. There would be a lot of foot-stamping when a newspaper referred to her as "Japanese-Canadian"." I am *not* a hyphenated Canadian," she would say and throw the paper down.

Canadian Senator Pamela Wallin knew Margaret as a boss almost fifty years ago. "It was her humanity. She was not defensive or cynical about all that had happened to her." Wallin shook her head and took a breath. "She just believed in public broadcasting. It was that Canada that she grew up in that had shut her out, that had excluded her, and all she did was embrace it more and say, we can be special, we can be different, we can make our mark, and she wanted to be part of that."

Margaret Lyons died in 2019. She took advantage of the amendments to the Criminal Code that legalized medical aid in dying. Margaret Lyons—always in charge.

Margaret and Mark Starowicz, 1984

# 10. VERA

*If you know you're right say nothing—you don't have to convince the other person...it never matters.*

—Vera Peters

Snowboarder Max Parrot stood on the podium at the Beijing Olympics in 2022 with a gold medal around his neck. He had flown high, twisted, turned; life was bursting from him, and it so easily might not have been. In 2018, Max Parrot was diagnosed with Hodgkin lymphoma, cancer of the lymph nodes most often found in the young and more often in young men than women—young men like Max Parrot at the peak of their form. There's little chance that he had ever heard of Vera Peters—she died the year before he was born—and she certainly was not famous in the sports world, but looking back, Max Parrot owes his life to Vera Peters. It was Dr. Vera Peters who showed back in the 1950s that Hodgkin lymphoma, then called Hodgkin's disease, was not fatal, that it could be treated, and when cellist Zara Nelsova was diagnosed with breast cancer in the late 1990s, it was the tumor that was removed, not her breast. She kept playing. That was Vera's doing as well.

That's what Vera Peters did—demonstrated that young men like Max Parrot need not be written off, and, for millions of women, treatment for early-stage breast cancer could leave them with a slight scar, a puckering of the skin, not a psychologically debilitating deformity. As the Medical Hall of Fame said, "…driven by the need to explain all she observed," Vera Peters "revolutionized treatment." Big changes in medicine seldom spring from the work of one person, and Vera Peters was not the only doctor working on treatments for Hodgkin's disease and breast cancer, but as much as others tried to push her out of the way, these were Vera Peters's triumphs.

She was so traditionally Canadian. When her colleagues and friends described her, they said that she was laid-back, obliging, nice, gentle, charming, mild-mannered, modest, friendly, even cute—and she lived up to every one of those adjectives. There was none of Margaret Lyons's combativeness or Zara Nelsova's imperiousness. She did not canoe thousands of kilometers and bear her babies on the trail like those eighteenth-century Métis women. Nor was she as blunt and outrageous as Paraskeva Clark, or as privileged as Alexandra Luke, as politically motivated as Isabel Crook, or as opportunistic as Mina Benson Hubbard. She did all that was expected of a woman of her era and more—unlike Trixie Worsley and Allie Douglas who remained single, she married happily and had children. She did not live a hardscrabble life like those women of Labrador. Vera Peters made it look easy, but it wasn't. The ideas and the research that she put forward were treated with skepticism, scoffed at; she was told to "go back and do her women's work." No, it wasn't easy. She just didn't make a fuss about it.

+++

The Springhill farmhouse in Ontario where Vera was born and grew up was two stories and built of brick. The posts holding up the porch

were capped with gingerbread trim and there were shutters on the upstairs windows. Springhill was a 150-acre dairy farm, making it nearly
eight times bigger than the berry farm in BC where Margaret Lyons
grew up. When Vera was born in 1911, Springhill farm was out in the
country in the township of Thistletown. Today, it would be smack dab
in the middle of the Rexdale neighborhood of Toronto.

Like Mina Benson Hubbard and Allie Douglas, she came from
Irish Protestant stock—her ancestors arrived in 1831—making the
Peterses more deeply rooted in Canada than any except the Métis
women. Her grandparents, her father's parents, became the victims
of progress, killed when a train hit their horse and buggy, leaving her
father to carry on with the farm. He was a responsible, dependable
man who did not marry until he was forty-five. Rebecca, his bride, was
twenty years younger. Charles Peters died at sixty-six, and Rebecca was
left a widow with four daughters and a son, Charles. Two other children had died in infancy. Vera was eleven when her father died. From
then on, Rebecca Peters sat at the head of the big table in the kitchen
and ran the family. There was a piano in the parlor and even a maiden
aunt, their father's sister, to oversee the piano lessons. Charles, the son,
took over the farm, and Vera fed the hens, milked the cows, drove the
hay wagon, and when she got a little older, learned to drive the tractor.
It was a hard-working and happy childhood. They, like Allie Douglas,
went on horse-drawn sleigh rides in the winter, there were strawberry
socials in the spring, the children took their prize calves to show at
the fall fair and swam in the river in the summer. Rebecca had been
a schoolteacher—their father was a member of the school board that
hired her—and above all, she believed in education, the more the better, for her daughters. That education paid off—Vera became a doctor,
Katherine a teacher, and Florence a physiotherapist.

They, like most country children, went to a one-room schoolhouse
with fifty-plus pupils (her mother had, as was expected, retired from
teaching when she got married). The smarter kids picked up what they
could from the older ones as they went along, and by the time she got
to high school, Vera had learned how to teach herself. Most telling,
when she graduated, she chose a quote from Shakespeare's *Taming of*

The Peters's family farm

*the Shrew* for the yearbook. "I'll not be tied to hours nor 'pointed times, But learn my lessons as I please myself"—a line not from the defiant, bold Kate, the "shrew," but from Bianca, the courteous, charming, yet firm sister. Vera knew who she was.

+++

I didn't feel I was in the right place.

Growing up among women—her mother, her aunt, and her sisters— during World War I, there was no man in the family telling her what to do and what not to do. (Her brother, if he ventured an opinion, was outvoted.) Women all around her were filling in for men and at least some held on to those jobs when the war ended. It was a relatively encouraging time for a bright young woman. White women had

The Peters family: Back row standing, Katherine, Rebecca (Mom), Vera, Charles (Dad), and son Charles. Front row: Helen and Florence.

won the vote in Ontario in 1917 and federally in 1918. Universities were opening up to more women, and following high school, her older sisters both went to what was called normal school for teachers' training. But Vera, without much discussion, started at the University of Toronto. It was 1928, and she was seventeen. Initially she signed up for math and physics, her strong suits, but within months she moved into medicine. All she said was, "Over the weekend I switched over to medicine," as though it was the most logical thing in the world, and she added, "because it was related to people and I was interested in people." The death of her father had been sudden. "The nearest neighbor was a mile away." She said, "We couldn't get a doctor." That might well have influenced her as well.

There were other choices, a few, at least, for a young woman "interested in people." She could have become a nurse like Alexandra Luke and Mina Benson Hubbard, but she aimed higher. Medical school in the 1920s was not as big an undertaking for a young woman as it had been a few decades earlier. When Vera Peters graduated in 1934, there

Vera, 1920s

were 10 women out of 105 graduates, almost 10 per cent. Surprisingly, there were proportionately almost as many women in her medical school class as there were in most law schools forty years later.

Vera was one of a small group of women, but she was not going it alone. Enrollment in medical schools was growing by leaps and bounds. At the University of Toronto, everyone who applied with their senior matriculation—that is, passed the high school leaving exams—got in, no interviews, no discussion. Most of these aspiring doctors were young, straight out of high school, and the children of professionals. Only 5 per cent were, like Vera, from farm families, but as a white Protestant, she was in the racial and religious majority. Emily Stowe, Canada's first woman doctor (second to be licensed), had applied for admission to University College in 1869, and the university turned her down flat. When Emily predicted, with vehemence and conviction, that one day there would not only be women in universities but women doctors in Canada, John McCaul, the president of the University of Toronto, responded, "Never in my life, madam." Never say never. Stowe was practicing in Toronto in 1883. McCaul died in 1887. Dr. Jennie Trout, the first woman doctor to be licensed, received her license in 1875.

Trout was a woman driven by her Christian zeal. She too had big aspirations. "I hope to live to see the day," Trout said, "when each larger town in Ontario will have at least one good true lady physician working *in His name*." Vera Peters had been brought up a churchgoing woman, but she was not motivated by a missionary spirit; she simply decided that doctoring was what she wanted to do. And so, she did.

Midway through her six-year program, Vera met Ken Lobb, the man she would marry. He was tall and handsome; she was pretty and lively, and they were equally smitten. Neither came from money and

U of T medical class of 1928, Vera Peters, third row from the front, sixth from the left

they were working summer jobs on one of the tour boats that sailed from Toronto to Kingston. Ken Lobb wrote in his diary, "We met in the dining hall July 2, 1931, at 4:00 p.m. We immediately fell in love." It was money, not reluctance, that got in the way of marriage, and they dated for the next six years. Vera by now was working at the hospital and bought herself a saucy little sports car, and when Ken got a teaching job, she would cruise by and pick him up. They spent a lot of time in the Ontario outdoors fishing and swimming; it was classic Canadian courtship. But it wasn't. Right from the beginning, Ken Lobb knew that Vera was on track to becoming a doctor, that he would be married to a woman with a profession, not something many, if any, of his friends had to contemplate. Ken Lobb put in ten years of night school and got his degree. Their daughter, Jenny Ingram, is convinced that Vera, without saying a word, pushed him to pull up his socks academically.

As often happened, several of the relatively few women in Vera's medical class were overachievers. Women in the 1920s, and for decades to come, entered medical school feeling that they were second best and had to try harder. They had to prove that they were every bit as intelligent as the men in the class and even more dedicated and infused with ambition. It was not enough to be good, they had to be better than the men. Vera was among the overachievers.

Another was Jessie Gray, who became the first woman to win the gold medal in her class. Gray was academically gifted—she had to be. Jessie Gray wanted to be a surgeon. She had no intention of being channeled into the womanly branches of medicine. She did not want to be a pediatrician, she did not want to be a family physician; surgery was what Jessie Gray wanted. It was common wisdom that surgery was only for the best and the brightest—the gold medal winners, and no woman had ever won the gold medal. Jessie Gray set out to trap the men in their own logic, worked hard and long, won the gold medal, and dared them to turn her down. Dr. Gray became Canada's "First Lady of Surgery," and one of the top four cancer surgeons in North America. In 1940, she became the first woman resident in surgery at Toronto General Hospital, and rose to become chief six years later.

The boat where Vera met her husband, Ken Lobb

Jessie Gray and Vera Peters finished medical school in 1934. Twenty years later, Lucille Teasdale graduated magna cum laude from medical school at Université de Montréal. Surgery was no more accessible for her in the mid-1950s than it had been for Jessie Gray in the '30s. Even today, surgery is a male enclave, and specialized surgery most of all—in 2018, 90 per cent of cardiac surgeons were men. But Teasdale was another born fighter. Like Vera Peters, she was one of seven children and the only one in her family to finish high school. Her father was a butcher from the east end of Montreal, and she got herself into medical school on a full scholarship. As a woman, Dr. Lucy Teasdale was pushed toward pediatrics. But it was surgery that she wanted—she applied to American hospitals for a surgical residency and every one turned her down, but finally she found a French hospital, in Marseilles, that would train her in surgery.

Vera could not afford the luxury of choice. She graduated as the Great Depression began and was surrounded by soup kitchens and destitute families who could not afford doctor's bills; there was no free medicine back then. Every day she passed lines of unemployed men looking for work. She too had bills to pay, and as with Lucille Teasdale, there was no family money. Medical school fees at one hundred fifty or two hundred dollars a year seem paltry today, but she was hard-pressed. Her sister Florence had been working as a teacher, but Florence too wanted something more and decided to become a physiotherapist, a relatively new profession. It was a bold and risky decision for a young, single woman. As Vera's debts were closing in on her, Florence put her own ambitions on hold, kept teaching, and gave Vera enough money to keep her in school. Vera returned the favor years later.

Family was important. As Vera was going into her final year of medical school, her mother Rebecca, the woman who held the family together, who had encouraged Vera to go to medical school and Florence to be brave and try something new, who had been behind all her girls, was diagnosed with breast cancer. In the 1930s, cancer was a diagnosis that almost always meant death. There was a pall over Springhill farm. Rebecca Peters had a radical mastectomy, standard treatment at the time; her breast, her lymph nodes, and the muscles in her chest wall were all removed. Vera saw her mother's chest, now concave and raw, and tried to have faith that the breast cancer was gone. It recurred. Rebecca Peters was then referred to Gordon Richards, one of the first therapeutic radiologists in the country and one of Vera's teachers at medical school. As a cancer therapy, radiation was in its infancy. Marie Curie and her husband Pierre had discovered radium in 1898 and, shortly after, begun work on its therapeutic properties. Gordon Richards was in almost on the ground floor and became head of radiology at Toronto General in 1917. Inevitably he, as good as anyone in the field, was operating by trial and error.

Rebecca Peters died in April 1933. Vera had been back and forth to and from the farm looking after her mother and trying to keep up with her work at medical school. Then, in 1934, she was called back, this time to nurse her sister. Helen had tuberculosis. It was another twenty years before antibiotics were used to treat TB, and when Vera came back to the farm, the only treatment for Helen was fresh air and rest. She was with her sister on the front porch of the farmhouse when she died. What Vera Peters saw at the hospital, and she had seen a lot, was one thing; to watch her mother and her sister die within a year of each other was something else again. She went back to school with a far more personal understanding of severe illness. Her mother's illness, what turned out to be the false hope and pointless suffering that came with a radical mastectomy, stayed with her. Vera Peters went back to medical school a more thoughtful woman. She made up her lost time and by December 1934, at twenty-three, was Vera Peters, MD.

Some people move straight as an arrow in pursuit of a goal that is undeniable. Margaret Lyons wanted to be a journalist and never wavered; Paraskeva Clark had "artist" engraved on her soul by the time she was a teenager; Jessie Gray and Lucille Teasdale wanted to be surgeons and would not settle for anything else. Vera Peters was not as single-minded. As is so often the case, she fell into the work that came to define her life. Serendipity.

Gordon Richards was a big, imposing, red-haired man, a former army medic—Vera maintained that the staff was scared of him. He had met Vera Peters when he treated her mother and he knew that she was smart, she asked the right questions about radiation, and she had shown that she was good with patients. He knew too that she needed work, and he needed an assistant.

Vera Peters did not have ambitions to be a country doctor delivering babies in the middle of a snowy night; she was not burning to go to Europe and study the newest techniques in heart surgery. She did not want to leave Toronto—with the deaths in her family, she was even closer to her siblings, and she had a fiancé. Therapeutic radiation was not even a recognized specialty, it was still proving itself, and any work she did would be more like apprenticing in a trade, but she wanted to know how it worked, what it could do, and now she had more than an academic interest in the treatment of cancer. When Gordon Richards said, "I need an assistant. What do you think?" she said yes.

✦✦✦

The Radium Spa and Zimmer Emanator—add radium to your drinking water! Try the Radium Ore Revigator, a water cooler lined with uranium and radium.

Newspaper ads were marketing radium-enhanced tonic water, nurses administered radium enemas, and there were uranium-enhanced dishes for sale—bright yellow-and-green phosphorescent cups and saucers painted with uranium. Marie Curie won *two* Nobel prizes, one in 1903 (which she shared with Henri Becquerel and her husband) and one alone in 1911, both arising from her work with radium and radiation. Mme Curie protested the radium water and the enemas, saying that the effects of radiation were not sufficiently well understood. Such protests fell on deaf ears. As late as the 1950s, smiling shoe-store clerks helped children stick their feet in big, stand-up X-ray machines painted in happy colors and told mothers that this would guarantee their children's shoes fit perfectly. Radiation was new and wonderful. It was enthusiasm that should have been tempered with caution.

Not for the first time, medical pioneers experimented on themselves and felt the effects. A dentist named Walkhoff took a twenty-five-minute X-ray of his mouth and head and said it was torture, and when he X-rayed some of his patients, their hair fell out; Marie Curie died of aplastic anemia as a result of radiation exposure; and it was the long-term effects of radiation that killed Vera Peters's mentor, Gordon Richards, in 1949. Remarkably, the jump from the destructive effects of X-rays to their therapeutic potential happened within months—the thinking went that if these X-rays could blister

Gordon Richards

hands and burn skin might they not destroy pathological conditions like cancer? Refining radiation therapy and controlling it was something else again. Gordon Richards aimed to turn radiation treatment into a science to standardize treatment. Vera's job was to monitor, to chart patients, and to analyze what radiation treatment did for those patients. She started working with Richards in 1936 and stayed with him for more than a decade. In that decade she also had her first baby, more reason to be very careful. One day in 1947, Gordon Richards steamed down the hall in the hospital, ran into Vera Peters, and said, "Dr. Peters, how would you like to review our experience with Hodgkin's disease? All the textbooks suggest it is a fatal disease but we seem to be seeing patients who are cured."

To "review our experience" meant to chart, to graph, to look at how patients did after treatment. Hodgkin's disease had been identified two hundred years earlier, and at the beginning of the nineteenth century, pathologist Thomas Hodgkin described the microscopic characteristics of the disease. (In 1831 Hodgkin, a Quaker and a social activist, wrote to Sir George Simpson, governor of the Hudson Bay Company, protesting the company's treatment of Indigenous people. Only months before George Simpson opened that letter, his friend John McTavish, at Simpson's instigation, had abandoned Nancy Mackenzie McTavish, his Métis wife, and their seven children.) Hodgkin's disease was not new, but the medical consensus was that there was no effective treatment. Hodgkin's disease was a fatal diagnosis. Gordon Richards had been treating Hodgkin's patients with radiation since 1924. When he had that conversation with Vera Peters in the hall of the hospital, he saw that some patients were getting better and he knew that radiation was working with other diseases. Was that what was helping his Hodgkin's patients? Was Hodgkin's a curable disease? Figure it out, please, Vera.

+++

Dr. Peters, researcher, c. 1948

*Vera was one of the great doctors of the world but perhaps the worst driver I had ever driven with.*

For Vera, cars had always been an indulgence. As soon as she had the money, she bought that sporty coupe; in the fifties, she took a shine to Cadillacs, later on there was a Mercedes. Vera Peters was also a lifelong smoker. Carolyn Bennett, who went on to be a federal government cabinet minister, was a medical school classmate of Vera's daughter, Jenny. Bennett remembers watching Vera, clearly with something on her mind, climb into her car, push a cigarette in the ignition, and throw the car keys out the window. As Bennett said, "She could be easily distracted."

◆◆◆

Vera Peters married Ken Lobb in 1937. It was a small wedding on the farm, and with great sartorial panache, they wore matching white suits. He was a schoolteacher; she was a doctor. Now that they were married, how would they handle things?

Vera Peters was not a strident feminist. She did not lobby for women's rights, she very seldom suggested when the recognition that was clearly her due did not fall her way, that it might have been because she was a woman, which is not to say that she did not advocate for women. Ken Lobb was clearly proud of his doctor wife and never anything other than supportive, and Vera never belittled her husband—yet whether Vera was instinctively downplaying her work or consciously protecting her marriage, she got out ahead of the issue. She created a dual identity. Dr. Peters drove herself home from the hospital every evening. As soon as she parked and swung her legs out of the car, Dr. Peters disappeared, and it was Mrs. Lobb who walked in the house. Dr. Peters reappeared the next morning as she walked into the hospital. At parent-teacher meetings—their first daughter Sandy was born in 1942, Jenny, their second, seven years later—she was Mrs. Lobb; when she went with her husband to a school basketball game, she was Mrs. Lobb; in the summer on holiday, she was Mrs. Lobb.

There were neighbors and parents of her children's friends who had no idea that she was a doctor, let alone a research doctor with a growing reputation. She was Sandy and Jenny's mother, wife of the schoolteacher. Ken Lobb never seemed to have been jealous of her success or considered himself a lesser man. When Ken Lobb went with her to medical gatherings, he was not surprised or upset when someone shook his hand and said, "Hi, Mr. Peters," but Vera was making sure. It's

Classmates. Left to right: Doctors Penny Watson, Carolyn Bennett, and Jenny Ingram.

Wedding day, 1937

said that she turned down a pay-raise to make sure that her salary did not exceed his.

Her job as a research doctor, at least in theory, gave her a nine-to-five schedule. After her children were born, there was always a nanny or housekeeper to look after the house and make dinner. In the evenings, she could come home, eat dinner, and then, like Margaret Lyons, unload her briefcase and start her homework.

The kitchen table at the farm had been the place where everyone came together. In the Lobb household, it was the dining room table. Vera would set up on one side of the table, the girls did their homework on the other side, and if Ken had papers to mark or lessons to prepare, he found a spot at the end. Vera has been praised for her work-life balance. At home, she went berry picking and made jam and fudge with her daughters. Mrs. Lobb did everything a mother was expected to do. Dr. Peters was equally generous with her time at work. It was a precarious work-life balance, with Vera always trying to put twenty-five or -six hours in a twenty-four-hour day. It was the only way to do what she did.

♦♦♦

*As soon as you demonstrate something that is not part of common thought, you run up against a lot of disbelief....*

—Vera Peters

Gordon Richards asked Vera Peters to look into their treatment of Hodgkin's patients, and she dug in and did not stop. She pulled all the medical files for patients who had been treated for Hodgkin's disease at the hospital for the past twenty-three years, loaded them in her briefcase, and lugged them home. It was 1947, and patient confidentiality was not what it became. After dinner, she sat at the dining room table going through file after file and making notes. What was the extent of the disease when treatment began? What was the treatment? How long did it last? How old was the patient? Man or woman? Was there improvement? Did the patient die? Did they die of Hodgkin's disease or something else? Epidemiology had only just been recognized as an academic discipline, there were very few rules on "how to do a study," and research doctors often designed their own system. Vera entered her data by hand on great wide pads of paper. Variables were matched,

Daughters Jenny and
Sandy with Vera, 1950s

Ken and Vera with paddle

calculations made; she excluded some patients, put others in different categories, and looked at how the disease had progressed, and, bottom line, had radiation treatment made a difference?

Vera Peters spent the better part of two years bent over those files and gradually she put order to what Gordon Richards had observed in his patients: the disease had responded to the treatment, some-times permanently. They could say that some patients were cured, that Hodgkin's was not necessarily a fatal disease. These were Gordon Richards's patients, this was his project, but Gordon Richards did not live to see the end of Vera's study. He died at the beginning of 1949. A few months later, Vera presented her results to the staff of the Toronto General Hospital. She had looked at 113 cases of Hodgkin's disease treated with radiation between 1924 and 1942. Then she looked at how far the disease had progressed—what became the "stages" of Hodgkin's disease. Patients who had been diagnosed when the disease had not gone past stage one had the highest chance of survival. It was the definition of those "stages" that were equally as important as proving that Hodgkin's could be cured. When Lilian Fuller, a therapeutic radiologist from Texas, heard about her work, she came to Toronto to meet this Vera Peters. "Peters's work set the world on fire," Lilian Fuller said, and she added, "No one related cure to stage and treatment as Vera Peters did."

Triumph should have followed. Not so. Gordon Richards was respected, his work trusted. Vera was an unknown quantity. The *Canadian Medical Association Journal* (CMAJ) refused to publish her paper saying that the many charts made it too complicated for their typesetting. It was not a convincing explanation. Thirty years later, Vera did say that she wondered if there was some bias because she was a woman. It was published instead by a major American journal. There was curiosity but skeptical curiosity, verging at times on ridicule. A Canadian doctor starting work in Britain was asked where he was from. When he said Toronto, the response was, "Oh, you are from that place where it is believed Hodgkin's disease can be cured"—followed no doubt by a hearty guffaw.

But there was enough curiosity that, in 1956, she was invited to speak at the Eighth International Congress of Radiology in Mexico City. The family turned it into a vacation, loaded the kids in the car, and drove to Mexico City. This was Vera's debut on the international cancer stage. Many in that audience, she knew, did not see any credibility in what she was saying, and to present her work also meant to defend it before leaders in the field. Now she was playing in the major leagues.

Never a dynamic speaker and always at least a little nervous, Vera Peters was not at her best standing in front of several hundred doctors from all over the world. For one thing, her image was all wrong. She did not appear bold and confident, instead, she was soft-spoken; she was not very tall; she dressed well but was not sophisticated. Vera Peters drank beer and liked country music. But in July of 1956, she took a deep breath and plunged in.

Sitting in that lecture hall in Mexico City in 1956 was the man

Henry Kaplan at the end of the table with Vera Peters and colleagues over shrimp cocktails, Mexco City, 1958

who became Vera Peters's *bête noire*. His name was Henry Kaplan— it was said of Henry Kaplan that he had accomplished by the age of thirty what it took others a lifetime, but he was never satisfied. His biographer, Charlotte Jacobs, wrote that while he could be gentle with his patients and some of his colleagues called him a saint, others called Henry Kaplan a "malignant son of a bitch" with a habit of stepping on his colleagues. On that summer day in Mexico City listening to Vera Peters, Jacobs says that Henry Kaplan thought this woman was advancing the treatment of cancer and he was not. By then, Vera had gone back to her data and was now talking about a "cure-rate" of 60 per cent in patients with early-stage Hodgkin's disease. Kaplan listened, went back to his university at Stanford California, and began to work with her findings. They continued to meet at international conferences. Kaplan vehemently disagreed with Peters's "stages" of the disease. What he was proposing was an approach to staging that involved surgery. Vera vehemently disagreed with what she considered unnecessary intervention, a position that would influence her later work. In 1965, nine years after they met, Vera had been invited to a multi-disciplinary symposium to decide on what would be the definitive "staging" or classification system. Kaplan had organized the meeting. Vera's reputation by now was well-established, and she was to give the forty-minute keynote address to explain her classification system. When she got to the podium, she discovered her time had been cut in half; at the twenty-minute mark, the mic went dead. Being Vera, she quietly sat down. At the end of the conference, the all-important classification committee was announced, and Vera was not included. That stung. "It was the worst slap in the face I ever got," she said. Who knows exactly why, but Henry Kaplan wanted Vera Peters out of Hodgkin's research and he was not subtle about it. By the early sixties, she was also involved in breast cancer research, and on another occasion when Henry Kaplan and Vera Peters met, this time in Paris, he invited her to dinner. As she reported back to her daughter, he said to her, "Why don't you go home and concentrate on your women's work, breast cancer?" Vera smiled, ordered an expensive dinner, and said, no, she wasn't about to back off.

It was not in Vera's nature, in her upbringing, to wage battle. "Don't argue," she would tell her daughter Sandy. "If you know you're right, say nothing. You don't have to convince the other person…. It never matters." Rather than argue, she wrote another paper. Kaplan believed in argument, that vociferous debate would lead to more knowledge. On a less altruistic level, he was a good self-promoter. One recent medical book points out that back in the 1960s, 95 per cent of patients with Hodgkin's disease died, and it goes on to say today "most are cured due mainly to the efforts of Dr. Henry Kaplan." And what about Vera?

The rejection and dismissal of her and her work upset Vera more than she let on, said her physician daughter, Jenny Ingram. But then, she had been brought up not to let her emotions show, to keep it all inside, and never draw attention to herself.

✦✦✦

Vera Peters stayed close to home. She saw patients, conducted her research, and fought for her position in her understated way on home turf. Lucille Teasdale, the Quebec woman who was determined to be a surgeon, had to move out to move on. She finished her surgical residency in Marseilles. It was 1960, she was fully qualified, and she knew she could not go home and work as a surgeon in Quebec. The Collège royal des médecins et chirurgiens du Québec did not permit women to head a surgical team until the late sixties. Dr. Lucy, as she became known, had met an Italian doctor, Piero Corti, when she was doing her internship in Montreal. She liked him. They both wanted to practice where it would do the most good—Lucille Teasdale had said when she was a little girl that she wanted to be a missionary. Corti, the son of an industrialist from Turin, had set up a medical mission in northern Uganda. Lacor was a thirty-bed hospital built around a dusty courtyard (fifty years later it had grown to five hundred and fifty beds). In 1960, Piero Corti needed a surgeon and looked at her longingly. Dr. Lucy flew to Uganda, they got married in the hospital chapel, and she never left. When Vera Peters was looking after Hodgkin's patients in Toronto, Dr. Lucy was scrubbing up and conducting surgery on anyone who staggered into her hospital. Lucille Teasdale-Corti was the only surgeon in thousands of square kilometers in sub-Saharan Africa. If she had stayed home, she would still be fighting for the right to pick up a scalpel.

Therapeutic radiation was more female-friendly, perhaps because it was new, and Vera Peters could do what she wanted and stay in Toronto. They were very different women. Dr. Lucy minced no words, called a spade a spade, even lost her temper. Not Vera. "Once," said a colleague, "Vera got so angry that she almost raised her voice."

One summer's day in small-town Alberta, Gert, a woman in her fifties, stood in her living room and shouted at the other woman in the room, a visitor, a woman she had never met, who had come by to ask some questions about breast cancer. Gert was angry. "Come here, come…," and she grabbed the other woman's arm and pulled her into her bedroom. "Come here." Then she stripped off her shirt and stood bare-chested in front of the mirror.

The bed sheets were rumpled, there were clothes on the floor. Gert flung open the closet door and pointed at the mirror on the back of the door. "Look! Look at that!" she said, and both women looked in the mirror at her scarred chest. "Nothing, that's what I've got. Scars. There's nothing left of me. Nothing!" The visitor stood behind Gert, looked over her shoulder, and saw what she saw. Gert pointed at the big red scars on her bony chest, the place where her nipples used to be, where her breasts used to hang soft and plump, and she wept and wept. It was six months since the surgeon took her breasts—"took 'em both off"—and she still could not believe that this was her body. Her husband wouldn't touch her; her family just wanted her to be quiet. Her arms were swollen and had no strength. She could not peg the washing out on the line, could not carry her groceries home, could not pick up her grandson. And she could not forgive what, as she saw it, had been done to her. Surely there was another way.

There are very few "perfect" operations in medicine, but the medical profession felt that it had found one in the radical mastectomy—the 1894 Halsted procedure, a milestone in breast cancer treatment. It appeared—no one had done any studies—to greatly increase the numbers of patients who survived breast cancer, but at what price? William Halsted, chief of surgery at Johns Hopkins Hospital in Baltimore, is credited with revolutionizing surgery in America. In his younger and more frenetic days, he researched the anesthetic properties of cocaine and became a lifelong drug addict, yet Halsted remained chief of surgery for thirty years. He is described as painfully

Vera Peters, 1960

shy, unapproachable, sarcastic, cruel, and a man most at ease with his patients when they were unconscious. Halsted had been dead more than a decade when Vera Peters began to practice, but he was a legend, and so was the radical mastectomy, and legends are difficult to dispel.

Rebecca Peters, Vera's mother, had a radical mastectomy in 1932. It was the surgery of choice, usually the surgeon's choice, for up to 90 per cent of breast cancer patients into the 1970s. Betty Ford, wife of US President Gerald Ford, had a radical mastectomy in 1974, and if the President's wife had a radical mastectomy, the thinking went, it must be the right thing to do. But as it was in the 1930s, a radical mastectomy remained psychologically debilitating; when the muscles in the chest were taken away, so was the strength in the arm, and many women had nerve pain or numbness and untreatable swelling in their arms or hands—none of that had changed.

Working in radiation oncology, Vera saw all kinds of cancer. When she began in the thirties, skin cancer was the most common referral, breast cancer was second. But given that there was a treatment for breast cancer—the radical mastectomy—other cancers took research focus. In the mid-1950s, along with her work on Hodgkin's disease, Vera Peters started looking at breast cancer. She understood why a woman like Gert, looking at her scars in the mirror, was more than angry. She had seen it too many times. Years later, she said that she was inspired to look for better methods of treatment by the "diverse devastations of breast cancer patients." She had changed her mother's dressings, seen the "diverse devastations" visited on her. It was twenty years ago but an image that did not go away.

Treatment gradually evolved, always depending on the type and stage of breast cancer and the surgeon, from the radical mastectomy to the modified radical mastectomy (the muscles of the chest wall were spared) and the simple mastectomy—only the breast was removed. Then in 1953, Vera Peters quietly suggested that there "might" be another way. "We are not entirely convinced that the [simple mastectomy] is the method of choice for all breast cancers," she wrote. "…we [the Institute of Radiotherapy in Toronto] have fallen heir to a small series of cases…and hope to report on it in the near future." Her "small series of cases" were patients who had not had a mastectomy—simple or radical—out of a concern that they might not survive surgery, because of age or other illness, and in a few cases, because they refused to have a mastectomy. Over time, more women began to refuse mastectomies, and some surgeons—Peters called them "rebel patients and missionary surgeons"—told their patients that in some cases removing only the tumor, what became known as a lumpectomy followed by radiation, could be as successful as removing the entire breast. Patients were pushing, they wanted more information, a bigger voice in their treatment, and they wanted more conservative treatment, less surgery. Increasingly, these women were referred to Vera Peters.

It was not only Vera who thought that radiation and less radical surgery could work. Geoffrey Keynes, brother of economist John Maynard Keynes, was convinced as early as 1937 that radium needles around the tumor, that is radiation and *no* surgery, could be as effective as radical surgery. There was a study out of Finland, and another out of London, showing that there was no difference in survival rates between the patients, depending on the type and stage of their cancer, who had had their breasts removed and those who had lumpectomies and radiation. It was time to look more closely at those Toronto patients.

Once again, as she left work, Vera Peters packed her briefcase with patient files, took them home, and piled them up, this time, her daughter Jenny remembers, on a card table in the basement. Fueled by coffee, cigarettes, and curiosity, there she sat working her way through seven thousand files, one for every breast cancer patient seen between 1935 and 1960 at the old Institute of Radiotherapy and, since 1958, Princess Margaret Hospital. More than once, Jenny came downstairs in the morning and Vera was still working. "Oh, is it morning already?" she would say. As with the Hodgkin's research, she entered the data by hand on wide pads of paper; she created huge graphs; and she did the calculations with a slide rule and an adding machine, this was still well before personal computers. Of those 7,000 patients, 852 had had lumpectomies, and 124 had no follow up treatment except radiation. Those were the women she wanted to study. And when she did, what she thought was borne out—after five years, among women with stage 1 breast cancer, there was no difference in the survival rates of the lumpectomy women and the women who had had mastectomies.

In 1968, she presented her findings at one national cancer conference in the United States and in 1969 at another. She never sensationalized, her data did not support a miracle cure, rather her conclusions were, like the treatment she was advocating, conservative. Lumpectomy and radiation she said, "*appears* to be *equally* as effective as other [radical] methods of treatment [emphasis added]." She was met with stony silence. It was déjà vu all over again.

+++

*...one woman in a household of men.*

—Barron Lerner

There was a steely determination about Vera. The reaction almost a decade earlier to her work on Hodgkin's disease had been lukewarm at best, and there were the ongoing battles with Henry Kaplan and others, that she neither anticipated nor wanted. If her work on Hodgkin's disease was a tough sell, what she was saying about breast cancer treatment would be even tougher. This time, Vera Peters was challenging what was seen as a highly effective treatment of the most common cancer in women, a cancer that was fifty times more frequent than Hodgkin's disease. But challenge she did. Not only was she opposed and refuted, she was shunned. One oncologist in the Netherlands, a woman, wrote to Vera Peters a decade later and said that she had referred to a Vera Peters's paper about lumpectomy and "was nearly killed for it."

There were allies, doctors at a hospital in Houston, who, convinced by her work, began conservative treatment of early-stage breast cancer, but the allies were few and far between. Opponents attacked her research. Hers was a historic study, looking back at patients from years past, and the criticism was that examples had been cherry-picked to make her case and that Vera's study had no control groups.

She went back to the files; there had been good and consistent record-keeping in Toronto. The card table was set up in the basement again, and this time she went through *eight thousand* files, manually charting, cross-referencing, matching patients treated by lumpectomy and radiation by age and stage of cancer, size of tumor, and year of treatment with women who had been treated by mastectomy and radiation. The lumpectomy was the only difference between these two groups. This time, the survival rate of the two groups was not equal, the lumpectomy patients had a slightly higher survival rate.

Vera Peters prepared to present her findings one more time. It was 1975, the annual conference of the Royal College of Physicians and Surgeons, and the venue was the ballroom of the Holiday Inn in Winnipeg. Jenny, Vera Peters's daughter and by then a newly qualified doctor, went with her mother. Vera was nervous, she practiced the night before, Jenny encouraged her, and Vera smoked a lot of cigarettes. The next morning, impeccably but quietly dressed as usual,

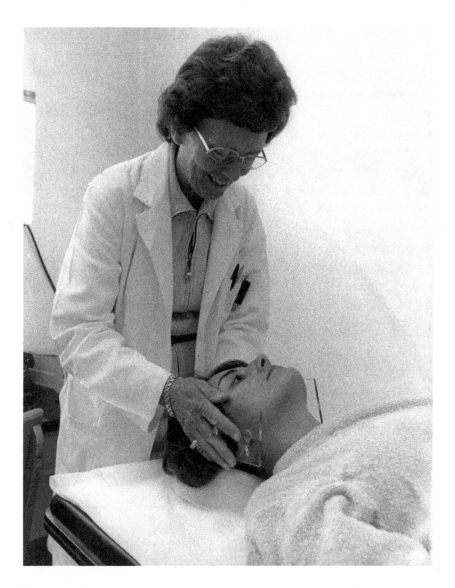

Dr. Peters with a patient

she and Jenny took the elevator down to the ballroom at the Holiday Inn and chatted and mingled with the four hundred doctors, nearly all of them men, getting their coffee and settling in. In the 1970s, women were never more than 6 per cent of any medical class, a smaller percentage than when Vera graduated, and Jenny and Vera had the women's washroom to themselves in Winnipeg.

Vera was the only woman presenting at that meeting and she knew that what she was about to say would not be popular. More than forty-five years later, Jenny Ingram shivers when she talks about that day. "You could feel the coolness in the room." When Vera finished and stepped away from the podium, there was polite applause, nothing more. Medical historian and bioethicist Barron Lerner, in his book *The Breast Cancer Wars*, asked, "…can you picture this woman standing up in a meeting full of surgeons in the 1960s and 1970s telling them they were doing the wrong operation…? [O]ne woman in a household of men."

♦♦♦

*As more and more conservative studies ripen, as more and more concerned physicians observe the adverse effects of excessive treatment, as more and more women become armed with knowledge, mastectomy, in early breast cancer, may become as old-fashioned as bloodletting.*

—Vera Peters

The Winnipeg paper was published in the *Annals of the Royal College of Physicians and Surgeons*, and was virtually ignored. Two years later, an updated version appeared in an international journal with a larger circulation. She ended that article with a graceful, polite battle cry and prediction that as more women are "armed with knowledge, mastectomy in early breast cancer" would become as "old-fashioned as bloodletting." She was reflecting what she was seeing and hearing from her patients. Vera Peters did her research work at night; her day job was her patients.

Vera Peters was a first-class clinician, respected for her almost intuitive ability to assess a patient. Her fingers could read a Hodgkin's patient and the state of their lymph nodes at first examination, and when it came to treating and diagnosing breast cancer patients, she became known for her compassion and her propensity to look at the woman—and those few men with breast cancer—and ask nonmedical questions in areas that few others in the 1960s thought to explore: Was she poor? Did she have children? What were her worries? What did she most dread in the treatment she was facing? Vera Peters became known for her patient-centered care before the term was invented.

When she received a medal from the American National Cancer Institute after she retired, in her acceptance speech, Vera chose to focus not on her research but on her patients:

> We seem to have become more and more removed from understanding the human condition or even recognizing that needs exist.... Little do we render less perilous the emotional journey of the cancer patient! The patients' cornerstone of trust rests on faith—faith that their rights, even those

Vera, the international presenter

unknown to them, will be recognized and honored by the physician. The right to seek consultation, the right to fully understand treatment, the right to know treatment alternatives, the right to know treatment ramifications, and the right to help with treatment decisions.

At the height of her career, there had been international trips—lectures, visiting professorships, appearances on expert panels, even a six-month sabbatical in England. Off went Vera, well turned out as always—Ira Berg, her clothing store of choice, knew her so well that she could double-park, and someone would run a garment bag stuffed with dresses and suits out to the curb. By the mid-70s, the travel, the events were trailing off, retirement was looming. There was mandatory retirement at sixty-five at Princess Margaret Hospital. Vera would turn sixty-five in 1976. More than thirty years later, after more than a dozen cases claiming mandatory retirement was discriminatory had been heard at Human Rights Tribunals and all the way up to the Supreme Court of Canada, the federal government finally said no, employers cannot dictate mandatory retirement—too late for Vera. She was tight-lipped, only letting the occasional remark slip, but she was being forced out when she still had work to do. She had laid the groundwork for conservative treatment of breast cancer and now, when it seemed about to be accepted, she was being cut out. There was talk in 1973 of a prospective study—a study that selected patients and monitored them *before*, not after, their treatment, comparing lumpectomy and radiation and mastectomy—being run out of Princess Margaret Hospital, but it came to nothing. The reality was that prospective trials were what it was going to take to put an end to the mastectomy-lumpectomy/radiation debate; it was what the science of epidemiology now required. Vera's steely determination could verge on stubbornness. She held fast to the validity of her historic studies. She was right, but did she resist the push for prospective studies because she was too committed to her results?

The year *after* her 1975 presentation in Winnipeg, when she had laid her cards on the table based on her historic research, an American researcher named Bernard Fisher launched a series of well-funded clinical trials in the United States involving five hundred different institutions and fifty thousand patients. In 1985, the *New England Journal of Medicine* published his findings, and the lumpectomy plus radiation in early stages of breast cancer was finally established as the treatment of choice in early breast cancer. Vera looked on from the sidelines. Bernard Fisher and Vera Peters were on the same side of the debate, and like Vera Peters, Fisher had been roundly attacked by the old guard, but look up "who invented the lumpectomy?" and the answer that comes up is Bernard Fisher with no mention of Vera Peters. Bernard Fisher's massive study was later shown to have included falsified data. A congressional subcommittee investigation acquitted him of

Daughter Jenny Ingram
with Vera, 1980s

scientific misconduct, but his reputation was ruined. *The Philadelphia Inquirer* described Fisher as "once a magnetic autocratic genius" now "tired, abstracted and ill-prepared" with "no trace of the fierce pragmatism which made him a hero of the women's health movement."

But Vera Peters was long dead when the last chapters of the Bernard Fisher story played out.

In 1975, she was made a Member of the Order of Canada, and sat at the same table for the ceremony as Ed Mirvish and his wife, Anne, who had earlier that year picketed the Arts and Letters Club in Toronto over its men-only policy. Vera would have been politely interested but such tactics were not her style. There were honorary degrees and medals. But in 1976, she was cleaning out her desk at Princess Margaret Hospital, handing in her office keys, and going home.

◆◆◆

Artists and musicians never retire—Paraskeva Clark slowed down but never got rid of her paintbrushes, and Zara Nelsova was planning her next concerts on her deathbed. Margaret Lyons peppered her retirement with projects and volunteer work, and Allie Douglas never stopped staring at the stars, nor, a hundred years earlier, had Charlotte Small. But what was there for Vera Peters?

Ken, her husband, had a heart attack and died suddenly in 1967. Now, two of the mainstays in her life, her husband and her job, were gone. Both daughters had moved away from Toronto, they had children, they were busy, and Vera struck up a friendship with a younger woman named Lila Jackson, who worked at the

Lila Jackson

*Toronto Star*. The friendship had begun when Vera was at Princess Margaret, and Jackson had been a friend of a patient. When Vera retired, she sold her house and found an apartment near Lila; they ran an antique store together in a little town outside Toronto; they co-owned a house in Florida, and when Vera bought her new Mercedes, it was Lila who drove it, saying to Vera's daughters, "Your mother should not be driving." Her daughters were not happy. They could not figure out what was going on and simply called it "the dark times."

Then, just as suddenly as it began, the relationship with Lila ended. Jenny, who was living and practicing medicine in London, Ontario, phoned her mother, almost out of desperation, and said, "I need help with the kids," and that was that. Vera left Toronto, took care of the children, and later became a consultant in her daughter's medical practice.

In the winter of 1984, she got another call for help, this time from a former colleague. "Vera, can you come to Ottawa?" Jeanne Sauvé, first woman elected to the House of Commons from Quebec, former cabinet minister, and tapped the previous December to become the next and the first female governor general. Somewhat mysteriously, Mme. Sauvé's swearing in had been postponed. Jeanne Sauvé was in hospital. "We're treating her for an infection," said the colleague, "but she isn't responding. I think it might be Hodgkin's. Can you come?" Vera Peters went to Ottawa, quietly visited Jeanne Sauvé, examined her, and confirmed the diagnosis. Treatment began, she recovered, and Jeanne Sauvé was sworn in as governor general. There had been a five-month delay between the initial announcement and her move to Rideau Hall, and no one outside a very small circle—that included Vera Peters— knew why.

It was curiosity and increasing dissatisfaction with the way things were that kept Vera Peters going. Surely it was not acceptable that the preferred way to treat breast cancer was to take off a woman's breast? Why was it accepted that there was no "cure" for Hodgkin's disease? And, as she had said matter-of-factly when she was asked why she had gone into medicine, "I was interested in people." She was also quite prepared to work long and hard in relative obscurity. In that she had more than a little in common with Lucille Teasdale, still, when Vera retired, working up on the Uganda-Sudan border. As Vera Peters had slogged away systematically compiling her charts and looking after her patients in Canada, Lucille Teasdale-Corti trained nurses and doctors, operated every day, and ran the Lacor Hospital in Africa. By the late '70s, Ugandan dictator Idi Amin's troops rampaged through the country, and the wounded were dumped at the hospital almost every day. Dr. Lucy put on another pair of thin, worn surgical gloves and swiveled between operating tables repairing war wounds. She and Piero decided it was 1979, when a piece of bone fragmented by a gunshot pierced Dr. Lucy's gloves, that she contracted HIV/AIDS. That was two years before HIV/AIDS was identified in North America.

Dr. Lucy continued to see patients for the next fifteen years. They would line up across the dusty courtyard as she set up her chair on the hospital verandah. There was a nurse behind her with patient records, and Dr. Lucy would see up to three hundred patients in a day. Vera Peters and Lucille Teasdale-Corti each looked after their patients with a regard and respect they had never known. Dr. Lucy died of AIDS

Left to right: Piero Corti, Lucille Teasdale-Corti, their daughter Dominic, and her husband, at Lacor hospital in Uganda, 1993

in 1996. Six years later, the butcher's daughter from the east end of Montreal was inducted into Canada's Medical Hall of Fame. She had performed more than 13,000 operations in Uganda. Had she stayed in Quebec, she would have barely got started.

Vera Peters, like her mother before her, was diagnosed first with breast cancer then lung cancer—she never stopped smoking. Her old colleagues, many of whom she had mentored, would drop by for a quick visit in the weeks she was in hospital—one would come by in the late afternoon, and they would have a glass of something together. Vera Peters died in 1993. It wasn't until 2010 that she was inducted into the Medical Hall of Fame. Vera Peters was never in it for the glory. Mild-mannered Vera—it had taken seventeen years before someone said, "Oh, yes, Vera Peters. She did important work; she deserves a place."

Vera in the last month of her life, surrounded by daughter Sandy and granddaughter Kelsey

# ACKNOWLEDGMENTS

I had a great deal of help writing this book, a great deal. Scholars, archivists, journalists, and librarians at a dozen different institutions, together with nieces, nephews, grandchildren, friends, and colleagues of each of the subjects of these chapters, have been more than generous with their time and their recollections, and I am most thankful to all of them. Any mistakes are my own.

It would be impossible to write about Mina Benson Hubbard were it not for the work of her biographer Anne Hart. Her Memorial University colleague, Roberta Buchanan, generously shared her unpublished work on George Elson and, as ever, Memorial archivists pointed me toward new material. Thanks as well to Mina Benson Hubbard's descendants for their reflections, and to Karen Levine for the original assignment that is finally coming to fruition.

There is a long list of people in the classical music world who each added a link in the chain of discovery of Zara Nelsova. My thanks to cellists Roman Borys, Margaret Gay, Judy Fraser, Denis Brott, Etan Cornfield, and bass player Peter Madgett; to Zara's former daughter-in-law Julia Bradford; to Loie Fallis and the archivist of the Toronto Symphony. My posthumous thanks as well to my former partner, Peter Schenkman, for a very keen understanding of the life of a cellist.

It would have been all but impossible to write about Beatrice (Trixie) Worsley were it not for the work of Scott M. Campbell at Waterloo University, and his patient explanation of the early world of computer science.

My thanks to Allie Vibert Douglas's nephew Patrick Douglas, her great-niece Marianne Douglas, and her great-nephews Stephen and Dan Douglas, for their recollections of their aunt and for the loan of her unpublished memoir. Ian Alexander and Marilyn Dalzell gave me on-the-ground help tracking down the final home and grave of Nancy "Matooskie" Mackenzie in Victoria, BC. Filmmaker Gail Singer shared her memories and her film about Paraskeva Clark, and both Alexandra Luke's grandson Peter McLaughlin and her granddaughter Wendy Moses were more than generous in helping me understand her and her work.

The connections between these women never ceased to surprise me. That Mina Benson Hubbard gave Zara Nelsova her first grown-up cello, that Allie Vibert Douglas walked past the grave of Charlotte Small every time she visited her mother's grave; the surprising discovery that Stephen Douglas, nephew of Allie Vibert Douglas, had met and spent time with Isabel Brown Crook in China; how Norman Bethune kept popping up in these women's lives—great-grandson of Louisa Mackenzie Bethune, lover of Paraskeva Clark, part of the lives of Isabel Crook and her husband David; that David Crook spied on George Orwell; and Margaret Lyons inherited his desk at the BBC—these were all nuggets that underlined the significance of these women and reminded me that our history is still fresh.

My thanks to Sarah Holland for introducing me to the Grenfell Mats and the work of Paula Laverty, and to Chris Brookes for his Newfoundland perspective on Wilfrid Grenfell. Again, there is a long list of men and women who talked to me about Margaret Lyons—particular thanks to Ruth Lyons, Michael McEwen, Harold Redekopp, Mark Starowicz, and Doug Ward. Charles Hayter has shared his thoughts on Vera Peters over the years, as has Jennifer Ingram. I am grateful to them and to Sandy Clark.

Finally—I owe a debt of gratitude to Mary Lou Fallis and other friends who listened to my endless talk about these women, and whose enthusiasm carried me forward. And, of course, there would not be a book were it not for my editor, Andrea Knight, and Melissa Kaita, Gillian Rodgerson, Margie Wolfe, and everyone at Second Story Press. Thank you.

# PHOTO CREDITS

Computer Science and Technology, University of Cambridge. Reproduced with permission.

Page 86 - Copyright Department of Computer Science and Technology, University of Cambridge. Reproduced by permission.

Page 87 - Public domain

Page 89 - Courtesy of Alva Worsley

Page 96 - Courtesy of Western University communications

Page 97 - Courtesy of Archives of Thisted Kommune

Page 99 - R2770 Vol. 151, CFUW Library and Archives Canada

Page 116 - Public domain

Page 117 - Smithsonian Institution

Page 119 - Courtesy of Douglas family

Page 120 - Public domain

Pages 121, 125, & 126 - Courtesy of Douglas family

Page 129 - Public domain

Pages 130 & 131 - Courtesy of Douglas family
Page 139 - Public domain

Page 146 - © Artist Melissa Jayne

Page 149 - © Sculptor Rich Roenisch

Page 152 - Public domain

Page 157 - Wikimedia Commons

Page 160 - City of Victoria Archives M09894

Page 170 - United Church of Canada Archives, Toronto. 1976.001P/645

Page 173 - United Church of Canada Archives, Toronto. 1976.001P/3182

Page 184 - Wikimedia Commons

Page 185 - © China Global Television Network

Page 186 - © China Global Television Network

Page 188 - Courtesy of Robin Engleman

Page 193 - © China Global Television Network

Page 197 - Courtesy of Stephen Douglas

Page 203 - © Estate of Paraskeva Clark
Page 204 - © Estate of Paraskeva Clark

Page 210 - Public domain

Page 211 - Public domain

Pages 213, 214, 218, 220 - © Estate of Paraskeva Clark

Page 222 - The Robert McLaughlin Gallery

Page 228 - The Robert McLaughlin Gallery

Page 230 - © Estate of Paraskeva Clark

Page 233 - © 2011 Lynda M. Shearer. All rights reserved.

Page 235 - The Robert McLaughlin Gallery

Pages 239, 245, 249, 253, 256 - Courtesy of The Rooms, provincial archives, NL

Pages 262, 263, 265, 267, 274, 275, 276, 277, 278, 281, 283, 286, 293, 295 - Courtesy of the estate of Margaret Lyons

Pages 299, 300, 301, 302, 304 - Courtesy of Peters family

Page 307 - Courtesy of Canadian Association of Radiologists

Pages 309, 310, 311, 312, 313, 315, 319, 323, 325, 327, 328, 330, 331 - Courtesy of Peters family

# ABOUT THE AUTHOR

Karin Wells grew up in BC, and now lives in Port Hope, Ontario. She is best known as a CBC radio documentary maker and is a three-time recipient of the Canadian Association of Journalists documentary award. Her work has been heard on radio networks around the world and has been recognized by the United Nations. Wells worked—briefly—as a line worker in a pea factory and an actor. She is also a lawyer and, in 2011, was inducted into the University of Ottawa's Common Law Honour Society.

Karin Wells is the author of *The Abortion Caravan: When Women Shut Down Government in the Battle for the Right to Choose*, winner of the Ontario Historical Society's Alison Prentice Award for best book in Ontario women's history, and short-listed for the Writers' Trust Shaughnessy Cohen Prize for best political writing.